The Fracture of Faith

The Fracture of Faith

Recovering Belief of the Gospel in a Postmodern World

Douglas Vickers

Mentor

© Douglas Vickers
ISBN 1-85792-6129

Published in 2000
by
Christian Focus Publications,
Geanies House, Fearn, Ross-shire,
IV20 1TW, Scotland, Great Britain

www.christianfocus.com

Mentor
is an imprint of
Christian Focus Publications

Printer and bound in Great Britain by
J W Arrowsmith, Bristol

Cover design by Owen Daily

Contents

To the faithful members
of the Sunday morning class
at Millers Falls

Foreword

"Doctrine and Life"

by

W. Robert Godfrey
President and Professor of Church History
Westminster Theological Seminary in California

Jesus said, "I am the way, the truth and the life." Christians ever since he made that statement have rightly recognized that their religion rests on biblical doctrine and genuine experience. Truth and life are the hallmarks of the faith.

The Protestant Reformation of the sixteenth century balanced truth and life in a remarkably fine way. While doctrine may have been somewhat more prominent in light of the errors of the medieval church, life was healthy and strong. Since the Reformation Protestants have often had trouble maintaining that balance. In the seventeenth century, for example, Puritan critics of the Church of England feared that while doctrine was formally right, vital religion had not prevailed among the people. The fear of a lifeless formalism shaped a number of religious movements in the centuries that followed. Experience became the central concern to demonstrate the reality of true religion.

In the nineteenth century the evangelical empire of the United States, while accomplishing much that was good, tended to ignore or downplay the significance of any sophisticated doctrinal system. A personal experience of Christ was what united, even where rather different conceptions of Christ prevailed. The stress on experience would give birth to a surprising variety of children of that empire in America. Liberalism, Fundamentalism and Pentecostalism can all trace their ancestry back to the experiential evangelicalism of the nineteenth century.

J. Gresham Machen in his important book, *Christianity and Liberalism* (1923), drew attention to the triumph of experience over doctrine in his day and the disastrous consequences for the church. He was responding to the claims of liberals in his day that their rejection of certain basic doctrines of Christianity did not touch the heart of Christianity, which was not doctrine, but ethics and life. The second chapter of Machen's book was entitled, "Doctrine," and in it, Machen asked, "Is it true, then, that Christianity is not a doctrine but a life?" He answered, "But if any one fact is clear, on the basis of this evidence, it is that the Christian movement at its inception was not just a way of life in the modern sense, but a way of life founded on a message. It was based, not upon mere feelings, not upon a mere program of work, but upon an account of facts. In other words it was based upon doctrine."[1]

While Machen's analysis won wide support among those called fundamentalists in his day, the triumph of experience is even greater in our day than in Machen's. David Wells exposed that reality with devastating clarity and ample evidence in his book *No Place for Truth* (1993) - a book not about liberalism, but about contemporary evangelicalism. He wrote, "...the vision of God in his otherness ... has now largely faded, a fact most obviously evidenced by the disappearance of theology in the evangelical Church."[2] Theology has retreated before the advance of various kinds of spirituality and activism.

Christians today need much help in reestablishing the importance of sound, biblical doctrine as the foundation and standard of their Christian experience. We need vital religion, but one of the ways in which vitality must be measured is by the rule of the truth. Douglas Vickers has provided the church with a book that will help significantly in that enterprise. He lays out the great doctrines of the Scriptures and shows their importance both to Christian life and to the world in which we live.

May we see in the twenty-first century a restoration of the balance of truth and life that Christians knew in the sixteenth century. Only the Spirit of God can accomplish that in our time. But books like this one can be instruments for the fulfilling of that hope.

---

[1] J. Gresham Machen, *Christianity and Liberalism*, Grand Rapids. Michigan: Eerdmans, 1977, 20f.
[2] David Wells, *No Place for Truth, or Whatever Happened to Evangelical Theology?*. Grand Rapids, Michigan: Eerdmans, 1993, 288

Preface

My objective in this book is to bring into prominence some features of the belief and life of the contemporary church. A pressing need exists to understand why, and the manner in which, the testimony of the church has been tarnished by the devaluation of its doctrine and the uncertainty that clouds its statement of the gospel. Professing Christians in both the pulpit and the pew are bewildered, unsure, and conceivably discouraged by the complex pressures of the age and by the apparent impotence and irrelevance of the church. As a result, many are tempted to abandon it as a tottering anachronism.

It is a commonplace to say that we live in an age without secure anchorage in thought or life or behavior, an age of postmodernist surrender of all claims to truth. But against that reality it is necessary to explain where it is the church, particularly in its evangelical expression, now stands, to be aware of the deviations from its Reformed doctrinal heritage that have occurred, and to consider again the biblical gospel that stands in need of urgent recovery.

I have endeavored to explain the several influences that have led to the contemporary condition: the capitulation of theological doctrine to alien thought systems and secular philosophic trends, the assumption of non-Christian thought that God, if he exists, is irrelevant, the consequent loss of clear directives for life and belief, and the accommodation of evangelicalism to secular cultural norms The development of my argument is set out more fully in chapter 1, where I have indicated the headings under which I discuss the doctrinal content of Christian truth and belief. The book's doctrinal exposition addresses such important questions as the being, the holiness, and the love of God, his covenantal-redemptive purpose, the realities of sin and the provision of redemption in Christ, the believer's entrance to eternal life, and the imperatives of the life and walk of faith.

In writing this book I have been indebted to many scholars in the Reformed theological tradition, as I have endeavored to acknowledge throughout the work. I mention at this stage only one point that is not only relevant to the heart of the biblical-Reformed construction of the gospel, but has become a subject of debate and of differing shades of understanding among theologians of good will and good evangelical-Reformed credentials. In the position I have taken in the matter of theological apologetics I stand in the tradition of presupposi-tionalism, as that has been instanced most articulately in the last century by Cornelius Van Til. That has influenced my state-ments and conclusions regarding the being, knowledge, and purposes of God, the knowability of God by man in both his unregenerate and his regenerate state, and the consequent meaning of the redemptive objectives of the gospel.

I am indebted also to several people who have encouraged and assisted in the production of the book. I owe a heavy debt to the Rev. Dr. Robert E. Davis for his support and constructive guidance in this and many other aspects of my work. My wife, Miriam, assisted in proof-reading and in the correction of some infelicities that found their way into the manuscript. As has been true for many books and many projects, Ann Hopkins has given me invaluable editorial assistance. To them all, and to many others who have influenced my journey in the Christian faith, I record my hearty thanks.

I appreciate deeply the careful and insightful reading of the manuscript by several other scholars and theologians and the evaluative comments I have received. My thanks and apprecia-tion are due, and are here sincerely recorded, to Dr. Robert Godfrey for the generous foreword he has subscribed to the book. I cheerfully absolve all those I have mentioned from responsibility for what deficiencies and infelicities remain, and I dedicate this book to the hope that God will be glorified in it, that the church will be benefited, and that it will contribute to the growth in grace and in the knowledge of God of those into whose hands it falls.

1

Three Triads and the Evangel

A triad is a group of three things among which, in general, some significant relation exists. Any things or persons or ideas, or statements of concepts and propositions, can be arranged, for purposes of inspection and argument, in triadic form. Musicians in particular, and frequently theologians, arrange their thought in a triadic manner. The musician who strikes on the keyboard the root note of a scale, say the scale of C-Major, and then strikes with it the third and the fifth notes of that same scale, produces a harmonious sound that is described as a "Major triad". If the third note had been reduced buy a half-tone, and if, simultaneously with the first and the fifth notes as before, the black key immediately below the third had been played instead of the white key, the very pleasing and perhaps winsome sound would be described as a "Minor triad". Triads provide structure to any number of musical formations.

This concept of "threeness" lies at the heart of what, as Christians, we believe. God exists as three Persons. When we first learned the Catechism, perhaps in early and far-off days, we knew that "There are three Persons in the Godhead: the Father, the Son, and the Holy Ghost; and these three are one God, the same in substance, equal in power and glory".[1] All that didn't seem very clear to us then, and with our advancing years the wonder has only increased and the mystery has not

---

[1] *Westminster Shorter Catechism*, Question 6.

diminished. In fact, as we gave closer attention to what was involved in Christian belief, we learned that all Christian doctrines terminate in mystery. But we have held to two things. First, while there is mystery for us, there is no mystery for God. And secondly, we have seen that in actual history God has declared and revealed himself in his triune Personhood. We have seen that in all of the actions of God external to the Godhead the three Persons of the Godhead are engaged.

In his self-disclosure in history, God sent his Son to "declare" the Father to us (John 1:18) and to be our redeemer, to live and die for us as our substitute, to "bear our sins in his own body on the tree" (1 Peter 2:24). And we have seen that God the Father has fulfilled the promise that he gave through the prophet Joel (Joel 2:28) and has sent his Holy Spirit to be with his people whom he has redeemed (Acts 2:16). The Father and the Son have sent the Spirit as Christ himself promised on the night on which he was betrayed. "I will not leave you comfortless", he had said on that occasion, "I will come to you" (John 14:18).

As we wrestled with Christian belief and doctrine, we learned to recognize the fact and the limitations of our finitude. We have understood that the being that God is, and the knowledge that God possesses within himself, are incomprehensible to us. We learned why it was that he said to us through the prophet Isaiah that "my thoughts are not your thoughts" (Is. 55:8). The very manner of God's knowing, we came to understand, is different from our knowing. For God exists and knows outside of time. He created time. But our knowledge and our knowing are bounded in time. Our knowing is sequential, and our knowledge is successively grasped and realized and organized. But God's knowledge is not, in any similar sense, sequential. God knows all things, about himself and about all created reality external to himself, in one eternal act of knowing. God did not have to wait to discover anything about himself or about created reality.

But the "threeness" that inheres in our doctrine of God, determining as it does all of the rest of our theology, is raised here only for illustrative purposes. We shall return to it. For the present, let us project the notion of "threeness" to consider the "three triads" contemplated in the title of this chapter. There is cause to fear that the evangel, as we referred to it there, has not always been clearly understood in its biblical form, and expressions of it in contemporary evangelism have compromised the meaning of it.

The evangel and evangelism

By the word "evangel" we mean the good news of the gospel. Its meaning is spread liberally across the pages of the Scriptures. We speak, all too easily and all too freely perhaps, of the evangelical church and of its evangelism. The terms we employ in those contexts may be designed to differentiate one form or style of theology from another. On one level, we might speak of "evangelical theology" as distinguished from other theological systems that do not hold as closely as evangelical theology does to the biblical terms of the gospel. On another level, we might use the term "evangelical" to differentiate one Protestant theological tradition from another. In such a way, evangelical theology has been differentiated from other expressions of generally Reformed traditions. Different systems and structures of doctrinal thought, though they appear under the guise of evangelicalism, present different understandings of the place of God and man, and the work of God and man, in the drama of redemption.

But at this point, a basic question presses upon us. If we believe what we understand the Scriptures to declare as the gospel, should we not then be interested in evangelism? Evangelism, after all, is the announcement of the evangel and the spreading, far and wide, of the invitation to life in Christ Jesus that the evangel contains. If we understand ourselves to possess the good news of the gospel, should we not be paramountly concerned to spread that good news as widely and as forthrightly as we can? That is the calling and the task of the church. The church has been raised to spread abroad the fact and the reality that, as the gospel states, God has redeemed sinners to himself by the substitutionary death of his Son. If such a statement is true, and if we believe the Scripture that tells us it is true, then evangelism would be reasonably concerned with spreading that good news to all who will listen. We should

13

spread abroad the good news of the salvific implications for all those who will believe.

But a troubling question persists. It strikes to the heart of the uneasiness we feel as we consider these issues. It is a short and simple question. In asking it, we are not setting out to be excessively fastidious. But before we can consider one's evangelism we are compelled to ask, What is his evangel? We are uneasy at the suggestion that all and anything that might be presented as the good news of the gospel is, in fact, true to, and consistent with, what the Scriptures have actually said.

The question can be put differently. The evangel, we may say, is prior to evangelism. What one believes, and what he sets out to present as the gospel, call for evaluation before we make a commitment to what it is that evangelism might be setting out to say or to do. The difficulty that confronts us can be put even more simply. Consider the teaching and the belief structures of the church in general. Let us take whatever form of ecclesiastical arrangement we wish, or whatever denominational structure or identity that we imagine to be relevant. The question we confront is that of deciding whether what is believed and taught and practiced is consistent with what, on grounds of conscience, we understand the Scriptures to declare. What, again, is the evangel, or what is understood by the church, rightly or wrongly, to be the evangel?

That is the basic question that disturbs us as we consider the church at this point of its history. The nature of the times does not need to be spelled out at any great length to see that the church, at the entrance to the twenty-first century, has lost its place of social and cultural hegemony. The Christian church, and the confessing Christians within the church, we have reason to fear, are not the salt of the earth that they were called to be. There is reason to fear that the world no longer looks at the church as the beacon on the hill that shines on the paths of social and cultural rectitude. The church is all too often ignored for its weakness, if not despised for its meanness. The issue before us is that of what has happened to the faith and belief and the teaching of the church.

Where does the church stand, we ask in our troubled anxiety, or where does the church imagine that it has a right and a responsibility to stand, in what we can only see as an age of cultural and moral dissolution? The thought structures and behavior norms that characterize the church pale in comparison with what our fathers held and believed and stood for. Harry Blamires, some thirty years ago, placed his finger on the emerging problem of the decay of Christian thought. He perceptively began his work on *The Christian Mind* with the provocative and challenging comment that "There is no longer a Christian mind".[2] He had placed that comment quite correctly in the context of his discussion of the Christian's "Surrender to Secularism". The condition that now exists appears to have resulted from a continuing decay, rather than from any improvement and a recovery of belief. When Mark Noll surveyed the scene thirty years after Blamires wrote, he began his work on the same note, "The scandal of the evangelical mind is that there is not much of an evangelical mind".[3]

The theologians have registered a similar complaint, as even a minimal review of trends in the theology of the church will disclose.[4] Not only the doctrinal stance of the church, but also its organization, in some instances its heavyweight and mega-

---

[2] Harry Blamires, *The Christian Mind: How Should a Christian Think?*, London: S.P.C.K., 1963; Ann Arbor: Servant Books, 1978, 5.

[3] Mark A. Noll, *The Scandal of the Evangelical Mind*, Grand Rapids: Eerdmans, 1994, 3.

[4] For a very minimal sample of relevant literature that addresses more than one side of the issues, see Hugh Ross Mackintosh, *Types of Modern Theology: Schleiermacher to Barth*, New York: Scribners, 1937; Paul Tillich, *Systematic Theology*, Chicago: The University of Chicago Press, 1951; John Macquarrie, *Principles of Christian Theology*, New York: Scribners, 1966; Stanley J. Grenz and Roger E. Olson, *20th Century Theology: God and the World in a Transitional Age*, Downers Grove: InterVarsity Press, 1992; and three works by Cornelius Van Til, each published by P&R Publishing, Phillipsburg, N.J., *The New Modernism: An Appraisal of the Theology of Barth and Brunner*, [1946] 1972; *Christianity and Barthianism*, 1962; *The Great Debate Today*, 1971. A masterly survey of developments in theology and in doctrinal commitments is contained in David B. Calhoun's two volume history of Princeton Theological Seminary, *Princeton Seminary: Faith and Learning, 1812-1868* and *Princeton Seminary: The Majestic Testimony, 1869-1929*, Edinburgh: The Banner of Truth Trust, 1994 and 1996. A prophetic and highly relevant work that has stood the test of time is that of J. Gresham Machen, *Christianity and Liberalism*, Grand Rapids: Eerdmans 1923.

church administrative structures, its frequently ill-judged forays into television evangelism, its capitulation to a business organizational ethos, its dalliance with doctrineless ecumenicity, and its cultural and political entanglements - these are all, it is clear, levels on which cause for concern for the church's understanding of its mission and its function arises.

But the most troubling concern is that of the way in which all of these aspects of the contemporary situation have spilled over to a surrender of the church's grasp on the content and meaning of the biblical evangel. It has implied, at the same time, the surrender of the biblically mandated worship that the church is called to preserve. These issues that generate our anxiety, complex and interdependent as they are, have been surveyed with well-documented scholarship by David Wells in his recent trilogy, *No Place for Truth, God in the Wasteland*, and *Losing Our Virtue*.[5]

We may contemplate these issues from the point of view of the person who sits in the pew. We may enter a plea from the pew that asks what we can and should safely believe, and what it is to which we can safely trust the eternal security of our souls. These are short questions. But they project issues of profound, and even eternal, significance. Many voices clamor for our attention. We see, disturbingly, that they are not all saying the same thing. Indeed, they are confusing to us on two counts. First, some quite bluntly contradict others. We see that readily. But second, some are so minimally differentiated from others that we are confused as to where our spiritual and intellectual allegiance should safely be placed. Surely the pew can properly appeal to the pulpit for clarity and guidance in these matters of eternal import.

With the questions and issues that we have raised in mind, and from the perspectives of a spiritual uneasiness and concern, the following chapters will consider the terms of the good news of the gospel. We wish to understand what the Scriptures have declared concerning it. Our discussion will be fairly wide-

---

[5] David F. Wells, *No Place for Truth, or Whatever Happened to Evangelical Theology?; God in the Wasteland: The Reality of Truth in a World of Fading Dreams; Losing Our Virtue: Why the Church Must Recover Its Moral Vision*, Grand Rapids, Eerdmans, 1993, 1994, 1998.

ranging and will address a number of areas of biblical doctrine: the meaning of the knowledge of God, of time and eternity, of sin, of the wrath of God against sin that made redemption necessary in the manner in which it was provided, of the love of God, of the meaning of the Christian life.

The questions we shall raise can be seen, for purposes of summary at this stage, in triadic form. We referred in the title of this chapter to three triads. They have to do with what it is that we can know as to Christian belief, as that turns on God's revelation and his self-disclosure; with how it is that we can and do know, and how we can know that what we know is true; and with what are the implications for life in the every-day. Let us take a preliminary look at the triads on which the gospel throws its light.

The three triads

The questions we are setting out to address will fall within the subject areas summarized in the following schema:

Triad 1: *Christian Doctrine*

    a. Creation
    b. Sin and the Fall
    c. Redemption

Triad 2: *Christian Apologetics*

    a. Being and reality - Metaphysics
    b. Knowledge - Epistemology
    c. Behavior - Ethics

Triad 3: *Christian Life*

    a. Effectual calling - Regeneration
    b. The benefits of effectual calling -
          Justification, Adoption, Sanctification
    c. The eschatological hope

Christian doctrine, Christian apologetics, and the meaning and hope of the Christian life provide the framework within which we shall examine the structure of Christian belief. The objective is to reflect on what it is that the evangel says to us in these respects.

The first triad

Triad 1 speaks of the fundamental questions of Christian doctrine. It contemplates the issues of Creation, Sin and the Fall, and Redemption. When we speak of creation, the focus of our thought turns to the very being, existence, character, and purpose of God who at first said "Let us make man in our image" (Gen. 1:26). When the Catechism asked, "What is God", it answered that "God is a Spirit, infinite, eternal, and un-changeable, in his being, wisdom, power, holiness, justice, goodness, and truth".[6] Our meditation turns, accordingly, to the existence in eternity of the Creator-Redeemer God, to his creation of time into which he has spoken all of reality external to the Godhead, and to the entry into time that he has made in the Person of his Son. We are arrested by the awareness of the holiness of God and the innate consciousness of the being and the existence of God that we have by virtue of our creation in his image. We know, with a consciousness that cannot be avoided and a conviction that cannot be erased, that God is. For in the very act of self-awareness we are aware of God. The *sensus deitatis*, the sense of God, is created within the human soul.

When the Catechism went on to say that "The decrees of God are his eternal purpose, according to the counsel of his will, whereby, for his own glory, he hath foreordained whatsoever comes to pass", it explained that "God executeth his decrees in the works of creation and providence".[7] In these catechetical statements we have the beginning of Christian doctrine.

The second element of Triad 1 speaks of Sin and the Fall. Here we encounter the very starting point of the explanation of

---

[6] *Westminster Shorter Catechism*, Question 4.
[7] Ibid., Questions 7-8.

the human condition. If we understand the Scripture to be true when it explains that our first parents were established in a covenantal relation to a Creator-God, we give the lie immediately to every form of philosophic materialism that tells us that we came from the mud, even though we aspire to the stars. The sorry reality is that in our first parents we fell from original righteousness into, as the Catechism puts it, "an estate of sin and misery".[8] The history of the human race is not one of upward progress on some evolutionary scale. The story of mankind, on the contrary, is one of initial bliss and a catastrophic Fall.

John Milton has spoken eloquently "Of man's first disobedience and the fruit of that forbidden tree, whose mortal taste brought death into the world, and all our woe".[9] The biblical revelation, from the record of that Fall in the third chapter of Genesis onwards, is the explanation of God's redemptive purpose. It was in no sense necessary that God, whose holiness had been outraged by Adam's sin, should have provided a redemption for any at all. His justice and holiness would have remained inviolate if he had left all mankind to bear the penalty of eternal perdition for their sin. But the glory of the gospel is that God did, in his mercy and by his grace, set forth a redemption for sinners.

Implied immediately, therefore, is the third element of the first Triad, which directs our attention to the purpose and the accomplishment of the redemption that God has provided. In order that redemption might be accomplished in a manner consistent with both the justice and the love of God, it was necessary, the gospel declares, that the Son of God, the blessed Second Person of the Trinity, should come into the world and take our human nature, yet without sin, into union with his divine nature. Sin having entered by the lapse of human nature, it was necessary that the penalty for sin should be paid in human nature. But it was at the same time necessary that it be paid in and by a human nature that had no necessity to pay a penalty for its own sin. Redemption was possible only if Christ should come as the Son of God in sinless human nature, should keep

---

[8] Ibid., Question 17.
[9] John Milton, *Paradise Lost*, lines 1-3.

the law of God perfectly as our substitute in human nature, and should die for us in his human nature. The gospel explains the realities of redemption in those very terms. Redemption is provided for sinners by the messianic accomplishment of the *incarnate* Son of God.

The urgency of our wrestling with the content of Christian belief makes it necessary that the more expansive questions that arise in these areas should be our first concern. We have spoken of God as he exists in himself in eternity, beyond the bounds of time that he had made, of his cognizance of our fallen wretchedness and sin, and of the provision of the rescue and redemption from sin that his grace has set forth. The largest part of the following chapters will be devoted to these closely related questions, and the content of our first Triad, that of Creation, Sin, and Redemption, will therefore be of principal concern.

The second triad

In the triadic outline summarized initially, Triad 2 was concerned with the rather broad subject of Christian apologetics. We are concerned there with the relevance of the evangel to three basic question areas, those of Being, Knowledge, and Behavior. The very sound of "Christian apologetics" might have a deterrent ring about it. But that should not be thought to be the case. For what we are concerned with here are a small number of reasonably straightforward matters that do, in several ways, stand in close relation to the content and the truth of the gospel.

The substance and the objectives of Christian apologetics can be readily grasped by recalling the admonition of the apostle, "be ready always to give an answer to every man that asketh you a reason of the hope that is in you" (1 Peter 3:15). That is the text on which John Frame has based his recent treatment of theological apologetics.[10] An older theological tradition has referred to apologetics as "Christianity defensively stated".[11] That is the essence of what is involved in the

---

[10] John M. Frame, *Apologetics to the Glory of God*, Phillipsburg, N.J.: P&R Publishing, 1994.

[11] A.B. Bruce, *Apologetics; or Christianity Defensively Stated*, Edinburgh: T.& T. Clark, 1892.

questions that apologetics addresses. Cornelius Van Til, one of the foremost apologetic theologians of the second half of the twentieth century, has discussed the relevant questions under the heading of "The Defense of the Faith".[12]

If, in the tradition of Van Til and Frame, we take apologetics to involve, essentially, a positive statement of Christian truth, we are concerned with the light that the evangel throws on the three elements of our second Triad. When we speak of the nature of Being, we are concerned with what the Scriptures explain to us as both the being of God and the being of all created reality external to the Godhead. We shall inevitably look at some aspects of those questions under the heading of Christian doctrine as we have already referred to it. We shall be looking further at what, in the language of philosophy, is understood as Metaphysics.

Then secondly, apologetics takes up the question of knowledge, meaning by that the related questions of how we know what we know, and how we know that what we know is true. We shall see that diverse answers have been given to these important questions, even within what purports to be the evangelical church, and even, also, among those who present their arguments as Reformed theology. But a very important and related question follows from this level to that of one's understanding of the gospel. It has to do with what is understood as the knowledge and the reasoning capacities as they exist in the individual who is subject to the disabilities that entered because of sin and the Fall. Philosophy has traditionally addressed these related questions of knowledge and the processes and validity of knowing under the heading of epistemology.

The third of the elements of Triad 2 has to do with behavior. That takes up and discusses the large question of Christian

---

[12] Cornelius Van Til, *The Defense of the Faith*, Phillipsburg: P&R Publishing, [1955] 1967. See also John M. Frame, *Cornelius Van Til: An Analysis of His Thought*, Phillipsburg: P&R Publishing, 1995. We shall have occasion to refer at greater length to the work of Van Til, who has presented what has become referred to as apologetic presuppositionalism. In that connection we shall refer also to a critically negative evaluation of Van Til (from which we shall dissent) by R.C. Sproul, John Gerstner, and Arthur Lindsley, *Classical Apologetics: A Rational Defense of the Christian Faith and a Critique of Presuppositional Apologetics*, Grand Rapids: Zondervan, 1984.

ethics, or the criteria of behavior and action. As we consider these issues we shall become aware very quickly of two things. First, if the Christian gospel is an address to the human person in the totality of his or her existence, then the question of how life should be lived with proper attention to what is right and what is wrong becomes paramount. If the redemption that we have already anticipated is designed to bring the sinner back to a state of reconciliation with God and to conform that person in all of his or her being and behavior to the righteousness that God requires, then behavior norms, or ethical criteria, must emerge as a crucial part of the statement of the evangel.

Secondly, an unavoidable relation exists among the elements of Triad 2. Being, knowing, and behavior can be properly understood only as the question of knowledge, or what we know, is understood to be dependent on the prior understanding of being, or of the nature of being as God has established it. The *what* of knowledge, in other words, is prior to the *how* of knowledge.

Because we have understood Christian apologetics to be essentially a defensive statement of the Christian faith, the questions to be addressed under that heading are interdependent with what will be said in relation to Christian doctrine and the meaning and progress of the Christian life. But in order to focus on the reasons for the disarray of faith that marks the church in this time, and on the important apologetic issues of knowledge and truth, we shall devote two chapters to those questions. In those chapters we shall examine certain modern, and what have come to be called postmodern, traditions in the matter of knowledge.

The third triad

The elements of Triad 3 refer to certain aspects of Christian life. The issues raised are concerned with the basic question of how, if at all, a person comes to a Scripturally consistent awareness of, and a belief commitment to, the truth of the gospel. It will be seen that the new-creating, regenerating work of the Holy Spirit of God in the soul of the sinner alone accounts for one's commitment in faith to Christ as his or her Redeemer. The reality at that point is as Christ himself put it to Nicodemus in that climactic nocturnal encounter, "Except a man be born again, he cannot see the kingdom of God" (John 3:3).

Beyond that work of regeneration, the Holy Spirit, in the discharge of the redemptive office that he assumed before the foundation of the world, applies to the regenerate individual all of the gifts and benefits that Christ purchased for him in his act of atonement. Among those gifts are the gifts of repentance and faith (Eph. 2:8), and the benefits that follow from them: justification, adoption, and sanctification.

From all of that follows, in terms that are again spread liberally across the pages of the Scriptures, the great eschatological hope of the Christian, the hope of the eternal destiny of the soul that is joined to Christ. It is a basic fact of Christian reality that the Christian is an eschatological person. By virtue of the creation of new life in the soul that the work of the Holy Spirit accomplishes, the person is now joined to Christ in a vital, organic, spiritual, and indissoluble union. The truth of the Christian's condition is as our Lord himself stated it when he said that "No man can come to me, except the Father which hath sent me draw him; and I will raise him up at the last day" (John 6:44). And in that remarkable discourse on his identity as the good shepherd who gives his life for his sheep, Christ said that "My sheep hear my voice, and I know them, and they follow me. And I give unto them eternal life; and they shall never perish, neither shall any man pluck them out of my hand" (John 10:27-28).

The apostle Paul has said the same thing in his remarkable peroration at the end of the eighth chapter of his letter to the Romans. "Who shall separate us from the love of Christ", he asks. And his answer confirms the impossibility of any such separation. "I am persuaded", he says, "that neither death, nor life, nor angels, nor principalities, nor powers, nor things present, nor things to come, nor height, nor depth, nor any other creature, shall be able to separate us from the love of God, which is in Christ Jesus our Lord" (Rom. 8:35,38-39).

We have thus spoken of three triads, whose contents address Christian doctrine, Christian apologetics, and Christian life. But the issues and questions that need to be raised under these headings are, we have said, very much interrelated and interdependent. What calls for discussion under Christian apologetics is heavily dependent on Christian doctrine. Again, the questions that arise as to the meaning and progress of the Christian life are answerable only by a clear grasp of Christian doctrine. In the following chapters, therefore, we shall allow the relevant doctrinal relationships and interrelations to emerge as the discussions develop. It will not be necessary or desirable to maintain an isolation between what needs to be said under the headings of the three triads we have established for purposes of initial definition, though our exposition will proceed in the order we have already contemplated.

We turn immediately in the following chapter to look again at the call of the gospel. We shall see its invitation clearly displayed in a remarkable incident in the life of our Lord in this world.

2

The Call of the Evangel

The gospel call has rung through the corridors of time, its verity untarnished and its promise of life undulled. "Come unto me, all ye that labour and are heavy laden", Christ had said, "and I will give you rest" (Matt. 11:28). The call to repentance and faith in Christ has ever stood at the entrance to life eternal. "I am the way, the truth, and the life", he claimed to a hesitant disciple (John 14:6), and through the centuries since the gospel has heralded the same declaration.

A remarkable incident marked the life of the Son of God in this world. It is one in which the chief priests, the Pharisees, and even Nicodemus, whose encounter with Jesus was pregnant with eternal meaning, are all involved in its criss-crossing tensions.

The time of the Feast of Tabernacles had arrived. It was the occasion of the Feast of Booths or Ingathering, when all of the males of the Israelites were required to travel to the temple in Jerusalem (Lev.23). The city was thronged. Christ also was there, teaching in the temple. There, as John records, on "that great day of the feast", Christ made his profound and life-promising declaration, "If any man thirst, let him come unto me, and drink" (John 7:37). Many believed on him, though others added their dissent to that of the priests and the rulers. But it is the sequel that engages us. The authorities were disturbed by what the ministry of Christ portended. They would have taken him captive then and wreaked their dark designs upon him. They had sent soldiers and officers to bring him to them. But the soldiers returned empty handed.

What then took place in a meeting of the Sanhedrin betrays the agitation of the rulers. In fact, it was only after Nicodemus had cautioned them that the law required an accused individual to be heard in person before he could be condemned, that the meeting quietly adjourned. The adjournment, the record suggests, was not without embarrassment to those concerned. But it did not occur before the sarcasm of the authorities had been vented on the soldiers who had failed to accomplish their mission. The Pharisees hurled at the soldiers the biting question whether they too had been deceived by the claims of the itinerant teacher from Galilee. But the soldiers had only one thing to say. It is that that arrests us.

Jesus unique among men

The soldiers answered, with, no doubt, a greater prescience than they knew, "Never man spake like this man" (John 7:46). They had probably heard the teaching of Christ, their conscience disturbed by his invitation to come to him and partake of the water of life. Such a statement as he made, the claims it implied, and the promise of life it contained, disturbed their settled convictions. We do not know the details of their encounter with the Lord on that occasion. We know only that they could not then fathom the meaning and implications of what they had heard. Their interest in what the teacher on that occasion said was heightened. Their conscience quickened, the statements of the Son of God and the Savior of sinners had arrested them. They knew there was a uniqueness about the occasion in which their role had been cast. There was a uniqueness about the man they had heard teaching and had planned to arrest.

But how the tables were turned! An arrest there was on that historic day. But what a difference it was from what had been planned by the rulers and expected by the soldiers. It was the soldiers who were arrested. They were arrested by a conviction that no man previously, at any time on the stage of history, had spoken in quite the same way as the Galilean teacher. The words they heard had a graciousness about them, a compulsion, a strange assurance of a penetrating and sympathetic understanding of the human condition.

To say that the soldiers were so taken aback that they could not accomplish their mission is to leave the explanation of that day incomplete. To say that the outcome was what it was because, as our Lord himself stated on other occasions, his hour had not yet come, is also to leave untouched an important point of the record. Simply put, the episode clarions the fact that here were men, hardened in the tasks of their profession, forced to testify to the most remarkable fact of all of history. The conclusion forced itself upon them that the man they heard teaching was not an ordinary man. Jesus was unique. There was a difference about him. That, they could not for the moment explain. They could only attest, against the responsibilities of their mission, that no man had ever spoken like the man they had heard that day.

The same conclusion had been reached on other occasions. In the very first chapter of his gospel record, Mark reports the reaction of those who had listened to our Lord's teaching in the synagogue at Capernaum. "They were astonished at his doctrine", Mark observes, "for he taught them as one that had authority, and not as the scribes" (Mark 1:22). Luke records in a similar fashion the reaction of Christ's hearers in the synagogue at Nazareth. Following his reading from the sixty-first chapter of Isaiah's prophecy and his applying it to himself in an act of self-disclosure, the people "wondered at the gracious words which proceeded out of his mouth" (Luke 4:22). The instances could be expanded.

The soldiers at Jerusalem, the worshippers in the synagogues at Nazareth and Capernaum, and many who heard his memorable declarations testify in unmistakable ways that there was a uniqueness, a compelling difference, about the man they were hearing. They heard him declare that he had come as the bread of life (John 6), that he was the good shepherd who would lay down his life for his sheep (John 10). The testimony that history has rung through the years, from that early first century through two millennia since, cannot be evaded. Jesus Christ, the Son of God and the Savior of men, was unique.

It is true that he partook of our humanity, that he took unto himself the likeness of sinful men, a true body and a reasonable soul, yet without sin. He was the Son of man and the Son of God. True it is that in his humanity he was tempted in all points like as we are (Heb. 4:15). He suffered and he was sorrowful. We are challenged by his sinlessness and his impeccability. We cannot avoid the fact that is clarioned by the testimonies we have culled from the sacred text. In the simplest of possible terms, Jesus the Christ is unique. That reality challenges our thought and reaction, as it did the soldiers and the worshippers of old.

Jesus, the teacher whom the soldiers could not arrest, was a divine person. He was not a human person. He was not a divine-human person. In him, human nature was not personalized. The uniqueness of Christ continues to disturb every human imagination. His hearers of old could not grasp its reality, and even his chosen disciples were reluctant to absorb its meaning. We have to do with the divine Person of the Godhead who assumed our human nature into union with his divine nature. He was, he continued to be, a divine person, but a divine person in whom the divine and human natures were joined.[1]

Our interest at this point is in that simple declaration that sets the compass for all our reflection on the Person and the work of Christ. Not only is it true, as the soldiers of old reported, that never man spoke as he did, but it is true that no one like him had ever appeared on the stage of history. He, and only he, in all of the uniqueness that characterized him, could be the mediator between God and man.

Even his executioners did not know who he was. In their consuming ignorance and consummate foolishness they

---

[1] The Council of Chalcedon (451AD) gave to the church what has rightly become known as the Christological settlement, that stated that in Christ the divine and the human natures are so related as to be "two natures, without confusion, without change, without division, without separation". See Cornelius Van Til, *The Defense of the Faith*, 16. Van Til observes that "the former two adjectives safeguard against the idea that the divine and the human are in any sense intermingled; the latter two adjectives assert the full reality of the union" (loc. cit).

crucified the Lord of Glory. The apostle Paul summed it up in precisely those terms. "None of the princes of this world knew", he concludes, "for had they known it, they would not have crucified the Lord of glory" (1 Cor. 2:8). What blindness and perverseness had corrupted the vision of that far off time. How true it was in all of its eloquent sadness that "He was in the world, and the world was made by him, and the world knew him not. He came unto his own, and his own received him not" (John 1:10-11).

Our Lord himself, who "needed not that any should testify of man: for he knew what was in man" (John 2:25), knew clearly the passion and intentions of those who crucified him. Did he not pray to the Father, "they know not what they do" (Luke 23:34)? And he prayed that for them the day of mercy would be extended and the opportunity for repentance would be pro-longed. But on that day, on which all the meaning of all of history converged, the cry of the crowd had had its way:

> "Barabbas, murderer, scoundrel, thief
> 'Tis bold Barabbas we'd release".
> "And what of Christ?" 'Twas Pilate's voice.
> But still Barabbas was their choice.
> Indeed it was the people's right
> That at the Feast the governor might
> Release to them a prisoner
> Whom they demanded. He incurred
> Their favor when with feeble sway
> He gave them Christ the King to slay.
> And bold Barabbas, he was free,
> While justice waits eternity
> To all its recompense to bring
> The maddened mob who killed a King.[2]

The Prince of glory died. He died unknown, except by the few who had grasped the truth that the centurion exclaimed in consternation at the cross, "Truly this was the Son of God" (Matt. 27:54). The prophecy had been fulfilled, and Isaiah's

---

[2] Douglas Vickers, "Barabbas", lines 1-14.

anticipation, that "he bore the sin of many" (Is. 53:12), had been realized. Our Lord's own declaration that "the Son of man came to give his life a ransom for many" (Mark 10:45), had come to its consummation.

Jesus the Christ was unique among men. The testimony of the soldiers who failed in their mission blazons the truth. The Christ, the arresting teacher of Galilee, was unique in his person, in the messianic mission he came to accomplish, and in what he said as he fulfilled that eternally ordained assignment. "There was no other good enough to pay the price of sin", as the hymnwriter has put it. "He only could unlock the gate of heaven and let us in".[3]

The call to belief

But we stay for the moment with the gracious words of the Lord of heaven who dwelt for a time among men. His ministry began with a call to repentance. In that again, he "spoke as never man spoke". Here the Son of God speaks in the language of men with a divine insight into the human condition. The gospel of Matthew records that following his baptism and his temptation in the wilderness Jesus began to preach. With a bluntness and economy of statement, Matthew states that "From that time Jesus began to preach, and to say, Repent, for the kingdom of heaven is at hand" (Matt. 4:17). The call to repentance establishes the meaning and purpose of his coming. He came as the Lamb of God, John observes, "to take away the sin of the world" (John 1:29). The promise that Abraham had given to his son Isaac on that fateful occasion in the land of Moriah had been fulfilled: "God will provide himself a lamb" (Gen. 22:8). Christ came that he might "save his people from their sins" (Matt. 1:21), that by his obedience he might satisfy the demands of the law of God against those he came to redeem. He calls his people to repentance and to newness of life in trust in him. The Scriptures are eloquent on the meaning and purpose of that

---

[3] From the hymn, "There is a green hill far away", by Cecil Frances Alexander, 1848.

divinely ordered mission and its covenantal objective.

The call to repentance with which Christ began his ministry stands at the very beginning of the meaning of the gospel. The apostles Peter, Paul, and John join their urgent appeals at that very point. In his magnificent sermon on the day of Pentecost, Peter had stated clearly the meaning of the work of Christ. He articulated that in terms of what God had ordained in his covenantal arrangements before the foundation of the world. It was what it was, he states, because it was established "by the determinate counsel and foreknowledge of God" (Acts 2:23). Peter responded to the Jews who were "pricked in their heart" with the simple declaration, "Repent, and be baptized every one of you in the name of Jesus Christ" (Acts 2:37-38).

Again Paul, in his discourse on Mars' hill, made it clear that "God now commandeth all men everywhere to repent" (Acts 17:30). In doing so, Paul was faithful to the command and the mandate that he had received at the time of his arrest on the Damascus road. The commission he received there from Christ was that he should go to the Gentiles "to open their eyes, and to turn them from darkness to light, and from the power of Satan unto God..." (Acts 26:18). And again in his response to king Agrippa, on his arraignment prior to his dispatch to Rome and to Caesar, Paul expanded the meaning of that commission. He stated again what his message was. It was that the Gentiles "should repent and turn to God" (Acts 26:20).

The apostle John reinforces the theme in a different context, one that will engage us again at length. In his first epistle his concern is that of the fellowship that can exist between God and the Christian believer. "If we walk in the light, as he is in the light, we have fellowship one with another" (1 John 1:7). The prospect in view at that point is that of fellowship between the Christian and God in his triune being and existence. But all of those high potentialities exist because, as John goes on to state and to underline, "the blood of Jesus Christ his Son cleanseth us from all sin" (1 John 1:7). Here again is the commanding fact. The thing that stood, and the thing that ever stands, between God and man is the sin into which, by Adam's fall and by its own deliberateness, the human race has descended. The cleavage and the dereliction that sin entailed was reparable only by the work of Christ.

John therefore goes on to say that "If we confess our sins, he is faithful and just to forgive us our sins ...and ... we have an advocate with the Father, Jesus Christ the righteous: And he is the propitiation for our sins" (1 John 1:9-2:2). The issue of paramount importance is that of the reality of sin and the remedy for it that God has provided in his Son. John's exposition brings into prominence again the need for repentance from sin.

That very call solicits from the human heart the commitment of saving faith in Christ. That faith involves the twofold elements of assent and trust. In saving faith the sinner gives his assent to what God has declared. He sees, with a clarity of vision that he once could never have imagined to be possible, his condition of guilt before the holiness and the righteous law of God. That guilt derives not only from the results of that first fall into sin by which Adam brought the race to destruction. The sinner knows, too, that he has, in his own conduct and throughout his life, turned his back in hatred upon God to whom he was obligated by virtue of his very creaturehood. He knows the burden of that guilt from which, apart from Christ, there is no escape.

Awakened now to his lost condition, the sinner sees and assents to the fact that God has provided in his Word the only real and true explanation of the condition that plagues him. Man apart from God is without any true explanation of himself. When at last he sees "the light of the knowledge of the glory of God in the face of Jesus Christ" (2 Cor. 4:6), he knows that only by obedience to the call to repentance that stands at the beginning of the gospel, and only then by committing his case to Christ, can he be saved. That, then, brings to expression the second element of saving faith. It is the element of trust in Christ as the only way of rescue and relief. The Lord of heaven, who in his human nature bore the penalty of our sin as our substitute and redeemer, is then seen as the only Savior.

The assurance of life

But what is the ground of assurance that a release from the

burden and guilt of sin is to be found in Christ? That assurance rests, the gospel declares, in the veracity of God himself. Let us observe the declaration to that effect that Christ himself has made. Let us recall, for this preliminary look at the meaning of life in him, three statements that he made, each in somewhat differing situations.

On a memorable occasion, when a multitude attended his teaching, he was concerned that they should be provided with food. But what could be done to satisfy the needs of five thousand men? The disciples were able to muster only "five barley loaves, and two small fishes" (John 6:9). But the sequel is familiar. Following our Lord's miracle of the feeding of the five thousand, his departure, his walking on the sea, and his ministry to the crowd again on the following day at Capernaum, he gave that immortal discourse in which he declared himself to be the bread of life. The people did not understand him at that time. They thought that he spoke of bread because he had fed them with bread on the previous day. But his meaning was much more profound. He was the very bread of life in the sense that, as he said, "he that cometh to me shall never hunger; and he that believeth on me shall never thirst" (John 6:35).

What remarkable new thing is this? Here is one who is speaking as never man spoke, telling us that he is not speaking of bread such as Moses had given to the people in earlier times. He is saying that trust in him, belief in him as the substitute Savior of sinners, is the only way to life. Only in that, he is saying, is there entrance to life eternal. But many, of course, did not believe. We have already seen their unbelief at work and their failure to grasp and understand who it was they were privileged to hear. The very words of life evaded them. Again the Savior of men was a man of sorrows. Again he was rejected. Again he had cause to reflect on the meaning of his mission, in the face of the discouragement and the obtuseness and perversity of his hearers.

But on that occasion our Lord responded to the discouraging reception of the crowd with a statement rich with eternal significance, one which has meant the assurance of life to thousands since. "You do not believe", he said in effect, "though you have seen me, but there is an eternal truth that I declare to you. It establishes and vindicates the whole of my mission and all that I am saying". And he stated that ineradicable reality, as John records it in his gospel, "All that the Father giveth me shall come to me; and him that cometh to me I will in no wise cast out" (John 6:37).

The second occasion we refer to from the ministry of our Lord again finds him confronting the discouragement of the unbelief of his hearers. We may look simply at the prayer he offered on that occasion. "I thank thee, O Father, Lord of heaven and earth, because thou hast hid these things from the wise and prudent, and hast revealed them unto babes. Even so, Father: for so it seemed good in thy sight" (Matt. 11:25-26). And then we hear from the divine lips of the Savior the gracious words that have rung true through centuries since. We have heard them often. And often our heedless, impatient anxiety has clouded their meaning. But to sin-burdened souls they resonate in responsive chords. There is rescue and relief in their salvific assurance. "Come unto me", the Master said, "all ye that labour and are heavy laden, and I will give you rest. Take my yoke upon you, and learn of me; for I am meek and lowly in heart; and ye shall find rest unto your souls" (Matt. 11:28-29).

In that promise and invitation, the sin-burdened and the heavy laden have found relief. The burden of the search for the meaning of life; the burden of the search for relief from the guilt of sin; the burden that renders heavy laden the wandering task to discover the explanation of oneself and his real condition; these cry out for relief. They find in Christ the only response that offers peace to the wretched soul. The cross of Christ is the place for the lifting of burdens. It alone is the refuge for sinners.

We hear on a third occasion the words of Christ that speak their volumed eloquence to burdened souls. It is the occasion on which he declared that he was the good shepherd who came to lay down his life for his sheep. The details are familiar, and John has recorded them at length in the tenth chapter of his gospel. We cull from that discourse only one statement that again assures us of the ground of our security in belief in Christ and trust in him. "I am not as the thief or the hireling who comes to steal", Christ says. "But I am the good shepherd and know my sheep", and "I am come that they might have life, and that they might have it more abundantly" (John 10:10-14).

Here the invitation of Christ contains a promise of life that could be multiplied in a thousand ways on the basis of the Scriptural data. Indeed, the canon of Scripture closes, in the final chapter of the book of Revelation, with the same invitation and promise, "Let him that is athirst come. And whosoever will, let him take the water of life freely" (Rev. 22:17). "Come unto me those who are heavy laden", Christ is here saying, "and you will find rest in me. If you come, and in coming trust in me, I will never cast you out. For I myself have come into the world that those who trust in me might have life more abundantly". What gracious words from the lips of the Son of God and the Savior of men.

Effectual calling

In all of those ringing declarations we hear the call of the evangel. The promise of God is fulfilled in Christ who came to give new life to those who trust in him. But clearly, not all those to whom the call to repentance comes do, in fact, turn to Christ and believe. Why, we ask, should that be so?

The answer can be stated briefly. The blindness that inhibits belief and commitment to Christ is due to the state of sin to which, as a result of Adam's Fall, we had all been reduced. That state of sin involves the blindness of mind (2 Cor. 4:4), the perversity of heart (Jer. 17:9) that makes the sinner a God-hater (Rom. 1:30), and the enslavement of the will that so orders the faculties of the soul that it is not possible for the sinner, apart from the revivifying grace of God, to turn to Christ.

Did not our Lord say clearly to Nicodemus that unless one is born again he cannot see the kingdom of God (John 3:3)? Did he not make it clear, in his magnificent discourse on his identity as the bread of life, that "No man can come to me, except the Father which hath sent me draw him" (John 6:44)? The reality is that in his natural state the individual is the captive slave of sin. For "whosoever committeth sin", Christ explained to the Jews, "is the servant of sin" (John 8:34). Or as an alternative translation has it, the individual is the "slave" of sin. The apostle Paul made the same point in his closely reasoned letter to the Romans.

35

"Know ye not", he says, "that to whom ye yield yourselves servants to obey, his servants ye are ... whether of sin unto death, or of obedience unto righteousness" (Rom. 6:16).

How, then, can any be saved? The answer is that only those will turn to Christ in saving faith in whom the Holy Spirit of God has created that new life of which our Lord has spoken. The renewing, regenerating, re-creating work of the Spirit in the soul, carrying along with it the gifts of repentance and faith, is the necessary antecedent of the sinner's turning to Christ and to the refuge of the cross.

The older theologians frequently discussed that important work of regeneration under the heading of "effectual calling", meaning by that the sovereign, unsolicited, effective call of God to the human soul that is otherwise lost and captive in sin. The authors of the *Westminster Shorter Catechism* stated that "Effectual calling is the work of God's Spirit, whereby, convincing us of our sin and misery, enlightening our minds in the knowledge of Christ, and renewing our wills, he doth persuade and enable us to embrace Jesus Christ, freely offered to us in the gospel".[4]

What more recent theology has referred to as "Regeneration" was in that way subsumed by older theologians under the heading of effectual calling. In fact, it has since been a matter of debate whether effectual calling and regeneration are to be adequately understood as synonymous or interchangeable terms so far as biblical doctrine is concerned. The question has been raised as to which work of God in the human soul is to be understood as prior. Does a proper construction of Scriptural doctrine require it to be said that effectual calling is prior to regeneration, or is it to be understood that regeneration, the creation of new life in the soul, precedes effectual calling? The debate has been addressed by John Murray[5] who has concluded that while no serious defect of doctrine is involved in which of the two possible orderings is preferred in doctrinal formulation, there is reason to judge that effectual calling is prior to

---

[4] *Westminster Shorter Catechism*, Question 31.
[5] John Murray, *Redemption: Accomplished and Applied*, Grand Rapids: Eerdmans, 1955, 97-133

regeneration and saving faith.

Some preliminary comments can be made on the doctrinal issues that are involved. First, when the parlous and perilous state of the natural, unregenerate soul in its captivity to sin is understood, the need for the sovereign, effective call of God to the soul becomes clear. Regeneration should be seen as standing in an intermediate place between the call of God on the one hand and the effective response of the sinner on the other. Many are called, we are told, but only few respond in saving faith.

Secondly, if the call of God to the sinner is to be understood as an "effectual" call, it cannot be said to be complete or effective until the response of the sinner is involved. It might properly be said, therefore, that the debate as to which is to be understood as prior in time, effectual calling or regeneration, is not completely to the point. Rather, we might regard regeneration as a necessary constituent element of the overall process of God's effectual calling. In that manner, the sovereignty of God in the call of the sinner to Christ is preserved in accordance with biblical doctrine, understanding that those are called in that effective sense whom God the Father chose to eternal salvation before the foundation of the world. For that is at the heart of the apostle's summary when he observed that "Whom he [God] did foreknow, he also did predestinate to be conformed to the image of his Son ... Moreover whom he did predestinate, them he also called; and whom he called, them he also justified; and whom he justified, them he also glorified" (Rom. 8:29-30). And at the same time, the doctrine is preserved that those who are in that effective manner called are precisely those who, before the foundation of the world, God the Father gave to the Son to redeem. "Thine they were", Christ prayed to the Father in his high priestly prayer on the night on which he was betrayed, "and thou gavest them me" (John 17:6).

These issues will be explored more fully when we see the meaning of God's promise that comes to us through the prophet Jeremiah, "I will give them an heart to know me" (Jer. 24:7). Life in Christ is the fulfillment of that promise of God to his people whom the Son of God and the Savior of men redeemed. We shall see that God is sovereign in all of the processes and benefits of the Christian life. It is he who makes Christ to be unto us "wisdom, and righteousness, and sanctification, and redemption" (1 Cor. 1:30).

We begin immediately in the following chapter to consider, against the perspectives we have now established, the doctrine of the being and the holiness of God, his existence in eternity and, in the Person of his Son, in time. It is to him that all of the parts and aspects of our salvation sovereignly belong.

3

The Holiness of God

The categories of Creation, Sin and the Fall, and Redemption radiate their meaning to the areas of Christian doctrine that we shall consider in this and the following four chapters. Behind the doctrine of creation stand the being and majesty, the sovereignty and the purpose of the Creator-redeemer God. We have looked in the preceding chapter at the invitation to life in him that God has given through his Son. We have heard his words of compassion and insight into the human condition. We have heard him speak as never man has spoken. We have known that only in trusting him could we find the entrance to life eternal. We have turned to him from the broken cisterns that failed us in our search for the water of life. The conviction and awareness has dawned that behind the divine redemptive purpose, and behind the determinate council of the Godhead that projected its objectives into the history of a fallen race, stands the holiness of God. We turn now to reflect on what it is that our arrest by the conviction of God's holiness implies.

In this and the following chapter we shall look at some aspects of the manner in which God has made his self-disclosure to us. He is "infinite, eternal, and unchangeable", the *Westminster Catechism* states, "in his being, wisdom, power, holiness, justice, goodness, and truth".[1] Our conviction of the holiness of God

---

[1] *Westminster Shorter Catechism*, Question 4.

leads us to an awareness of his essential character and being. He exists in eternity and, in the Person of his Son, in time. The consideration of the love of God for sinners opens for us the remarkable reality that God who created time entered into time, became man for fallen men, in the Person of his Son.

The person whom God has called to himself, the heart that knows God, knows something of the holiness of God. For it is the awakening awareness of the holiness of God that clarifies the meaning of sin and turns the sinner to the cross of Christ. Nothing conducts us more effectively to the meaning of the gospel than the perception of the holiness of God. In that perception the meaning of redemption comes to its sharpest focus.

The apostle John, in his first epistle, provides three propositions which, taken together, explain and expand the meaning of redemption. His propositions clarify what redemption means, both in its original process and in its significance for the Christian's life. First, John sets down at the beginning of his letter what is always the first statement of the gospel. "God is light, and in him is no darkness at all" (1 John 1:5). Second, he goes on to explain the meaning of the love of God for his people that set redemption's course. "God sent his Son to be the propitiation for our sins" (1 John 4:10). And third, the possibility of fellowship with God is contemplated as the end and objective of the redemption that God provided. "If we walk in the light, as he is in the light, we have fellowship one with another, and the blood of Jesus Christ his Son cleanseth us from all sin" (1 John 1:7). "Truly", John says, "our fellowship is with the Father, and with his Son Jesus Christ" (1 John 1:3). The possibility of that fellowship is embedded in the fact that "the blood of Christ cleanseth us".

These three propositions state that, first, whatever is to be said about the gospel of redemption and the knowledge of God is to be said against the initial awareness that God is a holy God; second, knowledge of him and fellowship with him is the Christian's highest good; and third, the meaning of the gospel and the possibility of fellowship with God turns on the propitiatory, substitutionary work of Christ.

We know, on the basis of the Scriptural record, that by his

initial sin Adam forfeited the fellowship with God that he had enjoyed. The Scripture records that as the curse of death fell because of sin, God "drove out the man" (Gen. 3:24). God drove him out, not only from the garden and from his paradisaic state, but from communion and fellowship with God. He was driven out from the blessed and beatific relation he had enjoyed. Now in delinquency and dereliction, he stood in need of one principal thing if he was again to enjoy the fellowship with God for which he was created. By some means a reconciliation with God must be established. A way of a renewal and a rediscovery of peace with God must be found. It was the blood of Christ that alone could atone for sin and open that way of reconciliation. It is Christ who is, John declared, the propitiation for our sin. The coming of Christ was necessary because no other way, consistent with the justice and holiness of God, could have been advanced to accomplish the end in view.

Let it be granted, then, that following the Fall, the curse of malediction that was inherent in the creation covenant fell with the weight of divine justice and judgment. When Adam sinned, moreover, that judgment fell on all those for whom he had stood as the federal head (Rom. 5:12-21). Let it be granted that by virtue of the divine wrath against sin and the sinner a way of reconciliation was necessary. Let it be granted, further, that the coming of the Son of God and the shedding of his blood was necessary in order to open the way of reconciliation and fellowship with God. All of that leaves open the question as to why the propitiation effected by the Son of God was in fact necessary. Why, in other words, was the wrath of God directed against the sinner and his sin?

The answer to that question returns us to the prefatory statement of the first epistle of John. He sets his entire argument there against the background of the statement that "God is light, and in him is no darkness at all" (1 John 1:5). God, it is being said, is holy. In John's summary statement that "God is light" he is saying that God is a holy God. He is sovereign, eternal, unchangeable. He called all of created reality into being by the word of his power. His grace upholds and sustains and preserves that reality. This he does in order that he might thereby be glorified. But what the apostle places before us is not only a statement of God's power and sovereignty and purpose and grace. These are very much implicit in the context that John establishes. But what he insists upon is something that shatters our complacent carelessness and destroys every possible thought of our own autonomy. He says, in profound but economical language, that God is light. God is holy. If we seek, then, for what lay behind the need for the propitiation provided by the Son of God, we find it in the fact that God is a holy God. The wrath of God against sin and the sinner proceeds from the holiness of God.

Here, of course, is the very heart of our confession. The declaration of the gospel is properly occupied with the proclamation of the love of God. The divine declaration of that love lies patent on the very surface of Scripture and is spread generously and liberally across it for all to see. "God so loved the world, that he gave his only begotten Son" (John 3:16). But the love of God is understandable for John, in the sense that its brilliance and extent and compass are displayed, when it is seen as expressed in the action of God that lies at the heart of redemption's plan. The love of God is displayed in the fact that God himself provided a way whereby his wrath against sin could be appeased and his justice satisfied. He himself set forth the necessary propitiation. The meaning of John's statement to that effect is that God set his love upon those who were the objects of his wrath. The love of God is coordinate with his wrath against sin and the sinner. Displayed as an aspect of the character of God, his wrath is not inconsistent with his love. Love is explained, in this remarkable case of the love of God for sinners, only as it is seen against the holy wrath of God.

The wrath of God and the love of God are coordinate aspects of the holiness of God. The wrath of God against sin proceeds from the holiness of God. It is a necessary expression of that holiness, apart from which God would not be God. Stephen Charnock, a distinguished theologian-scholar of the mid-seventeenth century, has addressed that relationship at length in his classic *The Existence and Attributes of God*. "God is so holy", Charnock observes, "that he cannot possibly approve of any evil ... but doth perfectly abhor it". "Thou art of purer eyes than to behold evil, and canst not look on iniquity" (Hab. 1:13).[2] The love of God that, as Paul observed, "constrains us" (2 Cor. 5:14), acquires its brilliance in coordination with the wrath of God against which it is displayed.

What, then, is the ground on which fellowship with God is again possible? The answer is the blood of Christ his Son (1 John 1:7). But why was the shedding of the blood of Jesus Christ necessary in order to provide the ground of redemption and fellowship? The answer is that it was necessary as a propitiation of the wrath of God against sin, and that in an expression of his love God provided that propitiation in the death of his Son (1 John 4:10). Further, then, why did the wrath of God thus come to expression against sin, and what is it that provides the explanation of that divine wrath? The answer is that the wrath of God against sin is the necessary expression of his own holiness (1 John 1:5).

In short, the blood of Christ was the necessary propitiation of the wrath of God that was inherent in the eternal reality of his holiness. It is in that final sense that John sees the necessity, at the beginning of his epistle, to set forth clearly and determinatively the reality of the holiness of God.

Holiness and the attributes of God

What do we mean by the Christian perception of the holiness of God? Let us ask initially a related question. What is the relation between the holiness of God and the attributes of God? Or the question may be posed by asking what relation exists between the holiness and the *other* attributes of God? That raises the further question of whether it is appropriate to conceive of the holiness of God as one among a number of his attributes. If, in our doctrinal construction, we regard the holiness of God as one among a number of his attributes, the question may properly arise as to whether an ordering, or in some sense a priority, should be seen to exist among those attributes.

---

[2] Stephen Charnock, *The Existence and Attributes of God*, Minneapolis: Klock and Klock Christian Publishers [1797] Reprint 1977, 455.

There is a long and distinguished tradition in theology that appears to place the holiness of God as one among a longer list of divine attributes. We have already noted that tradition exemplified at the beginning of the *Shorter Catechism* attached to the seventeenth-century *Westminster Confession*. It states that "God is a Spirit, infinite, eternal, and unchangeable in his being, wisdom, power, **holiness**, justice, goodness, and truth".[3] The question we are now asking, however, is what we are to understand as the place or the vision of the holiness of God. The statement of the Catechism does bring to proper emphasis the reality that God is infinite, eternal, and unchangeable in his being and in all of his attributes. He is infinite, eternal, and unchangeable in himself, in his being, and in his wisdom, his power, his holiness, and his justice, goodness, and truth.

In what is thereby said regarding the infinity, eternity, and immutability of God, we are aware of his possession of incommunicable attributes. They are his attributes which, by virtue of his Godness and the Creator-creature relation that he has established, cannot be communicated to his rational creatures whom he created in his image. But his attributes of wisdom, power, holiness, justice, goodness, and truth are communicable. According to his sovereign good pleasure and in the degree that he purposes, God communicates those attributes to his people. They determine the meaning and the purpose of the Christian life.

For we know that by the grace and the purpose of God, Christ is made unto us "wisdom, and righteousness, and sanctification, and redemption" (1 Cor. 1:30). The Christian, Paul further observes, has "the mind of Christ" (1 Cor. 2:16), he begins to think Christ's thoughts after him, and in his intellective life and in his behavior he is progressively conformed to the pattern of holiness in Christ. Similarly, God works in the lives of his people a measure of holiness, goodness, and truth. God creates in his people a power by which they can again, redeemed as they are from the disabilities of Adam's Fall, direct their lives to the glory of God. For this, the Catechism concludes in its very first question, is "the chief end of man", or the principal purpose and

---

[3] *Westminster Shorter Catechism*, Question 4.

objective of his life, "to glorify God and to enjoy him forever".

But as we consider explicitly the holiness of God and his attributes, we avoid the mistake of imagining that we are speaking of a list or a string of attributes or character qualifications in God that stand independently of each other.[4] Rather, we understand that all of God's attributes are interdependent and interrelated. Each of his attributes is involved with all other attributes in the unity of his essence. His attributes are the fullness of his essence coming to expression in his self-revelation. God's holiness, distinguishing as the apostle John has already stated it, God's essential being, determines the meaning of all of his attributes. That means that his wisdom is a holy wisdom. His power, justice, and goodness are holy. And his wrath against sin and the sinner is a holy wrath.

When that is said, however, there remains the twofold question: First, are we to conceive of the holiness of God as one among a series of characteristics that can be properly attributed to him; and second, in what does the holiness of God consist, and what are we to understand by our usage of the highly meaningful terms and designations we have already employed?

To ask these questions is to inquire what God has revealed to us in the self-disclosure he has made. On the basis of that disclosure, God's holiness is to be seen, not in terms of a separable aspect or attribute of his character, but as an all-comprehending description of the transcendence or separateness of God as God himself. The essential meaning of holiness, or the essential nature of the Godhead to which our thought is turned repeatedly by the Scriptures, is that of God's separateness. That truth can be put in other terms by referring to God's transcendence. That means that he exists before all of reality external to himself, that he is the source and origin and Creator of all reality, that he alone, as Paul stated it in his letter to Timothy, "hath immortality" (1 Tim. 6:16).

The separateness or transcendence of God, as that directs our thought to his holiness, may be contemplated under the threefold

---

[4] See Geerhardus Vos, *Biblical Theology: Old and New Testaments*, Grand Rapids: Eerdmans, 1948, 257ff., 268; L. Berkhof, *Systematic Theology*, Grand Rapids: Eerdmans, New Edition, 1996, 73.

THE FRACTURE OF FAITH

headings of, first, his separateness from all of reality, sentient and inert, external to himself; second, the respect in which his self-knowledge, purposes, and designs are consistent with the unity or oneness and the perfections of his character in which he exists as God; and third, the implications of his separateness for the complacence or pleasure with which he looks on what, external to himself, conforms to his own character. God looks with satisfaction on what conforms to his own perfections and righteousness, and he looks with displacence or abhorence upon what does not.

Stephen Charnock, in his "Discourse upon the holiness of God", has contemplated God as "glorious in holiness" (Ex. 15:11). "Holiness", Charnock says, "is a glorious perfection belonging to the nature of God; hence he is in Scripture styled the Holy One, the Holy One of Jacob, the Holy One of Israel, and oftener entitled Holy than Almighty, and set forth by this part of his dignity more than by any other. This is more affixed as an epithet to his name than any other; you never find it expressed, his *mighty name* or his *wise name*, but his *great name*, and most of all his *holy name*. This is his greatest title of honour; in this doth the majesty and venerableness of his name appear".[5] Charnock continues, "the nature of God cannot rationally be conceived" without holiness. Of all the characteristics or aspects of the Godhead, or of all of the respects in which God has revealed himself, "none is sounded out so loftily, with such solemnity, and so frequently by angels that stand before his throne, as this. Where do you find any other attribute trebled in the praises of it, as this? 'Holy, holy, holy, is the Lord of hosts; the whole earth is full of his glory' (Is. 6:3); and 'the four beasts rest not day and night saying Holy, holy, holy, Lord God Almighty' (Rev. 4:8)". Charnock continues: "Do you hear in any angelical song any other perfection of the divine nature thrice repeated? Where do we read of the crying out Eternal, eternal, eternal; or Faithful, faithful, faithful, Lord God of hosts!"[6]

By his holiness God has sworn his fidelity to his promises. "Once have I sworn *by my holiness*", he has said (Ps. 89:35). And

---

[5] Stephen Charnock, op. cit., 448.
[6] Ibid., 449.

again, the prophet Amos declares that "The Lord God hath sworn *by his holiness*" (Amos 4:2). God swears by the very Godness of his essential being. But we see, in these Scriptural statements, that it is his holiness that is advanced as the essential descriptive character of his being. That very aspect of God's relation to men, his swearing by his own holy name, came to focus in the initial covenant that he made with Abraham. When, as recorded in the fifteenth chapter of Genesis, God required Abraham to divide the animals at the inception of the covenant, God himself moved between the parts of animal flesh. He did so as a sign of the self-malediction that he warranted to himself, in the event that he should not be faithful to the promises of the covenant he gave to Abraham. God was there swearing that for him to be unfaithful would involve the surrender of his Godness.[7] That oath of faithfulness is brought before us, explicitly and articulately, in the letter to the Hebrews. The writer says there that "when God made promise to Abraham, because he could swear by no greater, he sware by himself" (Heb. 6:13). God therein "confirmed the immutability of his counsel by an oath" (Heb. 6:17).

These Scriptures make clear that the holiness of God is descriptive of the essence of God as he exists in himself. His holiness is best understood, and the category of God's holiness is best assimilated into doctrinal statements, not by considering holiness along with, or in series with, or parallel to, other attributes. Rather, holiness is the biblical category or expression that presents to us what God essentially is. All of God's being and attributes are characterized by holiness. The love of God is a holy love. The wrath of God is a holy wrath. The truthfulness of God is a holy truthfulness. His justice is a holy justice. Holiness is the comprehensive and summary characterization of God as he has revealed himself. It takes up and informs and determines the meaning and character of all of his attributes.

We have observed, however, that God's holiness radiates its meaning in the threefold terms of his separateness, his self-consistency, and his complacence with righteousness or rectitude

---

[7] A discussion of God's covenantal swearing is contained in Douglas Vickers, *Christian Truth in Critical Times*, Philadelphia Skilton House Ministries, 1989, 80ff.

in his creatures. In a comparable way, the meaning of his holiness radiates his displeasure and abhorrence against their sin. These important terms can be considered further by contemplating the nature of, and the relation between, God's holiness and his righteousness.

Holiness and the Creator-creature analogy

The terms *holiness* and *righteousness* are frequently understood and employed imprecisely in Christian discussion. They are frequently, but somewhat improperly, used interchangeably. Let us begin our approach to the holiness and righteousness of God by looking at the fact and the expression of these characteristics in the Christian person. In doing so we are not committing the error of arguing from the nature and characteristics of man to the nature of God and to who and what he is or must be. On the contrary, our argument is in the opposite direction. We begin with the observations that follow precisely because man in his existence, and regenerate man in the character he possesses, is an analogue of God. It is because God is holy and righteous that we see the reflection or the analogy of his holiness and righteousness potentially displayed in the people whom he has redeemed.

Our argument at this point is similar to that envisaged by the writer to the Hebrews. Consider his statement that "almost all things are by the law purged with blood; and without shedding of blood there is no remission. It was therefore necessary that the patterns of things in the heavens should be purified with these; but the heavenly things themselves with better sacrifices than these" (Heb. 9:22-23). The writer is here pointing to the better sacrifice of Christ. In doing so, he argues that certain things and activities and procedures were "patterns of things in the heavens". Certain things were to be understood as analogical of the things that pertain to God, and the proper understanding of them directs our thought to the fuller understanding of God himself and his being and purposes.

In the case we have just noted, we may ask why it was necessary that, as the text has said, all things should be purged by blood. Perhaps another question will throw its light on the answer. Was the shedding of the blood of Christ necessary simply or only because the sacrifices in the earlier age that anticipated his own sacrifice involved the shedding of blood? Or does the true nature of the relations proceed in the opposite direction.

It was because it had been ordained from before the foundation of the world that Christ should die, that he should shed his blood, that blood must also be involved in the types that preceded him. The one true and final atonement for sins was established in the eternal counsel of God as involving, of necessity, the death, the shedding of blood, of the Son of God who would come into the world for that purpose. It was therefore appropriate and necessary that whatever ordinances anticipated his coming and his atonement should also involve the shedding of blood.

In a similar manner we may look at the question of holiness and righteousness in the people of God. Again, we do so not to argue from what is characteristic of men to what must be true of God. Rather, we observe at this point certain aspects of human life and experience in order that, recognizing them to be analogical of what is true in an infinitely greater sense of God, we may be guided in the statements we make about the character of God himself.

The designation of "holy", as applied to persons and things in the Scriptures, means essentially that they are set apart or separated or consecrated to God. They are designated "holy" because their relation to everything else in the world is essentially different from what it could be conceived to be if that designation did not apply. The notion of separation or separateness is the root meaning of the word that is translated as "holy". It is also the root of what is translated as saints, and it is frequently used in that latter sense as a designation of God's people. Paul employs precisely that word in his opening addresses, for example, in the letters to the Ephesians, Philippians, and Colossians. The Christians to whom he wrote were saints. They were holy before God, because by the sovereign power of the Spirit of God they had been separated from the world and from their Adamic heritage to be peculiarly God's people. In designating them as saints, or as holy, the apostle is not envisaging any particular degree of conformity to the righteousness of God to which they had been called. Their sainthood consisted simply in the fact that by God's design and purpose they had been set apart for him. It was true that they would grow progressively into closer conformity to God's holy law and his perfect righteousness. They would grow in sanctification. Indeed the root word that we are now concerned with as meaning "holy" is at the root also of the word "sanctification". It appears, for example, in the Pauline statement that "this is the will of God, even your sanctification" (1 Thess. 4:3).

The basic notion of separateness that lies at the root meaning of holiness has always characterized the people of God. In the terms of the earlier covenant that lay behind the theocracy of the Old Testament age, God instructed Moses to "speak unto the children of Israel ... ye shall be unto me a kingdom of priests, *an holy nation*" (Ex. 19:6). They were a holy nation because they had been sovereignly set apart for God. They were his chosen people, to whom his inscripturated law was given as a "schoolmaster" (Gal. 3:24) to keep them until Christ should come. Separated for God and his purposes, they would be preserved by the grace of that law in the midst of the universal darkness and ignorance that had descended on the world as a result of Adam's sin.

But the very same designation that was applied to the Israelites in the light of their place in the purpose of God was later used also to designate the church. The apostle Peter addressed the church by saying that "ye are a chosen generation, a royal priesthood, *an holy nation*, a peculiar people" (1 Peter 2:9). Here again the root meaning of the "holy" nation, the holiness of the people of God, is that they are separated unto God for his peculiar glory and purpose. That holiness, of course, has always been, and continues to be in the case of the New Testament church, a separation and a separateness for a special purpose. In the latter case Peter makes it clear that the objective in view was that the people "should show forth the praises of him who hath called you out of darkness into his marvellous light". That is precisely the same statement as Paul had made to the Colossians. God had made them "partakers of the inheritance of the saints", Paul states, employing again the same word as is used consistently to designate the "holy" (Col. 1:12). As did Peter, Paul continues at that point by observing that God "hath delivered us from the power of darkness, and hath translated us into the kingdom of his dear Son".

Granted, then, that in relation to God's people as individuals and as the church, the notion and the concept of holiness refers essentially to their separation from one state and condition and their consecration to another. The essential content of holiness, on the level on which we are now considering it, is that of separateness. In what way, can the same notion of separateness as intrinsic to the concept of holiness be carried over to the explanation of the holiness of God? The answer is that by it we are led to the recognition that separateness again defines the character of God. But that separateness exists in his primary and eternal self-existence and transcendence. He is transcendentally before all things. He has spoken into existence all of created reality. All that is and exists external to his Godhead exists by virtue of his creative act. It is impossible, therefore, that his own existence could be in any sense dependent for its definition and being upon anything external to himself. For he alone is the source of all that external reality.

We may put that in another way. When we say that the holiness of God exists primarily and essentially in his separateness, we are addressing what we may refer to as the ontological reality of God. We are acknowledging, then, as descriptive of the holiness of God, the fact that holiness is the Scriptural term that is employed to designate his essential being and his essential differentness from all else that exists. That is an expression in another sense of what has been referred to as the two-layer explanation of reality or being.[8] Our doctrine of being is the two-layer explanation that says, in the first place, that God is. It says secondly that all else exists separately from, and because of, and is dependent upon, God.

The self-existence of God in his eternal independence was, of course, the precise characterization that he gave to himself at the beginning. We recall his encounter with Moses at the burning bush, his arrest of Moses at that time and his appointing him to his unique task. In response to Moses' asking for his name, God

---

[8] See Cornelius Van Til, *The Defense of the Faith*, 23ff.

replied with the designation: "I am that I am". Moses was instructed to say to the children of Israel, "I am hath sent me unto you" (Ex. 3:14).

Holiness and righteousness

In God's self-disclosure his holiness is exhibited also in what we referred to as his consistency, or his self-consistency. Separateness and consistency together connote the holiness of God. We know on the basis of Scriptural testimony that not only is God by his creative word the source of all things and all life. We know also that by his works of providence he preserves and governs all that he has made. In this latter sense God is immanent, he works immanently in his creation. Our thought therefore moves to the immanent entry into our lives and our affairs, and into the history of the world, of the transcendent God. Paul observed to the Ephesians that God "worketh all things after the counsel of his own will" (Eph. 1:11); and in his claim of "all things" he included all that eventuates in the life histories of the creatures of God, as well as all that happens to and for his people in the design and accomplishment of their redemption. The *Westminster Catechism* again has judiciously observed that "God executeth his decrees in the works of creation and providence"; and it goes on to claim that "God's works of providence are, his most holy, wise, and powerful preserving and governing all his creatures, and all their actions".[9]

When we turn, then, to the aspect of God's holiness that we have referred to as his consistency, we are concerned with the fact that all of God's thoughts, designs, actions, expressions, and revelations are consistent, as to their character and intention, with the nature and being of God as he has declared himself to exist. "God is not a man, that he should lie", Moses declared (Num. 23:19), and Paul similarly grounded his proclamation of the gospel in the veracity of God. We have the hope of eternal life, Paul declared, "which God, that cannot lie, promised before the world began" (Titus 1:2). We have, further, an intimation of the consistency of God in the statement that Jesus Christ is "the same

---

[9] *Westminster Shorter Catechism*, Questions 8, 11.

yesterday, and today, and for ever" (Heb. 13:8), a statement that is reflected by James in his reference to "the Father of lights, with whom is no variableness, neither shadow of turning" (Jas. 1:17).

That brings into prominence the fact and the doctrine of the immutability of God. The *Westminster Catechism* enunciated the doctrine in the claim that not only is God "infinite and eternal", but that he is also "unchangeable". This attribute of immutability is an incommunicable attribute of the Godhead. His veracity, the Scriptures declare, is inviolable. It provides the ground of our reception of, and our trust in and dependence upon, his revelation. He swore his veracity to Abraham, and by virtue of our participation in the benefits of the covenant he made with Abraham, God has also sworn his faithfulness to us (Heb. 6:13,17; Gal. 3:16,29). We have his own declaration and confirmation of the promise at the close of the prophetic revelation, "I am the Lord, I change not" (Mal. 3:6).

The aspect of the character of God that is addressed in this manner may be referred to as his righteousness. What distinction, then, is to be drawn between God's holiness and his righteousness? Again it will be useful to refer to the distinction between holiness and righteousness in the creature, notably, of course, God's redeemed people. We may again see in them analogies of the holiness and the righteousness of God.

Holiness has been seen to refer to the essential nature or being or state and condition, of the regenerate person on the one hand, and of God as he exists in himself in his own eternal separateness. Righteousness, on the other hand, refers not primarily to a state or condition, but to action that accords with a prior condition. It is a characterization of action, which in turn is said to be righteous insofar as it is consistent with the inherently holy nature and quality or character of the one performing the act. One is holy by virtue of the state in which he exists. He is righteous because his actions are of a certain kind or character as seen in relation to that state.

In the case of the individual person, this important distinction is crystallized by saying that one is righteous if, and insofar as, his or her relation to the law of God is what it ought to be. Holding, then, to the notion that righteousness in its essential reference to action consists in conformity to law, the question arises whether we can similarly conceive of the righteousness of God as being related to law. The answer provides further light on the holiness of God that we have just considered.

In the first place, it follows from what has been said already that it is impossible that God could be, or could have been, subject to, or answerable to, a law external to or higher than himself. If the contrary were true, and if a law higher than God and external to him existed, then the god to whom reference was thereby made would not be the God who has revealed himself in the Scriptures. It would be a lesser god of human construction and imagination.

But consistency of definition, and the nature of the analogies that are now in view, require us to say that righteousness as it is ascribed to God continues to inhere in consistency to law. But the law that is thereby in view is the law of God's own being and perfections. It is simply, in other words, the fact that in all that he thinks and determines and wills and performs, God is faithful to himself and to the requirements of his own holiness and glory. That being so, his holy attributes of justice, power, and wisdom, and his holy love for sinners that is coordinate with his holy wrath against sin, are in no way violated. The apostle has made precisely that claim in his statement that God "cannot deny himself" (2 Tim. 2:13). God's determinations and actions are consistent with the immutability of his character. In all respects they accord with the excellence of virtue that resides in him.

Further aspects of the holiness of God

These, of course, are high themes, and our examination of them must remain suggestive and incomplete. We have approached the conception of the holiness of God by suggesting the threefold aspects of his separateness, his consistency, and his complacence with righteousness and abhorrence against sin. We have explored in this chapter something of the significance of the first two of these three aspects. But it is necessary to take account of further implications of all we have said or pointed to in connection with the separateness of God. The relation of God to time, to the temporal process that he created and into which he came for our redemption in the Person of his Son, is of primary importance for the understanding of biblical doctrine. In the next chapter, therefore, we shall consider the significance of the fact that while the creature's history, awareness, life experience, and knowledge are temporally bounded, the eternal God exists outside of time.

But also, we have not in this initial consideration of the holiness of God inspected the fuller meaning of the third of the three aspects of God's holiness, namely his abhorrence of, and his wrath against, sin. That, we have seen, made necessary the entire process of propitiation that is at the heart of the accomplishment of our redemption. We shall therefore return to that important relation when we consider in a later chapter the declaration of John's epistle that the love of God is declared and exhibited in the fact that he gave his Son to be the propitiation for our sins.

4

God in Eternity and Time

It would be a brave man or a fool who would propose to solve the mystery of time or of God in relation to time. We are engaged here in a very different task. The issues we shall raise in this chapter are related to the propositions we have observed in the first epistle of John. These are first, that God is a holy God; second, that his holiness has come to expression in his wrath against sin and has raised the need for the propitiatory offering of his Son; and third, that in making that propitiation it is the blood of Christ that cleanses us from sin.

The issues to which we turn in this chapter bear forcibly on the meaning of the gospel of redemption. They do this by virtue of the mystery of the incarnation that they involve. God, we shall endeavor to see a little more clearly, is outside of time, though it will be necessary to take at least a brief notice of the argument in contemporary Reformed-evangelical literature that dissents from the timelessness of God. In the incarnation of his Son, in the union in the divine Person of Christ of the human and divine natures, he entered into time. But this he did in a way that caused no rupture in the meaning of either eternity or time. The eternal and the temporal could not be commingled, or joined in a way that gave rise to a mixture of them that violated the one or the other. No greater fact or mystery challenges our contemplation than this, that God in his Son entered into time for our redemption.

Summary propositions

The propositions we shall look at briefly, though not in detail in the order in which we now summarize them, may be stated as follows. *First*, God is outside of time by virtue of his transcendent eternity and his aseity or his independent and underived, or uncaused, existence.

Second, God created time and thereby established a temporal structure and environment in which all of reality external to himself exists and has its history.

Third, God in his being and his knowledge, referring in that to his knowledge of himself and his knowledge of all that exists and that eventuates in created reality, is timeless.[1]

Fourth, there are, therefore, no successions of moments in the knowledge of God or in the being of God. While he has knowledge of sequences of time events[2] he does not know those

---

[1] See Robert L. Reymond, *A New Systematic Theology of the Christian Faith*, Nashville: Nelson, 1998, 172-77 for a dissent from the "timelessness" of God, and Cornelius Van Til's statement that "It [time] is God-created as a mode of finite existence", *Introduction to Systematic Theology*, Phillipsburg: Presbyterian and Reformed, 1974, 66. In his reliance on Dabney's *Lectures in Systematic Theology*, Grand Rapids: Zondervan [1878] 1975, Reymond does not acknowledge Dabney's distinction between God's "existence without succession ... existence not related to time" and "the divine consciousness of his own subsistence". See Dabney, op. cit., 39-40. But see this implied distinction in Reymond, op. cit. 176-77. He comments there on the "ontological" and the "epistemological" categories in terms of which reference is made to God. But Reymond has not confronted us with the "timeless self-conscious God" to whom Van Til illuminatingly refers in his classic discussion of the differences between Idealism and Theism (see Van Til's essay on "God and the Absolute" in his *Christianity and Idealism* [Phillipsburg: Presbyterian and Reformed, 1955, 22]). See also the reference to Dabney in note 2 below. It is relevant and salutary to consider Van Til's comment on the position taken by the Arminian theologian, Watson, "with respect to the knowledge that God has of temporal events". Van Til observes that "if we introduce time or succession of moments into the consciousness of God in order that we may understand how God is related to time we have to ask ourselves in turn how the consciousness of God is related to the being of God. Thus we should have to introduce succession of moments into the being of God", *The Defense of the Faith*, Phillipsburg: Presbyterian and Reformed, 1963, 35-36. See also n.8 below.

[2] That proposition might be considered in the light of the observation of Robert L. Dabney that "Since all God's knowledge is absolutely true to the

sequences sequentially. He therefore has no memory of what has been, in the sense of his having become aware of it, or expectation of his own future that he must wait to discover.

Fifth, God has nevertheless ordained becoming and the eventuation of history and the awareness of history in his creatures, and in the light of that he eventuates all historical sequences and outcomes by his works of providence.

Sixth, God has entered into time in the incarnation of his Son. Our redemption is played out within the orbit of temporal boundedness in which, by our natures and by the nature that he assumed in Christ, our existence and awareness are conditioned.

Seventh, by virtue of the nature of our existence as that is derived from God, it is impossible that we should transcend our finitude, and that we should ever acquire the incommunicable divine attributes of infinity, eternity, and immutability. Our existence in the eternal age of the kingdom of God will therefore continue to be a temporal existence.

The immortal God

Paul, in his letter to Timothy, doxologically ascribes honor and glory to "the only wise God ... the King eternal, immortal, invisible" (1 Tim. 1:17) And he focuses our thought on "the King of kings and Lord of lords; who only hath immortality ..." (1 Tim. 6:15-16). John Calvin, in his comment on the apostle's statement, directs us to the twelfth book of Augustine's *City of God*. Augustine had wrestled at length with the mystery of time. In his *Confessions* he addressed the question of the relation between time and eternity.[3] In *The City of God* Augustine sets the tone of his examination of these questions in a conclusion

---

actual realities known, wherever he knows one thing as destined to depend on another thing, there must be a case in which God *thinks a sequence*. Let the distinction be clearly grasped. The things are known to God as in sequence; but his own subjective act of thought concerning them is not a sequence". *Discussions: Evangelical and Theological*, London: Banner of Truth [1890] 1967, Vol. 1, 294. Cf. Jonathan Edwards' comment that "[T]here is no succession in God's knowledge", *The Freedom of the Will*, 144.

[3] Augustine, *Confessions*, Trans. H. Chadwick, Oxford: Oxford University Press, 1991, 229.

that echoes in the propositions we have advanced: "Accordingly we say that there is no unchangeable good but the one, true, blessed God; that the things which he made are indeed good because from Him, yet mutable because made not out of Him, but out of nothing".[4]

Our primary concern at this point is with the apostolic reference to God as the One "who only hath immortality". When we speak of the immortality of God we are taking up aspects of what we have referred to as his aseity. We mean by that that God is independent in his being and existence, and that his existence is not derived from any more ultimate cause than himself. God is, we say, uncaused. He is, as Paul remarked to the Colossians, "before all things" (Col. 1:17). But we do not mean by such a statement that God is before all things in a temporal sense. On the contrary, God is before all things because it is he who called all things into being and established the temporal structure of their existence. He is their cause.[5]

When we say that God alone has immortality we are directing our thought to two things. First, the immortality of God has reference not primarily to time and its possible ending or non-ending, but to a condition of God's existence outside of time. Second, God himself is accordingly the creator of the immortality which, as analogical of his own existence, he has bestowed on those of his creatures whom he has made in his image. For them the temporal process in which they exist will, in fact, be non-ending. The prefix "im" in immortality as it is here referred to God, a translation of the negating prefix "a" or alpha in the Greek text, is designed to convey our thought away completely

---

[4] Augustine, *The City of God*, Trans. Marcus Dods, New York: Modern Library, 1950, 381.

[5] The question of time has been addressed in characteristically expansive fashion by Francis Turretin, the distinguished theologian of Geneva in the early post-Reformation period, in his *Institutes of Elenctic Theology*. Trans. G.M. Giger, Ed. J.T. Dennison, Jr., Phillipsburg: P&R Publishing, 1992, Vol.1, 170-71. In the same volume, 202-204, Turretin discusses in an illuminating manner "The Eternity of God", and he raises there the question of God in relation to time. Turretin observes that "the eternal duration of God embraces indeed all time - the past, present, and future, but nothing in him can be past or future ... God is called 'the ancient of days' ... as before and more ancient than days themselves and the birth of time" (ibid., 203-204).

from the region in which mortality or death in time can be contemplated. Our contemplation of God, on the contrary, cannot legitimately raise the category of mortality in the sense that, in relation to him, the ending or non-ending of time could be contemplated as possible or not possible. The prefix has removed us completely from any such level of consideration. The awareness of God, as the apostle here directs us to it, has reference to a plane of God's existence that has nothing at all to do with the dimensions or possible structures, or the beginning or ending, of time.

The reality of God's immortality rests, in the second place, in the eternity of God, in the sense that only because God has, and is, life in himself can he be the giver of life to his creatures. "In him was life", John observes (John 1:4). Because God is himself uncaused life, he confers derivative, analogical life on his creatures. If it were necessary, on the other hand, to contemplate a possible beginning or ending of God and of the life of God, then no absolute being would exist, all would then be relative, meaning would have capitulated to contingency, and blank and brute chance would be king. The Scriptures stand against all such arguments.

God, the source of life, is life in himself, and he exists as the locus of all meaning and as the source of the possibility of all creaturely apprehension of meaning. God, the one personal, self-existent, supreme, gracious, and self-disclosing God, is our only absolute. As to our life, and the possibilities we have of temporal experiences, the apostle observes that "God made the world and all things therein, seeing that he is Lord of heaven and earth ... [and] in him we live, and move, and have our being" (Acts 17:24, 28). God is our ultimate cause. He is the ultimate environment in which we live and have our being. He is our ultimate authority.

We could speak of the immensity of God, and with Solomon we could acknowledge that "the heaven and heaven of heavens cannot contain thee" (1 Kings 8:27).[6] The same recognition of the

---

[6] The question of the immensity of God, along with that of other of the attributes of the divine essence, has been widely discussed in the theological literature. Accessible discussions are contained in L. Berkhof, *Systematic Theology*, Grand Rapids: Eerdmans, 4th ed., 1949, 60; W.G.T. Shedd,

transcendent being of God is reflected in the words of the Chronicler (2 Chron. 2:6). The prophet Isaiah takes up the theme of God's immensity and observes in the final chapter of his prophecy, "Thus saith the Lord, The heaven is my throne, and the earth is my footstool" (Is. 66:1). Again, Jeremiah conveys to us the divine self-disclosure, "Can any hide himself in secret places that I shall not see him? saith the Lord. Do not I fill heaven and earth? saith the Lord" (Jer. 23:24).

The omniscience, the omnipresence, and the omnipotence of God are thus brought clearly before us. They are contemplated also in that magnificent prayer of David: "Whither shall I go from thy spirit? Or whither shall I flee from thy presence? If I ascend up into heaven, thou art there: if I make my bed in hell, behold, thou art there. If I take the wings of the morning, and dwell in the uttermost parts of the sea; even there shall thy hand lead me, and thy right hand shall hold me" (Ps. 139:7-10).[7]

But a realization of the immensity, the omniscience, and the omnipresence of God acquires its meaning because God as he exists in himself and orders all things by his power is outside of, and is independent of, the time and the temporal processes that he has created. Daniel the prophet has glimpsed this in his claim that God "changeth the times and the seasons" (Dan. 2:21). God orders the very passing of time and the structure of its events. This he does because he is himself the designer and creator of time. He is the originator and architect of it, and he is not himself conditioned by it. He himself exists in his uncaused eternity outside of, and apart from, time.

John the apostle, on the isle of Patmos, has reported a significant statement by the angel who visited him. "The angel sware by him that liveth for ever and ever ... that there should be time no longer" (Rev. 10:5-6). This statement regarding the cessation of time undoubtedly refers to the ending of the afflictions of the church that occupied much of the revelation to John, or to the point in time at which the predictions reported in that book would be fulfilled. But we may see in this statement

Dogmatic Theology, 3 Vols., Grand Rapids: Zondervan, n d., Vol.1, 339; Francis Turretin, op. cit., Vol.1, 196-201.
[7] See the very valuable discussion of this Psalm of David in E.J. Young, *Psalm 139: A devotional & expository study*, London: Banner of truth, 1965.

THE FRACTURE OF FAITH

also a pointedness in the apposition of the "liveth for ever and ever" in reference to God and the "time no longer" in reference to the history of the world. Here we have, in an anthropomorphic reference to the existence of God, a statement that the "for ever and ever" of God is entirely outside of the very time lapse and process in which the history of men and the world is being played out, and which God in his sovereignty orders.

We may note briefly the argument of Augustine on this point. In his contemplative address to God Augustine argues: "How could those countless ages have elapsed when you, the Creator, in whom all ages have their origin, had not yet created them? What time could there have been that was not created by you? ... You are the Maker of all time. If then, there was any time before you made heaven and earth ... you must have made that time, for time could not elapse before you made it ... Furthermore, although you are before time, it is not in time that you precede it. If this were so, you would not be before all time ... Your years neither go nor come, but our years pass and others come after them ... Your years are completely present to you all at once ... Your years are one day, yet your day does not come daily but is always today ... Your today is eternity. And this is how the Son, to whom you said 'I have begotten you this day', was begotten co-eternal with yourself. You made all time; you are before all time, and the 'time', if such we may call it, when there was no time was not time at all".[8]

---

[8] Augustine, *Confessions*, Penguin edition, 1961, 262-63. The contemporary British philosopher, Paul Helm, has addressed the question of God in eternity and time in an illuminating way in *Eternal God: A Study of God without Time*, Oxford: Clarendon Press, 1988. Helm, who presents his work as controverting the positions of an "analytic philosophy of religion" notes that "with few exceptions philosophers of religion in this tradition are united in dismissing the idea of God's timeless eternity". Helm observes that "The classical Christian theologians, Augustine of Hippo, say, or Aquinas or John Calvin, each took it for granted that God exists as a timelessly eternal being. They accepted it as an axiom of Christian theology that God has no memory, and no conception of his own future, and that he does not change, although he eternally wills all changes, even becoming, when incarnate in the Son, subject to humiliation and degradation". xi-xii. Contra Helm, and against such reformed theologians as Charles Hodge, Robert L. Reymond, in his *A New Systematic Theology of the Christian Faith*, states that "I remain unconvinced ... that God's eternality necessarily entails the quality of supratemporality or

God exists, Augustine acknowledges, in an eternal present. There is no before and after in his being and self-realization, no memory of what has been, and no waiting for what is to come.

The knowledge of God

When we refer to the knowledge of God, we mean the knowledge that God has, first, of himself, and secondly, of reality external to himself. The nature of God's knowledge is determined by the nature of his essence and being. We have just observed that God as he has revealed himself exists in a timeless eternal present. There is no succession of passing moments that determines his being. It follows, therefore, that there is similarly no succession of moments that determines his knowledge. God knows himself in one single eternal act of knowing.[9]

That is confirmed by his self-designation as the "I am". God did not wait, and in his timeless being he could not wait, for any development or events or awarenesses to provide for him an understanding of himself. God did not wait to discover any aspect of himself or the meaning and character and potential of any of his attributes. If we concluded to the contrary, we should be denying the being of God as we have already understood it. We should thereby reduce God from the level of being to that of becoming. We would then no longer be speaking of the God of the Scriptures.

That leads to a corresponding conclusion regarding the knowledge that God possesses of men and things and of created reality and their histories. Again we must conclude that God

---

timelessness" (xxi). (See ibid., 173ff. for Reymond's comment on Dabney and Hodge). The view of Van Til on this important question is implied in his statement that "Time ... is God-created as a mode of finite existence", *An Introduction to Systematic Theology*, (Phillipsburg: Presbyterian and Reformed Publishing Company, 1974), 66. This and other aspects of Van Til's apologetic are discussed insightfully and extensively in Greg L. Bahnsen, *Van Til's Apologetic: Readings and Analysis*, (Phillipsburg: P&R Publishing, 1998), passim.

[9] See the discussion of the knowledge of God in Cornelius Van Til, *The Defense of the Faith*, 31ff. See also Cornelius Van Til, *A Christian Theory of Knowledge*, Phillipsburg: P&R Publishing, 1969, passim.

knows all things in one eternal act of knowing. In this, of course, lies the essential difference between the what and the how of man's knowledge on the one hand, and God's knowledge on the other. Christian philosophers have discussed at length whether the difference between God's knowledge and man's knowledge is essentially qualitative or quantitative. A qualitative difference exists because the relationships that determine the meaning of the facts are fully defined in the mind of God, but are less than comprehensively conceivable for man.[10]

That long and important discussion can in a sense be reduced to a recognition of the facts that we have just adduced. The point of most basic importance is that man's knowledge is knowledge within, and is structured by, a temporal process. God's knowledge, on the other hand, is, for all the reasons we have seen, not temporal at all. God, we have said, knows all things in one eternal act of knowing. God does not know as the result of a process of investigation. He does not, and could not, wait to discover. He does not hold, therefore, any expectation of possibilities as to what might or might not eventuate.

The Scriptural data that bear on the point are expansive. They do not call for extensive review. "Known unto God are all his works from the beginning of the world", James declared at the Council of the church at Jerusalem (Acts 15:18), though variations of reading and textual difficulties do exist at that point of the text.[11] But the truth of the statement turns on the predestinating foreordination of God whereby God "worketh all things after the counsel of his own will" (Eph. 1:11). Somewhat more expansively, the purpose of God, in the predestination, calling, justification, and glorification of his elect, is laid out in the classic Pauline passage (Rom. 8:28f.) that recognizes all of God's eventuation of the histories of his people as suspended on his foreknowledge and purpose.

God knows all things, not only as to his own being, but as to the history of created reality that he has purposed and that he eventuates, in one eternal act of knowing. We distinguish

---

[10] See Douglas Vickers, *Cornelius Van Til and the Theologian's Theological Stance*, Wilmington: Cross Publishing, 1976.

[11] See J.A. Alexander, *Commentary on the Acts of the Apostles*, Edinburgh: Banner of Truth, [1857] 1980, Vol.2, 82-83.

sharply, therefore, between the nature of God's knowledge and the nature and the process of man's knowledge. Man knows sequentially. His epistemic capacity, or what he knows as well as what is capable of being known, is different on, say, Thursday from what it had been on the preceding Monday. For Thursday has a different history from Monday. It holds within it different possibilities and potentialities of subsequent events and therefore of the knowledge of them. Man perceives and contemplates and knows the objects of knowledge as they become sequentially available for knowing. He knows sequences sequentially. God, too, knows sequences, but he does not know them sequentially. He knows them in a single timeless act of knowing, because he ordered them and ordained them and structured their processes and outcomes.

We may put the point differently. There is no possibility beyond God. God has not confronted and considered the possibility of eventuation that he has not ordained. Or, from our point of view, possibility exists for man, but only that is possible which God has already thought and ordained.

The redemptive offices of the Persons of the Godhead

The proper understanding of possibility bears on the meaning of the redemption that God has set forth in his Son. A Scriptural understanding of God's knowledge precludes a "possibility" theory or doctrine of redemption and the atonement. Christ did not die simply to make salvation possible, in the sense that a sovereign decision as to whether the redemption he provided would or would not be accepted remained within the autonomous capacities of individual men. On the contrary, in his death Christ actually and definitively saved his people.

But in our present context the knowledge of God bears on two remaining questions that impact on our understanding of the gospel of redemption. First, if we were to conclude that there was in fact a succession of moments in the knowledge of God, that would imply that there was a succession of moments in the being of God. For if we fracture the knowledge of God, we thereby fracture the being of God. For his knowledge is determined by his being. If the error we have confronted were made, we should in effect destroy the unity of the being of God. God would then, according to that conception, be a sum of parts, the parts being each separately and momentarily identifiable by whatever succession of moments we have in view. Such a conception of God's being and knowledge is rejected by the *Westminster Confession* which concludes that the "one only living and true God is ... without body, parts, or passions ...".[12] The spirituality of God, and his singularity as to his essence, preclude us from such a fracturing theology.

Second, what has been said concerning the knowledge of God is relevant to our understanding of the Persons of the triune Godhead and of their offices in the accomplishment of our redemption. There is only one God. "Hear, O Israel: The Lord our God is one Lord" (Deut. 6:4). Christ himself makes the same claim. He has declared that "I and my Father are one" (John 10:30). "The Father is in me", he says, "and I in Him" (John 10:38). Moreover, our Lord's references to the Person and the coming of the Holy Spirit, notably in the supper discourses and his high priestly prayer (John Chs.13-17), make it clear that the Spirit, with him, is one with the Father. As Christ himself is the only begotten Son, begotten as we observed Augustine to say, in the eternal "today" of God, so the Spirit "proceedeth from the Father" (John 15:26),[13] as we know from the same context that the Spirit is sent into the world by the Father and the Son (John 15:26).

In the history of theology much has been written concerning the works of God internal to the Godhead. They have been referred to as the *opera ad intra*, as distinct from the works external to the Godhead, the *opera ad extra*.[14] In the latter, consistent with the various ways in which they mutually and jointly covenanted in the eternal council of the Godhead, each of the three persons is engaged. As to the *opera ad intra*, on the other hand, though the veil of mystery has not been lifted for us

---

[12] *Westminster Confession*, Chap. II.
[13] See note 15 below and Robert L. Reymond's discussion in loc. cit regarding the interpretation of John 15:26 in relation to the doctrine of the Spirit's spiration. The statements of Christ in John 14:26 and 15:26 may be understood as referable to the Spirit's salvific mission.
[14] See W.G.T. Shedd, *Dogmatic Theology*, Vol.1, 285, 304.

to the same explanatory extent, theologians have referred to those works as "generation" on the one hand and "spiration" on the other. In this way, reference is made to the generation of the Son and the setting forth of the Spirit.[15] We bow before the mystery of God's works internal to his own Godhead and we hold to the revelatory datum of the unity and the oneness of God.

But what has been revealed to us regarding the being of God, the oneness in substance of the three persons of the Godhead, has implications for the knowledge that is possessed by the Father, the Son, and the Spirit. It is not the case, for example, that there is a divine mind in the Father and a divine mind in the Son, and that those divine minds confer and concur in the purposes and works of God. Rather, our doctrine of the unity of God requires us to say that there exists a divine mind that is wholly in the Father and wholly in the Son. "I and my Father are one", our Lord has declared. The essence of the Godhead resides fully in each of the Persons of the Godhead. It follows that there is a divine knowledge that is wholly in the Father and wholly in the Son and wholly in the Holy Spirit. This will in turn determine our understanding, as we shall see in a moment, of the Person and presence of the Son of God in this world and of his messianic self-awareness and impeccability.[16]

The unity of God, the oneness of the Father and the Son, and the identity of the knowledge and purpose with which they designed our redemption, has further implications for the work

---

[15] See the discussion in Robert L. Reymond, op. cit., 324, on "The Father's Eternal Generation of the Son", in which he distinguishes between the elements of subordinationism implicit in the doctrinal formulation of the Nicene Fathers and that of Calvin, Warfield, and Murray. See also the observations of William Cunningham on "The Nicene Creed - the Eternal Sonship" in his *Historical Theology*, Edinburgh: Banner of Truth, [1862] 1960, Vol.1, 293ff. With further reference to the *opera ad intra*, note should be taken of Reymond's discussion of "The Niceno-Constantinopolitan Creed's Pneumatology" which points, he argues, to the denial "to the Holy Spirit the attribute of autotheotic self-existence", op. cit., 331ff.

[16] For a discussion of the impeccability of Christ see Douglas Vickers, *Christian Truth in Critical Times*, 98ff. See also W.G.T. Shedd, *Dogmatic Theology*, Vol. 2, 330ff., and Jonathan Edwards, *The Freedom of the Will*, 156ff.

of the Father and the Son in effecting that redemption. It will suffice for the present to focus on only one of the questions that arise in that connection. Let us consider the eternal decree of God to redeem. We ask at this point the question, "Who were the subjects of that eternal decree?"

To answer that question we need to see the Covenant of Redemption coming to expression in its several dimensions and intentions. First, God decreed to elect to salvation a certain people who were, in their natural state apart from his grace, the fallen children of Adam. Second, he decreed to redeem them by the substitutionary death of Christ, in that Christ undertook to bear on their behalf the penalty for their sin and thereby satisfy the demands of divine justice. And third, he decreed to call to himself, to regenerate, to sanctify, and to bring to glory those for whom Christ died. "Thine they were", Christ prays to the Father, "and thou gavest them me" (John 17:6). The predeterminate council from which those decrees issued involved a covenantal agreement between the Persons of the Godhead. In the outcome, God the Father elected his people to salvation and designed a redemption for them; God the Son came into the world and accomplished that redemption; and God the Holy Spirit applies to those for whom Christ died the benefits of the redemption that he accomplished.

The single point to be grasped at this stage relates to the identity of the subjects of these separate decrees. We can say in summary that those who were the subjects of the decree to elect were, in their particularity and individuality, the same as those who were the subjects of the decree to redeem. In turn, they were also the subjects of the decree to call and sanctify and glorify. The importance of this conclusion, and the reason why it is raised in our present context, can be grasped by noting the implications of its contrary.

If we were to say that those for whom Christ died were in any respect different in their individuality and particularity from those whom the Father decreed to save, then we should be driving a wedge between the work of the Son and the work of the Father. Similarly, if we claim that the subjects of the decree to call and sanctify and glorify were in any respect different from the subjects of the decrees to elect and redeem, we should be driving a wedge between the work of the Holy Spirit and the work of the Father and the Son. But if, in these ways, we drive a wedge between the works of the Persons of the Godhead, we are thereby driving a wedge between the knowledge of those respective Persons. And if in such a manner we fracture the knowledge of the Persons of the Godhead, we thereby fracture the being of the Godhead. Our doctrine of the being, the unity, and the knowledge of God avoids and guards us against such a doctrinal error.

The Scriptures stand against all such fracturing of the being and the knowledge of God. For if such a fracturing is allowed and implied by our doctrine, then we are no longer speaking of the God of the Scriptures. We are no longer speaking of the God who has revealed himself. That means, then, that we have no effective redemption from sin at all.

The incarnation of Christ in historical time

No more profound mystery deserves our contemplation than that of the incarnation of the Son of God. If there is any point at which we stand in awe and wonder and amazement at the "mystery of godliness" (1 Tim. 3:16), surely it is here. At this point we "see through a glass, darkly", we "know in part", and we hold to the hope of the fuller revelation that is yet to come (1 Cor. 13:12). But we assent to the statement of the apostle John that here we confront the very touchstone of Christian confession. "Every spirit that confesseth that Jesus Christ is come in the flesh is of God" (1 John 4:2). We know that the Word, who was with God and was God "was made flesh, and dwelt among us ... full of grace and truth" (John 1:1, 14).

The fact and the doctrine of the incarnation bear on our present discussion in several respects. First, we take note of the Scriptural data regarding the Person of the Lord who thus, coming from the eternal bosom of the Father, entered into the time that he had made. Second, we observe the sense in which the eternal and the temporal are thus brought into relation, without the rupture that would have occurred if the eternal and the temporal had become commingled and confused. Third, we observe the significance of the fact that the process of redemption was actually played out in historical time. The atonement that accomplished our redemption was a real-time, definitive, historical atonement.

Who was it that walked in this world as the Messiah and Redeemer, who healed the sick and the lame, who wept with compassion at human distress, and who pursued the dusty and often derisive way to the cross? We have said, on the basis of more abundant Scripture than we need to recall, that this was the Son of God.

But let us look closely again at Jesus Christ of Nazareth as he makes his messianic claim. Here is one who clearly partakes of our full, though sinless, humanity. We say that here is the Son of God, and we say, too, that here is the man Christ Jesus. What are we to say of the Person of Jesus Christ? Was he, then, a human person? To say that he was would be to say that not only did he come from the eternity that he knew with the Father and the Spirit, but that by a transformation about which the Scriptures do not speak, he ceased to be God. Such a claim, moreover, would belie the necessity of his coming and the respect in which that necessity determined the very possibility and definition of our redemption. For it was impossible that a human person could have wrought our redemption. The realities of the Fall and of sin, the damning inheritance that Adam's dereliction projected to all his posterity, stand in the way of any possibility of our redemption by a human person.

Are we to say, then, that Jesus Christ of Nazareth was, in some sense which we should then endeavor to unravel, a divine-human person? Presumably, the meaning of such a claim would be that he was a person in whom the divine and the human natures were commingled or blended together in a manner that, by virtue of their interpenetration, rendered it impossible to say that the one confronting us was either uniquely divine or uniquely human. Again our answer must be in the negative. Jesus Christ was not a human person. He was not a divine-human person. We are required to say that Jesus Christ was a divine person.

The eternal Son of God did, in fact, come into this world and take unto himself a truly human nature, being born of the virgin and thereby truly man. He took into union with his divine nature a truly human nature, but in thus combining the two natures in his one person, that person was, and continued to be, a divine person. In him, the human nature was not personalized.

He has been called the theanthropic person, combining the Greek words *"theos"* meaning God and *"anthropos"* meaning man. He was the God-man. The designation is appropriate, provided it is understood to imply the careful distinctions that orthodox theology has found it necessary to make. The biblical doctrine of the Person of Christ was brought to clear formulation in the early church, following the heresies that had developed in relation to it. That doctrine quickly came under attack even in the apostolic times. In his letter to the Colossian church Paul was concerned to refute certain heresies that were akin to what later became a more fully developed Gnosticism, and John in his epistle was very much concerned with the same problem. Gnosticism in its many expressions and aspects was essentially a heresy that denied the reality of the deity and the divinity of Christ. It argued, for example, that there could not have been a true union of spirit with matter. Divinity, in which essential goodness inhered, could not come into union with humanity and matter in which, as it was supposed, evil inhered. It was impossible, therefore, it was claimed, that Jesus Christ could be both divine and human. One expression of Gnosticism argued that Jesus Christ was a man on whom and to whom the Spirit of God came at an early stage of his life, but that the Spirit departed from him before his death.

The many-sided aspects of such heresies as these need not detain us. The important fact is that at an early stage in the history of the Christian confession attacks were made on the biblical revelation of the Person of our Redeemer. It is understandable that this should have occurred. For if the reality of the Person of Christ is destroyed, then the reality of our redemption is destroyed, and the entire Christian gospel and the hope that it holds for our eternal security is also destroyed.

In the post-apostolic age similar problems arose. The Sabellians, named after their founder Sabellius, argued that the Son and the Father were not distinct persons, but only different aspects or emanations of the one Being. The Arians followed their founder Arius, an Alexandrian priest, in maintaining that

71

the Son was not equal with the Father, but that he was created by him. Orthodoxy was thus forced to articulate the doctrine of the Person of Christ in such a way as to avoid the Sabellian heresy on the one side and that of the Arians on the other.[17]

The Arian heresy was condemned by the church at the Council of Nicea in the year 325 A.D.[18] An important figure in the early history of the church, Athanasius who became Bishop of Alexandria in 328, argued strongly for the Nicean orthodoxy. The church steadily adhered to that position. The continuing problems surrounding what we can refer to as the church's Christology, or its doctrine of the Person of Christ, were confronted and settled definitively at the Council of Chalcedon in 451 A.D. That Council has become justly famous for its achievement of what has become referred to as the Christological settlement.[19]

In its judicious formulation, the Creed of Chalcedon expressed the doctrine of the Person of Christ by stating that the divine and the human natures were so related in him as to be "two natures, without confusion, without change, without division, without separation". In the first two of these explanatory statements, without confusion and without change, a safeguard is erected against the idea that the two natures are in any sense intermingled. The last two explanatory statements assert, on the other hand, the full reality of the union of natures that existed.

The reality of the incarnation, notwithstanding the mystery of it, and the reality, at the same time, of the divine Personhood of our Lord, bear in further ways on the meaning of our redemption. We have spoken of the holiness of God and, as intrinsic to his holiness, his separateness from all of created reality external to himself. That implies his eternal separateness from time. That has significance for the knowledge that God possesses, not only of himself, but of all of the eventuation of all of the histories of created entities. God's foreknowledge and

---

[17] See William Cunningham, *Historical Theology*, Edinburgh: Banner of Truth [1862] 1960, Vol.1, 307ff.

[18] See Philip Schaff, *The Creeds of Christendom*, Revised by David S. Schaff, Grand Rapids: Baker Books, Vol.1, 24ff.

[19] See Philip Schaff, ibid., 29ff.

foreordination of all such eventuation imply the certainty and the security of the redemption that is our main concern at present.

We have spoken earlier in this and the preceding chapter of the attributes, the holiness, and the knowledge of God. It follows from that discussion that the Person of Jesus Christ, as he walked in this world as the eternal Son of God, remaining as he did very God of very God, continued to be characterized by those same attributes, holiness, and knowledge. In short, in his coming he did not lay aside his divine identity and glory. He did, as the Scriptural data make clear, lay aside in many respects the insignia or the demonstrable signs of his glory. But he was, and continued to be, one with the Father. Staggering as the realization is to our unpracticed ears, we may observe something of the significance of it.[20]

It has been claimed that when our Lord came into the world he did, in some sense, lay aside his divine attributes. That false doctrine has gone under the name of the kenotic theory. It has acquired currency, unfortunately, in the well-known hymn that states that when Christ came he "emptied himself of all but love".[21] But such a teaching is in no sense supported by a sound exegesis of the paragraph in the second chapter of Paul's letter to the Philippians on which it is supposedly based. Our Lord, as Paul there says, "made himself of no reputation, and took upon him the form of a servant, and was made in the likeness of men; and being found in fashion as a man, he humbled himself ..." (Phil. 2:7-8). Where both the KJV and the NKJV state that Christ "made himself of no reputation", the Greek text has the word "ekenosen" in the aorist tense, which means literally, "emptied" himself. The "kenotic" theory derives its claim from that Greek

---

[20] The statement in John 3:13 regarding "the Son of man which is in heaven" raises the important doctrine that following his incarnation Christ was, as to his human nature, in this world, but as to his divine nature he was both in this world and in heaven. The text referred to, which appears in the *Textus Receptus*, has been omitted from the modern or reconstructed text. But as to the doctrine to which it is addressed, an illuminating and positive statement is contained in William Hendriksen, *New Testament Commentary: Exposition of the Gospel According to John*, Grand Rapids: Baker Books, 1954, Vol.2, 500-501.

[21] Charles Wesley, "And can it be ...".

word. It would not serve any purpose to discuss further the various degrees in which different forms of the kenotic theory imagine Christ to have "emptied himself" of his deity, or his divine attributes. Suffice it to say that the Philippian passage does not address such a conception. That text is plainly concerned with the manner in which the Second Person of the Godhead humbled himself that he might be our redeemer.

Many aspects of the life and experiences and actions of our Lord that are clearly and uniquely attributable to his human nature are attributed in the Scripture to his Person. Similarly, many actions and expressions and realizations that are as clearly and uniquely referable to his divine nature are also attributed to his Person. But what should be understood in considering those facts is that his Person, in all its uniqueness and individual identity, was determined essentially by his divine nature. By this we mean that the divine nature dominated and determined and controlled the human nature.

That becomes clear from the inspection of only one point of fact in relation to him. We know that he was sinless. We know that as to his human nature he grew, that he was ignorant of certain things, and learned, and developed to maturity. How, then, could it have been true that in his human ignorance he remained free from sin? Are we to say that he was not humanly ignorant of anything? We should contradict the Scriptures if we were to do so. And yet we say that he did not sin. Do we say, then, that he was impeccable, meaning by that that it was impossible for him to sin? On the basis of Scriptural testimony as to his Person we have to say that that was so. It was impossible for him to sin.

The claim of impeccability is a claim that is made of the Person of Jesus Christ. He was an impeccable Person whose human nature was tempted and was in itself capable of sin. But in Christ the human nature was in no sense the isolated human nature in which Adam's posterity as created entities exist. In Christ the human nature was joined in union with a divine nature. And the divine nature so dominated and determined the scope of action of the human nature that it was impossible that in his Person Christ could sin. What the human nature might have been capable of in and of itself, it was incapable of when it was joined with the divine nature in the divine Person of Christ. We observed in an earlier context that while our Lord took unto himself a human nature, that nature was not in him personalized. In his very valuable discussion of "the unipersonality of Christ", Berkhof has made the same point.[22]

That important doctrinal issue can be considered further. We have said in effect that the divine nature did not permit the human nature to sin, not even as Jesus of Nazareth in whom the natures were combined grew and learned until his maturity. But there did, of course, come a point in time at which the divine nature permitted the human nature to suffer in a unique and eternally significant sense. In his human nature Christ suffered for us when he bore the penalty for our sins on the cross. At that point he knew, in his cry of derelicton, that he was bearing the wrath of the Father, that he was thereby satisfying divine justice on behalf of the sinners for whom he died. It was only thus that their redemption could be secured.

The Scriptural data that bear on the Person of Christ imply that the divine mind was wholly in the Father and the Spirit and wholly in the Son. We have seen that it was the eternal divine identity of the Son that was incarnate in Jesus Christ. He came into this world from his pre-existence with the Father. In his divine nature he continued, in all his Godhood, his divine existence outside of time. When he walked in this world Christ was, as to his divine nature, in this world and also continually present with the Father in heaven. As to his human nature, he was present on earth.[23] That is the mystery of the incarnation. We bow before it and acknowledge that its truth establishes the reality of our redemption and our reconciliation with God.

Implications for the atonement of Christ

In the incarnation there did not occur, and there could not have occurred, any commingling of the eternal and the temporal. In

---

[22] See L. Berkhof, *Systematic Theology*, 321-22, "[T]he Logos assumed a human nature that was not personalized, that did not exist by itself". See also W.G.T. Shedd, *Dogmatic Theology*, Vol.2, 330ff. Christ's impeccability is established by the promise in Is. 42:1f., 49:7f.. Cf. Is. 50:7, Ps. 2:7-8; 110:4.
[23] See n.20 above.

the Person of Christ there was no commingling or intermingling of the divine and the human natures, and for that reason no commingling of the eternal and the temporal. It follows that in God's design and implementation of the plan of our redemption there was similarly, at all points and in every respect, no commingling of the eternal and the temporal.

The eternal and the temporal remained unimpaired. That is, the eternal remained timeless, and the eternal character of Christ remained unchanged, with all of the attributes of the Godhead essential to it. And the temporal, or the human nature of Christ, that was itself created by the divine agency of the Holy Spirit, retained its temporal character. Because that was so, the eternal and the temporal were not commingled at any stage of the redemptive process. It follows that there was no such commingling at the atonement that Christ made. It was in his human nature that he assumed in time that Christ bore our sin.

But now we must pursue the implications of that further. We say now that neither could the eternal and the temporal be commingled at the point of the sinner's transition from wrath to grace, or, that is, at the point at which the sinner is translated by the work of God from the kingdom of darkness into the kingdom of his dear Son (Col. 1:13). What that implies can be put in two respects that will clarify its meaning.

First, our salvation is all of grace. It is by the grace of God that we are saved (Eph. 2:8). It is by the grace of God set forth in the divine Person of his Son that salvation in all its parts is provided for us. It is God himself, in that gracious provision, who makes his Son to be unto us "wisdom, and righteousness, and sanctification, and redemption" (1 Cor. 1:30). Only by the sovereign grace of God, reaching from eternity beyond the createdness of time in which we are bound, are we rescued from the ignorance, guilt, pollution, and misery into which we had fallen by Adam's sin.

But second, when we say for that reason that there is no commingling of the eternal and the temporal in the sinner's transition from wrath to grace, it follows that the creation of the new life in the soul is completely and solely the sovereign, unsolicited work of God the Holy Spirit. Or to state the implication in a different way, we say that the very faith by which the sinner believes in Christ is itself the gift of God. The sinner, that is, is passive in his regeneration and has no part in it.

Or we may put that important point still differently. Regeneration is prior to faith. It is not the case that a person is born again because he has faith in Christ. If that were true, then salvation would depend, at the crucial point of regeneration, on a joint work of both God and man. And contrary to our doctrine, that would imply that the eternal (the grace of God) and the temporal (the activity of the sinner) would have been, to use our expression, commingled. That, however, we reject. The reality is that a person believes in Christ because he has been born again by the sovereign grace of God. The correct understanding of our doctrine on that important point is to clarify the difference between the Arminian and the Reformed doctrines of salvation. We shall return to that most important point of doctrine in a later chapter.

Final implications of the doctrine of the Person of Christ

The final point we anticipated at the beginning of this discussion has by implication now been made. The mystery of redemption, we have said, involves the mystery of the relation between God outside of time and sinners in their created temporality. That mystery has come to its sharpest expression in the incarnation of the eternal, divine Son of God. In him the divine and the human natures were not changed and confused, but their union was, nevertheless, a real union. We understood that to mean that there was no commingling or mixing of the eternal and the temporal. That was seen to imply that there was similarly no such commingling in the atonement that Christ made. For it was in his human nature that he died, as it was in his human nature that he suffered and learned obedience. He could not die in his divine nature. It was as our incarnate high priest that he discharged his messianic assignment for us in this world, and it is now as our incarnate high priest that he continues for ever to discharge his heavenly high priestly office.

Two things, however, are clear and can be safely concluded. First, in the incarnate Son of God eternity and time have been brought into a new relation, one that will itself continue throughout the eternal age that is still ahead. Having assumed our human nature to himself, our Lord has not divested himself of it. Nor will he do so. "In like manner as ye have seen him go into heaven", the angels declared, "this same Jesus shall come" (Acts 1:11). "It doth not yet appear what we shall be; but ... when he shall appear we shall be like him" (1 John 3:2). It is not possible that we shall transcend our humanness or our finitude. But in our humanity we shall see our Savior in the humanity that he assumed to himself, and we shall be like him.

When we say that in Christ the eternal and the temporal have been brought into a new relation, we recognize that it was in actual and real historical time that Christ accomplished our redemption. The glory of the gospel is that the atonement is a real historic atonement. Christ, in the human nature that he assumed in historical time, died for our sins in historical time. Now in his mysterious supervision of the becoming as well as the being of his redeemed people, God by his works of providence and the ministry of his Spirit is immanent in historical time to bring us to glory.

The relation to the holiness of God

Our discussion in this chapter of God outside of time can now be seen in relation to our preceding consideration of the holiness of God. God's holiness subsists in what we called his separateness, or his distinction from his creatures, both as to being and as to the time or temporal process in which his creation has been established. God's knowing and acting and ordaining and redeeming are all in themselves consistent with the holiness of his being. His righteousness in what he does accords consistently with the holiness that characterizes him and in which he exists.

But we have stated also that the third aspect or implication of God's holiness that engages our thought is his holy revulsion against sin, his holy abhorrence and detestation of sin. His holiness is necessarily expressed in his wrath against sin. The basis for a clearer understanding of that important aspect of God's self-disclosure has now been laid. On it turns both the necessity for, and the meaning of, the redemption which, in real historical time, the eternal Son of God accomplished. We shall begin our consideration of those important issues immediately in the following chapter.[24]

---

[24] In the light of our discussion in this chapter of the Person of Christ, it may be observed that a tendency has recently emerged among theologically conservative scholars to refer to our Lord as a "human being". See, for example, John Blanchard, *Does God believe in atheists?* Darlington, UK: Evangelical Press, 2000, 555, 558ff. Robert A. Peterson, in his *Calvin's Doctrine of the Atonement*, Phillipsburg: Presbyterian and Reformed, 1983, presented a very valuable discussion of the fact that "God Became a Man for Our Salvation", 11 et seq. In the second edition of his book, however, published under the title of *Calvin and the Atonement*, Fearn, Scotland: Christian Focus Publications, 1999, Peterson has amended all such references to Christ as a "Man" to refer to him as a "Human Being" (25ff.). But Peterson does not give any explanation of that change of designation. In our discussion of the results of the Council of Chalcedon and the Christological settlement (see pp.28, 72 above), and in the context of our conclusion in this chapter that at the incarnation (and similarly at the atonement and at the sinner's transition from wrath to grace) there was no commingling of the eternal and the temporal, we have stated that our Lord was not a human person. That is to say, he was not a human being. Nor can he be said to be a divine-human person. He was, we have said consistently, a *divine Person*, that is to say a divine being. He was a divine Person (Being) who took a truly human nature into union with his divine nature. Our argument coincided with that of Berkhof who has made the relevant point by observing that "the Logos assumed a human nature that was not personalized" (p.75 above). We suggest, therefore, that the requirements of Christological doctrine and of doctrinal terminology point away from the designation of our Lord as a "human person", or a "human being", and make it necessary to preserve the designation of him as a divine Person (divine being). See the judicious discussion of these doctrinal issues in Cornelius Van Til, *The Defense of the Faith*, 16. Turretin, in his extended discussion of "The Person and State of Christ" in his op. cit. Vol. 2, 271ff., refers to "the union of the two natures in the one person in the incarnation" (310) by stating that "the human nature ... was destitute of proper personality ... because otherwise it would have been a person" (311), a conclusion that is reflected in the statement of Berkhof referred to above. It is clear that the terms of our salvation and the achievement of our Lord in the accomplishment of redemption turn on the reality and identity of his divine Personhood and on the mystery of his entering, in his incarnation, into the time that he had made. We shall return to the important implications of these facts in a later chapter when we discuss the satisfaction for sin that Christ provided.

5

Sin

One of the most remarkable developments in contemporary Christianity, and even in contemporary evangelicalism, is that the church has lost its doctrine of sin. What has been put in its place is not our immediate concern. The stance of the church, its message and methods, its deviation from its doctrinal heritage, and its excursions into a new administrative ethos, have been discussed by recent authors. We have taken note of some of those discussions in our first chapter. But we leave all that aside for the present. Our immediate concern is with a rather different and straightforward question. We ask, "What is the meaning of sin"? The question itself strikes to the heart of the church's reason for being and to the center of its message.

We shall endeavor in this chapter to understand something of the nature, the origin, and the character of sin, its entry into the world, and its effects on the human condition. But in its essence and in its most pointed characterization, sin is an outrage of the holiness of God. It has caused an estrangement between God and man. It has ruined the soul and shattered the harmony of its faculties. One of our Puritan fathers has examined the seriousness of sin and concluded that it is "The Plague of Plagues".[1] In its origin and its effects, sin implies the

---

[1] Ralph Venning, *The Plague of Plagues*, London: Banner of Truth [1669] 1965.

dereliction of the sinner from the covenantal obligations that his creation in the image of God established.

Sin is always an inversion of God's order. By his sin, man makes his own god in his own image. Sin cuts man off from the true source of meaning and the true explanation of his existence and his relations with the world in which he finds himself. For there is no possibility of the discovery of meaning unless we take as our presupposition God as he has revealed himself. But sin is a denial, a repudiation, of our responsible relation to God. That conviction is ineradicable in the human consciousness.

A sense of God, a *sensus deitatis*, resides in the human soul. Every man knows that he is the creature of a Creator-God infinitely higher than himself. He knows, as a result, that he is under an obligation to the law of God. He knows, moreover, that he has failed to honor that obligation and that he is therefore guilty before God. He knows that he is justly exposed to the wrath of God. In that final sense, therefore, there are no atheists. There are no agnostics. No man can say that knowledge of God is impossible. Every man knows that God is. Practical atheists there may be, and undoubtedly are, people who live as though there were no God. But there can be no psychological atheists, none who can deny the impression of God on and within the soul. In the very act of self-awareness, the individual person is aware of God.

The state of sin to which we were reduced was the result of Adam's Fall. That carried with it, the Scriptures explain, the imputation to us of the guilt of that first sin and the corruption and deprivation that followed from it. The implications of that fatal breach are described most clearly in the first chapter of the letter to the Romans. "When they knew God, they glorified him not as God ... but became vain in their imaginations, and their foolish heart was darkened ... who changed the truth of God into a lie, and worshipped and served the creature more than the Creator ... God gave them over to a reprobate mind ... haters of God ... covenant breakers ..." (Rom. 1:21-31).

It is true that after his Fall man continued to be, though in a sadly marred and tarnished condition, the image of God, the *imago Dei*. His intellective faculty is now such that he retains a cognition of the true God. The testimony of the *sensus deitatis* within him is to the effect that God is. God has not left himself without witness to men. But, the apostle observes, "when they knew God they glorified him not as God". Henceforth, in the darkness of their heart, men "suppress the truth in unrighteousness", and it is on those grounds that "the wrath of God is revealed from heaven against all ungodliness and unrighteousness" (Rom. 1:18).

It follows that we shall understand the meaning of sin only as we are able to grasp something of the meaning of the holiness of God to which, as we have said, sin is an affront.

The holiness of God and the reality of sin

In the preceding two chapters we have been concerned with the holiness of God as meaning, first, his separateness, and second, his self-consistency or immutability and the righteousness inherent in all his actions, purposes, and ordinations. The integrity of the divine nature is expressed in the conformity to it, and the conformity to the law of his own excellence, of the affections and the will of God. He is immutably conformed to the perfection of the eternal law of his own being and holiness. We have spoken of the transcendent majesty-holiness of God, his supreme perfection and his essential glory. But we have said also that God's holiness comes to expression in an abhorrence and hatred of sin. The relation between the holiness of God and the reality of sin in the presence of that holiness now calls for discussion.

The majesty-holiness of God is clearly exhibited throughout the Scriptures. The song of Moses moves to its climax with the confession, "Who is like unto thee, O Lord ... who is like unto thee, glorious in holiness" (Ex. 15:11).

The strain is taken up in the song of Hannah following the birth of Samuel, "My heart rejoiceth in the Lord ... There is none holy as the Lord; for there is none beside thee" (1 Sam. 2:1-2). The prophet Isaiah knew that he bore the words of "the high and lofty One that inhabiteth eternity, whose name is Holy" (Is. 57:15); and we are familiar with Isaiah's report of his vision of God's glory: "I saw also the Lord sitting upon a throne, high and lifted up [and] the seraphim [who] cried 'Holy, holy, holy, is the

Lord of hosts; the whole earth is full of his glory'". We recall, also, Isaiah's reaction to his realization of the majesty-holiness of God: "Woe is me! for I am undone: because I am a man of unclean lips, and I dwell in the midst of a people of unclean lips: for mine eyes have seen the King, the Lord of hosts" (Is. 6:1-3,5).

The Scriptural data could be multiplied. But at this point we consider the specifically ethical aspect of God's holiness. We encounter at this point the holy wrath of God against sin. We have already confronted that aspect of God's holiness by speaking of his revulsion from sin, his abhorrence of sin, and the incompatibility of sin and uncleanness with his holy character. This ethical aspect cannot be dissociated from the majesty-holiness of God. For we are speaking of the one God, the infinite, eternal, and unchangeable God who reveals himself to us in the various aspects of his character. God's ethical holiness follows from his immutability and the consistency of his untarnishable righteousness with his own eternal being and moral excellence.

When we refer to the ethical holiness or the righteousness of God, then, we acknowledge and speak explicitly of God's holy separation from sin. We need, therefore, a clear grasp of the Scriptural statement of the attitude to sin that is implicit in God's holiness. And we need a firm understanding of what follows as the meaning of sin in itself. We take the first point first.

Elihu, in his disputation with Job, propels our thought from the being and the purity of God to the consistency with his perfections of all his attitudes and actions. "Far be it from God, that he should do wickedness; and from the Almighty, that he should commit iniquity" (Job 34:10). The prophet Habakkuk has observed: "O Lord my God, mine Holy One ... Thou art of purer eyes than to behold evil, and canst not look on iniquity" (Hab. 1:12-13). Those statements establish a negative attitude to sin, meaning by that God's separation from sin. But they carry with them also the positive aspect of God's own moral excellence or ethical perfection, in that they hold before us his disapprobation of sin.

We recognize at this point, therefore, God's abhorrence of

sin. Coming into focus, as a result, is the attitude to the sinner of the holy and all-righteous God. If, as the Scriptures attest, God "is of purer eyes than to look upon evil" (Hab. 1;13), and if it is true that God has therefore had dealings with sinners only as he has dealt with them through the mediation of his Son, it follows that all of those relations are what they are because the wrath of God is directed, justly and irrevocably, to the sinner and his sin. The wrath of God is directed to the sinner irrevocably, that is, unless the grace and mercy of God intervene in the sinner's plight.

We speak, then, of God's vehement hatred of sin. He hates what he sees as the very beginnings of sin in the hearts and imaginations of his creatures. The prophet Zechariah has observed: "Let none of you imagine evil in your hearts ... for all these are things that I hate, saith the Lord" (Zech. 8:17). In his holy revulsion from evil God uses the strongest of language, "I hate, I despise" (Amos 5:21); and through the prophet Isaiah he says, with reference to the sins of his people, "My soul hateth; they are a trouble unto me... I am weary to bear them" (Is. 1:14). Again he speaks through Jeremiah to the sinful idolatry of the people and says "Oh, do not this abominable thing that I hate" (Jer. 44:4). The sin of his people "vexed His Holy Spirit" (Is. 63:10). Moreover, God makes it abundantly clear that his detestation of sin involves a hatred whose implications are directed against the person of the sinner who commits it. "Because thou hast not remembered the days of thy youth, but hast fretted me in all these things; behold, therefore I also will recompense thy way upon thine head, saith the Lord God; and thou shalt not commit this lewdness above all thine abominations" (Ezek. 16:43).

The Psalmist underlines the gravity of sin in his address to God: "Thou hatest all workers of iniquity" (Ps. 5:5). In such statements as these it is clear that sin is the object of God's abhorrence, revulsion, detestation, and hatred. We are therefore concerned to discover the meaning of sin as the object of his displeasure. The sinner as a sinner, absorbed as his character is by the sin that came not from God but from himself, is the object of God's wrath. God, with a necessity that expresses his own glory and holiness and purity, is infinitely angry, with an infinite hatred, against sin. His anger and hatred projected against sin is, in its own direction, as infinite and holy as his love and mercy directed to the sinner whom he has redeemed in Christ. There is, and there can be, nothing in sin as sin that could alleviate God's detestation of it.

Stephen Charnock, in his work on *The Existence and Attributes of God*, observes that "God being the highest, most absolute and infinite holiness, doth infinitely, and therefore intensely, hate unholiness; being infinitely righteous, doth infinitely abhor unrighteousness; being infinitely true, doth infinitely abhor falsity, as it is the greatest and most deformed evil. As it is from the righteousness of his nature that he hath a content and satisfaction in righteousness, 'the righteous Lord loveth righteousness' (Ps. 11:7), so it is from the same righteousness of his nature that he detests whatever is morally evil. As his nature therefore is infinite, so must his abhorrence be".[2]

The curse of God and the transition from wrath to grace

The aspect of God's holiness that implies his revulsion from evil and his wrath against sin is reflected in the argument of the apostle in his letter to the Galatians. In his discussion there of the curse of God that followed as a result of sin, Paul states that "Christ hath redeemed us from the curse of the law, being made a curse for us" (Gal. 3:13). That statement projects its meaning to the redemption of both the Gentiles and the Jews. All had fallen under the curse of God by virtue of their Fall in Adam. As a result of the process of redemption that Paul referred to, it is God's wrath against the sinner whom he has brought to himself in Christ that is removed. But his hatred of sin has not been removed or abated. God's hatred of sin, including his hatred of sin in the life of the believing Christian, explains the depth of his love. In that love, that set forth the rescue in Christ, God's justice and righteousness remained inviolate. Therein, as the Psalmist sang, "Mercy and truth are met together; righteousness and peace have kissed each other" (Ps. 85:10).

Statements to the same effect are spread liberally throughout

---

[2] Stephen Charnock, *The Existence and Attributes of God*, 456.

the Scriptures. John explains the love of God by stating that Christ has been set forth as "the propitiation for our sins" (1 John 4:10). The testimony of John the Baptist is clear and to the same effect. "He that believeth on the Son hath everlasting life: and he that believeth not the Son shall not see life; but the wrath of God abideth on him" (John 3:36). If one does not believe on Christ, then the wrath of God remains on him. It has not been removed. His non-belief is testimony to the fact that he remains dead in his sin (Eph. 2:1). He is still blinded in his mind by the "god of this world" (2 Cor. 4:4). He still walks "according to the course of this world, according to the prince of the power of the air, the spirit that now worketh in the children of disobedience" (Eph. 2:2). Of those who let the day of grace and mercy pass unheeded, it can only be said that the wrath of God remains on them. That wrath has not, in their case, been removed. It was not placed, for them, on the Savior and substitute, the Son of God incarnate. The wrath that was addressed to all men by reason of their participation in Adam's Fall has not, for them, been lifted. It remains. It remains, with all its damning implications, not only for time but for eternity.

The apostolic testimony could not be clearer than in Paul's quotation of the Deuteronomic curse, "cursed is everyone that continueth not in all things which are written in the book of the law to do them" (Gal. 3:10; Deut. 27:26). Paul spoke in his epistle to the Romans of the state and prospect of those who do not repent. They "treasured up" for themselves, he said, "wrath against the day of wrath and revelation of the righteous judgment of God" (Rom. 2:5). The final judgment of God against sin and against those who have not been judged already in their participation in the death of his Son, is an integral part of the apostolic gospel proclamation.

Paul referred, on the other hand, to those who had "turned to God from idols to serve the living and true God". The significance of their case lay in the fact that by the work of Christ they had been "delivered from the wrath to come" (1 Thess 1:9-10). The difference in the two cases Paul makes explicit again at the end of the same letter to the Thessalonians: "For God hath not appointed us to wrath, but to obtain salvation by our Lord Jesus Christ" (1 Thess. 5:9). In Christ there is, for his people, a transition from wrath to grace. But the wrath of God against sin remains on those who do not come to him.

John the Baptist had made the same rejoinder to the Pharisees and the Sadducees who came to him as he baptized: "O generation of vipers, who hath warned you to flee from the wrath to come?" (Matt. 3:7). The wrath of God comes to expression in the fact that the destiny of the wicked is, as the epistle of Jude observes, "the blackness of darkness for ever" (Jude 13).

But for those who are redeemed by the grace of God, for those who know the transition from wrath to grace, the song of the Psalmist rings clear: "I will set no wicked thing before mine eyes. I hate the work of them that turn aside" (Ps. 101:3). The redeemed react with joyous approval to the admonition, "Ye that love the Lord, hate evil" (Ps. 97:10). They have, by the mercy of God, begun to see something of the meaning of the apostle's "be ye holy, for I am holy" (1 Peter 1:16), as he echoes the early Levitical admonition (Lev. 11:44).

But we must look more closely at the meaning of sin. This is so for two reasons. First, it is possible and necessary, against the background of God's hatred of sin, to look with some care at the meaning of sin in relation to that hatred. It is necessary to understand the meaning of sin in relation to the holiness of God from which that hatred ensues. And second, a clearer understanding of sin will itself be conducive, in the life of the Christian person, to the development of that holiness to which God's people are called.

Sin and the law of God

We do not need to discuss at length what sin is not. We noted previously the Gnostic heresy that carries with it a false understanding at this point. It claims that there exists an eternal principle of evil, and that a division exists in man between that principle of evil and a principle of good. The spirit, it is argued, represents the latter, while the body represents the principle of evil. It is not necessary to stay with these or other kinds of dualism that deny the meaning of the gospel explanation of sin. Nor is it true to say that evil inheres in man simply by virtue of a privation that exists because of the limitations of his creature-hood and his finitude. Our concern here is a positive under-standing of the Scriptural doctrine of sin. Sin, in its clearest and its shortest definition, is properly understood to be the trans-gression of the law of God. But it is precisely that brief definition that needs explanation. What is the law of God? Why is it what it is? And why does the transgression of it constitute sin?

In its question as to the meaning of sin, the *Westminster Catechism* replies that "Sin is any want of conformity unto, or transgression of, the law of God".[3] That, moreover, is the definition of the epistle of John: "Whosoever commiteth sin transgresseth also the law: for sin is the transgression of the law" (1 John 3:4). It follows that sin is sin because of its relation to God, his law, and his preceptive will that is consistent with that law. Our attention is focused by those statements on what we might call a formal definition of sin, or sin as an ethical defect or deficiency. But the Scriptures hold before us a further understanding of the meaning of sin.

The universal declaration of the Scriptures is that the es-sence of human goodness is love for God, and that sin, or moral evil, consists in the opposite of love for God. Sin is to be understood, then, as opposition to God. In the same way as holiness involves, at the core of its meaning, the idea of separation, the same concept of separation is again the essential component of the meaning of sin. In this case, however, sin is sin because it involves, as Berkhof has put it, "separation from God, opposition to God, hatred of God [that] manifests itself in constant transgression of the law of God in thought, word, and deed".[4]

The Scriptures attest that sin is the transgression of the law of God, a transgression that entails a separation from God and from communion and fellowship with God. What, then, is the meaning of that law? In his letter to the Galatians, in the context of his statement that Christ had redeemed them from the curse of the law, the apostle looked beyond the ceremonial structure

---

[3] *Westminster Shorter Catechism*, Question 14.
[4] L. Berkhof, *Systematic Theology*, 232.

of the Mosaic administration to the law in its moral aspect. The sanctity and perpetuity of the moral law establish it as the rule of life for God's people. That law was in itself a republication and a rearticulation of the law of morality that had been given to our first parents at the beginning. The meaning of the Decalogue, the ten words of the moral law, cannot be properly understood, nor can their imperatives as the rule of life be rightly perceived, unless they are understood as the republication of the law of God as it was originally communicated.

For that reason, both the Gentiles and the Jews were understood to be law breakers. They both stood in need of the benefits of the substitutionary work and sacrifice of Christ if they were to be redeemed from the curse of that law. But beyond that, the law as it was initially given, and as it was rearticulated in inscripturated form, was what it was because it was a setting forth of the reflection of the divine perfections that inhered in God the law-giver himself. In the law as promulgated, in his earliest communication to Adam and in his literary as well as verbal communication to Moses, God has said what he has in order to place before us what the pattern of conduct and life must be if, as is required of us, we are to be like God.

That implies that God, in setting forth the law of moral obedience, has communicated the requirements that would conform human conduct to his own holiness. In doing so, he has defined goodness in itself and has declared that he loves what he has revealed to be the good. But that goodness consists in a resemblance of God himself, his own Person, and his own being. In shorter terms, we are here face to face with what we may refer to as the self-love of God. That self-love comes to expression in a concern for his own glory.

God's jealousy for his glory is reflected in the judicious statement of the Catechism that "The decrees of God are His eternal purpose, according to the counsel of His will, whereby, *for His own glory*, He hath foreordained whatsoever comes to pass".[5] For this reason the law is summarized in the comprehending directive that "thou shalt love the Lord thy God with all thy heart, and with all thy soul, and with all thy mind" (Matt.

---

[5] *Westminster Shorter Catechism*, Question 7. (Eph. 1:4,11 Rom. 9:22-23).

22:37). If we have done that we have kept the law. If we have not done that, the condemnation of God and his law rests upon us. In the latter case our only rescue and relief, the ground of our hope for reconciliation and peace with God, is the substitutionary work and obedience of Christ.

Charnock, again, has an insightful understanding of sin, the glory of God, and the relation between them that we are now examining. The "love of holiness", he observes, "cannot be without a hatred of everything that is contrary to it". And in the same context he traces out the implications of what we have referred to as God's self-love. "As God necessarily loves himself, so he must necessarily hate everything that is against himself; and as he loves himself for his own excellency and holiness, he must necessarily detest whatsoever is repugnant to his holiness, because of the evil of it. Since he is infinitely good, he cannot but love goodness, as it is a resemblance to himself; and cannot but abhor unrighteousness, as being most distant from him, and contrary to him. If he have any esteem for his own perfections, he must needs have an implacable aversion to all that is so repugnant to him, that would, if it were possible, destroy him, and is a point directed not only against his glory, but against his life. If he did not hate it, he would hate himself; for since righteousness is his image, and sin would deface his image, if he did not love his image, and loathe what is against his image, he would loathe himself, he would be an enemy to his own nature".[6]

The condition and the guilt of sin

Two final points need to be made in our understanding of the meaning of sin. The Scriptures make clear that the guilt of the first sin of Adam, our federal head, was imputed to all of his posterity (Rom. 5:12f.). At that point sin entered the world, and death by sin, and all mankind were involved and implicated in it. The Catechism is expressive: "The covenant being made with Adam, not only for himself, but for his posterity, all mankind, descending from him by ordinary generation, sinned in him, and

---

[6] Stephen Charnock, *The Existence and Attributes of God*, 455.

fell with him, in his first transgression". Moreover, "the sinfulness of that estate whereinto man fell, consists in, the guilt of Adam's first sin, the want of original righteousness, and the corruption of his whole nature, which is commonly called Original Sin; together with all actual transgressions which proceed from it". [7]

Sin, then, as it is presented to us in the Scriptures, does not have primary reference to our actions and to what we do or do not do. That aspect of its meaning must, of course, be clearly acknowledged and understood. But sin in its essence has primarily to do with the state and condition in which, as a result of Adam's Fall, we actually exist. That state is one that is characterized by both deprivation and depravation. By our fall into the "estate of sin", we were deprived of our original holiness and righteousness, and we were depraved in the corruption of our whole nature. Now, in the darkened and blinded state of sin (2 Cor. 4:4) we are implacably opposed to God, we are God-haters (Rom. 1:30; Jer. 17:9), naturally enemies of God (Rom. 8:7), and slaves of sin (Luke 11:21; John 8:44).

In its initial entrance into the human condition and in the conduct that follows from it, sin is an ethical lapse, a dereliction from obligation on the level of behavior and conduct. In saying that, we are saying that the entrance of sin did not effect any change in man's essential being as, in creaturely finitude, he stood before God and under obligation to God. Sin, in other words, did not represent a fall to a lower level in some imagined chain of being. Sin, in its initial act and in the actions that proceed from it, has reference to behavior, not to being.

But the ethical lapse that constituted our first sin did have implications for the soul, in that it brought upon it the spiritual death that God had promised would be the result of sin. Because of that spiritual death (Eph. 2:1), a newness of life in which the holiness of God again characterizes the person must await the renewing, regenerating work of the Spirit of God. For until that sovereign new birth by the Spirit, it is impossible, as our Lord has said, even to see the kingdom of God (John 3:3) or to enter into the enjoyment of the things of God.

---

[7] *Westminster Shorter Catechism*, Questions 16 and 18.

The same understanding of sin as condition and behavior is summarized by the apostle when he says that "they that are after the flesh do mind the things of the flesh; but they that are after the Spirit the things of the Spirit. For to be carnally minded is death; but to be spiritually minded is life and peace" (Rom. 8:5-6). Again, "the natural man receiveth not the things of the Spirit of God: for they are foolishness unto him: neither can he know them, because they are spiritually discerned" (1 Cor. 2:14). That is pointing to, and focusing our attention upon, the disabilities and the moral incapacities that characterize the state of sin.

By his fall into sin man not only forfeited and lost his communion with God, but he became, by that fatal act, enslaved to Satan and sin. The starkness of the fact should serve only to clarify our understanding of the scope of our fallen condition. When the Jews insisted to Christ that they were "never in bondage to any man", Christ replied that "whosoever committeth sin is the servant of sin" (John 8:33-34), or the slave of sin, or in bondage to sin. The apostle Peter made the very same point in his argument that "of whom a man is overcome, of the same is he brought in bondage" (2 Peter 2:19). Paul had explained to the Romans that "to whom ye yield yourselves servants to obey, his servants ye are to whom ye obey; whether of sin unto death, or of obedience unto righteousness". He went on to say, "But God be thanked, that ye were the servants of sin, but ye have obeyed from the heart that form of doctrine which was delivered you" (Rom. 6:16-17).

Involved in these statements is the fact that at the Fall, at the point of his capitulation to sin, man lost his free will. He became the blinded slave of the Devil. Henceforth he is not free. Either he is, in his natural, unregenerate state, the slave of Satan and sin, or he is, by the renewing, recreating work of God in the soul, the slave of Christ. Both Satan on the one hand and Christ on the other demand a totalitarian allegiance. Both, moreover, obtain it. Until his rescue by Christ from Satan, the "strong man armed who keepeth his palace [and] his goods in peace" (Luke 11:21), the individual is enslaved to sin. He is not free to turn to God. He is, as Christ again responded to the Jews, of his "father the devil" (John 8:44).

We may consider the Scriptural case further. If it is true that as a result of the Fall the mind of man is blinded so that he cannot see or understand what is good (2 Cor. 4:4); if the heart is naturally bent and inclined away from God and altogether propense to evil so that it cannot love what is good (Jer. 17:9); if, as a result, the mind cannot present to the heart a knowledge of the good and the heart cannot therefore love the good, then the will is not free to do the good. If the mind cannot see the good, and the heart cannot love the good, then the will is not free to do the good. The case is indeed a sorry one. The more is it true that the grace of God is magnified in the salvation of the sinner.

Many questions, of course, swirl in the context we have now raised. Is man not in any sense free? Is he not a free, responsible agent? Yes, we can say, man is a free agent. We can hold, under the Scriptures, to free agency and responsibility. But within the orbit of redemption, of sin, salvation, and eternal security, we are not talking of free agency. We are talking of what we have referred to as free will. Man has free agency in the sense that he is free to be consistent with his own nature. In the same sense all creatures are free to be consistent with their natures. A horse is free to be a horse, a cow a cow. Or, in the expressive language of the apostle Peter, a sow is free to be a sow, but only a sow. One can take a sow and wash it, Peter observes. But all one will have will be a washed sow. It will always be a sow, nothing other than a sow. And the only expectation we can have of it is, as Peter says, that it will return to its "wallowing in the mire" (2 Peter 2:22).

In the same sense, man has free agency. The crux of the matter is that man in sin, man in his unregenerate nature, is free only to be consistent with that nature. And that nature, the Scriptures clearly attest, is a sinful nature. Man in sin is free only to be sinful. It is his nature to be such. He can therefore never be anything but a God-hater, a covenant-breaker, and a suppressor of the truth. Every breaking, awakening awareness of the truth he will suppress. He necessarily does that by very reason of the fact that by nature he hates God. When we expand our conceptions beyond free agency to the state of the will and its significance for salvation, we simply have to conclude that man is not free at all. At the Fall, we hear the Scriptures say, man lost his free will. As he now exists in this world, he is not a sinner because he commits sin. Rather, he commits sin because he is a sinner, a slave to sin. He was constituted a sinner by Adam's Fall. It is only by the intervening, redeeming, renewing, recreating grace of God that any sinner is saved.

The self-direction of sin

We refer now, in a final reference to the meaning of sin, to what we call the *self-direction of sin*. As sin takes hold of a man, the passions and the energies of his soul are directed, in all of their potentialities for action and expression, not towards his Creator to whom he is obligated, but towards himself. That is so in a number of respects.

The Scriptures have made it clear that we are called to love the Lord our God with all our heart and soul and mind. "This is the first and great commandment", our Lord has said (Matt. 22:37-38). In his state of innocency, the faculties of his soul were such that man naturally loved God, he loved the communicated law of God, he enjoyed communion with God, and he directed his life, short though it may have been before the Fall, to pleasing God. In his initial and paradisaic state, man existed in a condition of knowledge, righteousness, and holiness (Eph. 4:24; Col. 3:10).

With the mind, the intellectual faculty, man in that pristine state knew God and knew the will and the law of God that were clearly communicated to him. God walked with Adam "in the cool of the day" (Gen. 3:8). With the mind he had a true apprehension of the perfections of God. He had, also, a true knowledge of the conditions of his own existence, and of what, in accordance with the benefits, obligations, and promises of the creation mandate, God required of him. In his unfallen state the mind was the prince of the faculties of the soul. God's communication was a reasoned, rational communication. The entire significance and implications of it were meaningful to man because of God's contact, through the mind of man, with the image of himself in which he had created man. When we say that the mind, the rational or the intellectual faculty, was the prince of the faculties of the soul, we are saying that man's loving, or the exercise of his emotional faculty, and his acting or behavior, or the exercise of his will or volitional faculty, were guided and determined by the presiding activity of the mind.

We have referred, in addition to the mind or the intellectual faculty, to the heart or the emotional faculty, and the will or the volitional faculty of the soul. Addressing again man's existence in his unfallen condition, we may say that not only with the mind did he naturally know God, but that with the heart he naturally loved God, and with the will, therefore, he naturally served God. There existed a primeval harmony in the faculties of the soul. But what, in this perspective, is to be said of the Fall and its implications for the soul?

The reality, as concerns the impact of sin on the faculties of the soul, is twofold. First, at the Fall the harmony of the faculties of the soul was shattered; and second, after the Fall, and as a result of the Fall, the mind no longer reigned as the prince of the faculties. At the Fall, we hear the apostle say, "the god of this world hath blinded the mind" (2 Cor. 4:4). As Christ said to Nicodemus, as a result of the blindness that descended at the Fall it is no longer possible for man in his unregenerate state even to see the kingdom of God or to possess any true apprehension of the things that pertain to it (John 3:3). Paul had argued in the same manner to the Corinthians: "the natural man receiveth not the things of the Spirit of God: for they are foolishness unto him: neither can he know them, because they are spiritually discerned" (1 Cor. 2:14). Our Lord stated the matter once and for all when, in the synagogue at Nazareth at the beginning of his ministry he stated that the very purpose of his coming was that he might bring "recovering of sight to the blind" (Luke 4:18). His parabolic ministry is explained in large part by the blindness of his hearers (Luke 8:10). The Scriptures are replete with the statement and the explanation of the blindness of man in sin.

But not only is that so. Man in sin, the apostle has concluded, is naturally a God-hater (Rom. 1:30). "The heart", the prophet Jeremiah explained "is deceitful above all things and desperately wicked" (Jer. 17:9). Men in sin, Paul explained to Titus, are "hateful and hating one another" (Titus 3:3). Again the Scriptural data could be multiplied. At the Fall, the heart of man was turned implacably against God. After the Fall and as a result of the Fall, man hates God, he hates the things of God, and he hates the law of God. Indeed, so profound is the hatred of God that naturally surges in the human heart that man spends his energies in the pretense that God does not exist. As Paul explains to the Romans, man in sin "suppresses" every wakening awareness of God (Rom. 1:18).

The mind is blinded in the state of sin and does not know and cannot see the goodness of God and the perfection of the law of God. The heart is naturally in hateful opposition to the goodness and the perfections of God. The mind and the heart are no longer able to instruct the will to do the things required by God. The will is therefore no longer free to serve God. The sorry condition of man in sin is that he is the blinded slave of the Devil. For precisely that reason Christ responded in the manner he did on one dramatic occasion: "Ye do not understand ... because ye cannot hear my word. Ye are of your father the devil, and the lusts of your father ye will do" (John 8:43-44).

Not only is the state of man in sin such that in these ways the energies and passions and faculties of the soul are directed against God. The harmony of the faculties is shattered to the extent that now the heart rather than the mind has assumed hegemony in the soul. Now, in a sadly perverse sense, the heart is the prince of the faculties. That, in shortest compass, is the meaning of sin and the state of man in sin. It means that in his unregenerate state he no longer does what he does because a mind that reflects the holy character of God instructs him. Now he does what he wants to do. The passions, the heart, the desires are in command. That is the explanation of the disordered disruption of the human condition. There is no restraint now, apart from those external restraints of conduct that civilization, due to the common grace of God, establishes. The heart is wicked and unruly. "Who can know it?" Jeremiah asks (Jer. 17:9). Reason has capitulated to passion in the human condition. There is no longer a holy law before the minds of men. Ignorance, guilt, and misery disguise their seductions and pretenses and degrade men's souls. Only the rescue and relief that Christ our Redeemer has provided can meet the sorry case.

When we speak of the self-direction of sin we mean, further, that now, in the state of sin, man's essential and motivating love of self has replaced his love of God. He has now become a god unto himself. Or in other terms, he has made gods for himself in his own image, gods he has found within the world of reality that he should have dedicated to the glory of the true God. Or he has manufactured his idols from within his own distorted and alienated imagination.

At the Fall, man asserted his autonomy from God. It was, of course, a false assertion, or the assertion of a false and spurious autonomy. For man the creature has remained subject to the providence of God, both for his continued being and for his actual life history. The apostle attests precisely that when he claims that it is in Christ, in his providential government of reality and its history of which he is King, that "all things consist" or are sustained and cohere (Col. 1:17).

The state of sin into which man has fallen is connoted by his assertion of autonomy as to his being and existence. The claim is made that man exists independently of God, that he has not come from the hands of a holy Creator, and that he is not therefore under any obligation to God. Man has in effect denied his creaturehood. That is the fundamental lie of his life. To make the lie bearable, he persists in the fiction that God does not exist. But what that means in our present context is that man has here, at the most fundamental level of meaning and of the possibility of knowing, turned in upon himself. That is the fundamental expression of what we have referred to as the love of self that absorbs the human soul. The love of self, the false assertion that the self can explain man to himself, is the fundamental lie of Satan in which man has been entrapped in his fallen condition. The love of self, in this all-determining way, has displaced the primeval love of God.

Because of this, the state of man in sin involves the false assertion of autonomy on the level of the possibility and the process of knowledge. That is the assertion that man can discover within himself, or within the structures of reality in which he exists, all necessary and efficient criteria of knowledge and truth. From that follows the false assertion of autonomy as to the criteria of behavior or conduct. That is the claim that man is capable of discovering within himself, or in collective opinion in the world around him, all necessary rules or criteria or mandates of proper behavior. No longer, for the sinner, is the perfect law of God the rule of life. Man in sin, in a sadly comprehensive and all-determining sense, is a law unto himself.

The gospel remedy

Against the meaning of sin, against the realities of the fallenness of the soul, the good news of the gospel confronts the sinner with the redemption that is in Christ. That redemption is grounded in the love of God. God set his love upon his people, and against the demands of his holy justice and law he set forth a propitiation in Christ. In him the repentant, believing sinner is a new creation. The old has passed away. All things for him are new (2 Cor. 5:17). Of course, as John the apostle engages the thought in his epistle, the new man in Christ is a saint who is a sinner. The very issue and problem of the sin that remains in the life of the believer demands a wrestling and an understanding that should itself conduce to the life of righteousness to which the believer is called. It is the task of Satan, as he pursues his designs, to deface the newly-created image of God in the life of the Christian. But for the one who is now joined to Christ, that Satanic design is ineffective.

We turn immediately in the following chapter to the grounding and foundation of all of our felicity, and to the security of the Christian in the love of God set forth for sinners.

6

The Love of God

Across the darkness of sin and the terror of wrath shines the love of God for sinners. Shut out by his sin from communion with God and from the tree of life (Gen. 3:24), the sinner again finds hope, a renewal and reconciliation in Christ the Son of God his Savior. Again the way to the tree of life is opened (Rev. 22:2). Again the joy of communion with God is established. Again, for the heart that knows God, the sinner looks, with Abraham, for that "city which hath foundations, whose builder and maker is God" (Heb. 11:10). The love of God has set forth a redemption for his people in Christ.

The love of God projects redemption's plan against the background of sin and the lostness of Adam's Fall. The Psalmist had seen through the arch of time that "mercy and truth are met together; righteousness and peace have kissed each other" (Ps. 85:10). Against the holiness of the wrath of God and the wrath of his holiness, the apostle John has grasped the meaning of the love of God. "Herein is love", he writes, "not that we loved God, but that he loved us, and sent his Son to be the propitiation for our sins" (1 John 4:10).

The obstacle that lay in the way of the salvation of sinners was that the justice and the honor of God must remain inviolate. If any were to be redeemed and brought to eternal security, two profound problems must be dealt with. First, the penalty for the breaking of God's holy law must be paid. And second, the law itself must be kept, and its demands and requirements must be honored and fulfilled. The only way in which that twofold requirement could be met was by God's sending a sinless substitute to stand in the place of the sinners he decreed to save. Christ the Son of God came from the eternal bosom of the Father to be the sinner's substitute. By virtue of his obedience on the sinner's behalf, the redemption that God provided could be freely extended. By his active obedience in keeping the law on behalf of his people, and by his passive obedience in paying on the cross the penalty due to their sin, Christ actually and definitively saved his people. Now, in him, their title to heaven is secure.

The gravity of sin and the propitiation of Christ

The biblical doctrines of sin and the Fall, the divine decree of redemption, and the propitiatory work of Christ are encapsuled in the Catechism attached to the *Westminster Confession*. "The estate into which the Fall brought mankind" was "an estate of sin and misery".[1] The Catechism continues: "The sinfulness of that estate whereinto man fell, consists in, the guilt of Adam's first sin, the want of original righteousness, and the corruption of his whole nature, which is commonly called Original Sin; together with all actual transgressions which proceed from it".[2] A deprivation and a depravation mark the sinner's condition. His deprivation consists in his loss of original righteousness and the primeval naturalness of his communion with God his Maker. And his depravation consists in the fallenness that destroys the harmonies and tarnishes the capacities of all of the faculties of his soul. It follows that "All mankind, by their fall, lost communion with God, are under his wrath and curse, and so made liable to all the miseries of this life, to death itself, and to the pains of hell for ever".[3]

Perhaps no clearer delineation of the biblical doctrines exists than the summary of them contained in the subsequent state-

---

[1] *Westminster Shorter Catechism*, Question 17.
[2] Ibid., Question 18.
[3] Ibid., Question 19.

ments of the Catechism. First, "Did God leave all mankind to perish in the estate of sin and misery?". The answer drives to the very foundation of our belief: "God having, out of his mere good pleasure, from all eternity, elected some to everlasting life, did enter into a covenant of grace, to deliver them out of the estate of sin and misery, and to bring them into an estate of salvation by a Redeemer". And "the only Redeemer of God's elect", the Catechism continues, "is the Lord Jesus Christ, who, being the eternal Son of God, became man, and so was, and continueth to be God, and man, in two distinct natures, and one person, for ever".[4]

Christ, the Catechism continues, became our Redeemer by his undertaking and discharging "the offices of a prophet, of a priest, and of a king".[5] It explains that in his redemptive office "Christ executeth the office of a priest, in his once offering up of himself a sacrifice to satisfy divine justice, and reconcile us to God; and in making continual intercession for us".[6] Here we have the foundational truths of the gospel. Here again is the meaning of the redemption that God has provided. In another perspective, this summary explains the transaction that occurred between the Father and the Son in that terrible moment on the cross when Christ bore our sins. In that atonement our redemption was secured, because the demands of divine justice were satisfied. A transition from wrath to grace was effected for the people that God the Father, from before the foundation of the world, had given to his Son to redeem (Eph. 1:4, John 17:6).

It was necessary that the wrath of God against sin and the sinner should be appeased. That, precisely, is the meaning of the necessity and the fact of propitiation. Propitiation means setting at peace. The work of Christ was both an expiation for our sin and a propitiation of the wrath of God. We do well to keep clearly in view the perfection of the expiation that Christ provided. But expiation has to do with the condition of guilt in which, because of our sin, we stood before God. Expiation is addressed to our guilt. By the expiation of Christ we are set free

---

[4] Ibid., Questions 20,21.
[5] Ibid., Question 23.
[6] Ibid., Question 25.

from the guilt that fell upon us by the imputation to us of Adam's sin, and from the guilt that clings to us by reason of our continuance in sin.

But at issue here also is something other than expiation, though numerous translators have substituted the word "expiation" for the word "propitiation" in the classic statement in 1 John 4:10 that we are now examining. In that textual statement the apostle is speaking of the work of Christ, not in its expiatory aspect, but as a propitiation for our sins. The fact and doctrine of propitiation directs our attention to the necessity that God should again be set at peace with man. It was necessary that the wrath of God against the sinner and his sin should be turned aside. But that could result only if the demands of that wrath were perfectly and completely satisfied. Peace must again be established between God and man. And the doctrine of propitiation directs our thought to the fact that it is God our Maker and Judge who must be at peace with man the sinner, quite apart from the subjective peace that accrues to us as the benefit of our union with Christ.

Propitiation and the gospel of peace

The doctrine of the effects and results of the propitiatory work of Christ are spread across the Scriptures. A classic and familiar statement is contained in Paul's letter to the Ephesians. In the sixth chapter of that letter the apostle urges his readers to "put on the whole armour of God, that ye may be able to stand against the wiles of the devil" (Eph. 6:11f). We do not explore at this point the meaning and significance of all of the six pieces of armor that the apostle refers to. He speaks of having one's "loins girt about with truth", of putting on the "breastplate of right-eousness", of having one's feet "shod with the preparation of the gospel of peace", of the "shield of faith", the "helmet of salvation", and the "sword of the Spirit, which is the word of God". We look particularly at the apostle's reference in that context to the "gospel of peace".

What, in the context of the apostle's argument regarding the putting on of the armor of God, is the primary meaning of the "gospel of peace"? Two possibilities present themselves. First, the "peace" may refer to the subjective peace that, as is made clear in the Scriptures and in the Christian's experience, accrues to the Christian by virtue of his union with Christ. Or second, it may refer, in a primary sense, to the fact that God is now at peace with man. God, that is to say, is now at peace with those sinners whom he gave to his Son to redeem.

It is beyond doubt that the sinner who is aware of his redemption in Christ enjoys, among the other evangelical gifts that accrue to him, peace with God. God is referred to in the Pauline texts as the "God of peace" (Rom. 15:33; Phil. 4:9). And this conveys the fact of the subjective peace, the peace that the Christian has by reason of his knowledge of God and his union with him in Christ. Paul reinforces the point in his statement to the Philippians that "the peace of God, which passeth all understanding, shall keep your hearts and minds through Christ Jesus" (Phil. 4:7).

But the question we have asked is the following. Is the apostle, in that familiar and famous exhortation in the sixth chapter of the letter to the Ephesians, where he speaks of the "gospel of peace", focusing our attention on the subjective peace we may possess, the peace that the Christian knows in his heart? Or is he directing our thought to the fact that by virtue of the work of Christ, by virtue of the "gospel" as he refers to it, God is at peace with his people?

The latter, we conclude, is in view. The primary reference, or the thrust or focus of the apostle's thought, has to do at that point with the fact that by virtue of the propitiatory work of Christ, God is now at peace with his people. So much is that so, that Paul refers to that complex of issues and circumstances at that point as precisely the "gospel". That is the good news that the gospel represents and conveys.

That is clear from a review of the structure and objective of the paragraph in which the apostle's reference to the gospel of peace occurs. That paragraph contains the apostle's reference to the fact that the "preparation", or the "equipment", of the gospel of peace is a vital and necessary piece of the armor of God that the Christian is exhorted to put on. These six pieces of armor are the "armor of God". They are armor provided by God. As such, they are provided to enable the one who bears them to "stand against the wiles of the devil". They are each, in their own way, defensive. They are what they are in order that they might enable us to stand "in the evil day", in the midst of our temptations and against the onslaughts of the devil.

Satan, of course, cannot destroy the certainty of the Christian's salvation and his eternal security. But Satan can, and he does, drag the Christian down to lower levels of spiritual awareness than he is entitled to share by virtue of his union with Christ. He can, and he does, make the Christian behave in ways that are unworthy of the Lord who redeemed him. He can, in short, trap the Christian in acts and occasions of sin. Satan sets out to deface the image of Christ in the redeemed sinner. Notwithstanding the security of the believer's position in Christ and the fact, as our Lord himself has promised, that "I give unto them eternal life, and they shall never perish, neither shall any man pluck them out of my hand" (John 10:28), Satan can and does, to our sad discredit, disturb the joy and the peace that Christ gives to us.

Sin, in short, is stronger than the Christian. It is stronger than what the Christian in himself, and apart from the grace of the Spirit of God, is able to stand against and surmount. Only by the ministry of the Spirit of God and by the "putting on" of the armor that God has provided can the Christian "withstand in the evil day". But here, precisely, is the Christian's defense. In this paragraph from the Ephesian letter the apostle is describing six pieces of defensive armor. What, then, are we to understand as that defensive piece of armor referred to as the "gospel of peace"? The question may be put in an alternative form.

When the attacks of Satan come, is it, or would it be, a proper or adequate defense to reply to him that he cannot touch us because we have a subjective peace by virtue of our knowledge of God? Would a reference to our subjective peace be an adequate line of defense against Satan and his subtle, deceiving angels? Let us suppose we were to make such a defense. Might it not be quite simple for Satan then to respond to us in such a way as to question the depth or constancy or continuity or the genuineness of the peace that we have just professed? Could he not thereby call in question what we profess to be our standing in Christ? Is there no way in which

Satan could then cause us to question the reality of the peace we have professed? Do not his attacks ever take that form? To say that they do not is to betray an unfamiliarity with the wiles of our adversary.

But let us restate the question. What is it in which our security and our effective line of defense against Satan exists? Is it to be found in something subjective within ourselves? Or is it not rather to be found in something objective that God himself has done and provided? The latter is true. The only sure defense against the evil one is the fact that God himself has done something about the case and condition in which Satan had previously held us bound. Now one stronger than Satan has come (Luke 11:21-22) and has rescued and released us from his terrible grasp. The security of what the gospel introduces us to resides in the grand objectivity of what God has done.

The apostle claimed that exultantly in the second chapter of his letter to the Ephesians. We were "dead in trespasses and sins" (Eph. 2:1-3), but God did something at that very point. God the Father designed a redemption and put that plan of redemption into effect in the person of his Son. The apostolic exclamation at that point, at which he declares "But God ...", captures the meaning and the glory of the gospel of grace.

We ask again, would it be an adequate line of defense to state to the tempter that he cannot touch us because we have a peace within ourselves? That peace is not irrelevant to our position in Christ. But is that the defense against Satan that the apostle refers to as one of the pieces of defensive armor in that important paragraph of the Ephesian letter? To the contrary, we may conclude that the "gospel of peace" is precisely the gospel, the good news, that God is now at peace with us. He is at peace with us because he now sees us joined to himself in Christ his Son. That is our defense. We can respond to Satan with the unalterable and untarnishable verity that God is at peace with us. We take refuge, not in what we think or feel within ourselves. We take refuge in what God has done and guaranteed to us. A hymnwriter has put it perfectly in his claim that "I may my fierce accuser face and tell him, Thou [Christ] hast died".[7]

---

[7] Philip Doddridge, "There is a way for man to rise ..."

The expansive love of God

We recall the Johannine text: "Herein is love, not that we loved God, but that he loved us, and sent his Son to be the propitiation for our sins" (1 John 4:10). We do not expand further at this point on the propitiatory aspects of the atonement of Christ. Nor do we stay with the transaction between the Father and the Son at that terrible moment of dereliction on the cross that led to our Savior's declaration that "It is finished" (John 19:30). Our redemption was there completed. The Covenant of Redemption that had been formed in the council of the Godhead before the foundation of the world was then brought to full effect. At that moment "the veil of the temple was rent in twain from the top to the bottom" (Matt. 27:51) by the hand of God, and the old order of preparation had passed away. The fulfillment of all the promises of God, to us his people and to Christ his Son in whom he has chosen us, was at hand.

Do we wish to know something of the expansive love of God that set forth the redemption that Christ accomplished? If, the apostle is here saying, we can grasp or measure the terrible extent and the wretchedness of our sin that made the propitiatory work of Christ necessary, we begin to glimpse an awareness of the love of God. If, that is to say, we can grasp the reality and the meaning of the holiness of God that came to expression in a holy wrath against sin that made propitiation necessary, then we begin to glimpse the love of God.

Or let us put the point in another way. If we can form an understanding of the extent of the journey that the second Person of the Godhead took, from the glory and the bliss of his eternal existence with the Father to his humiliation in this world and the agony of the cross, then we may begin to realize something of the meaning of the love of God. Or we may say that if we can be aware of the holiness and the wrath of God that made the setting forth of a "gospel of peace" necessary if his people were to be redeemed, then we begin to glimpse something of the love of God.

Or we may reflect on what we discovered in the preceding chapter of the meaning of sin. If we can measure the extent of the journey that Christ took in order to deal with our sin we may begin to understand the exceeding sinfulness of our condition. We may thereby grasp the terrible affront and outrage that our sin offered to the holiness of God. And reflecting on what we have understood of the holiness of God that our sin had outraged, the expanse of the love of God will begin to dawn upon us. The love of God is of such an unfathomable nature that we can begin to understand it, the apostle is saying, only as we see it and realize it against the fact of our sin and the wrath of God that made propitiation necessary. "Herein is love, that God sent His Son to be the propitiation for our sins".

Well might the poets and the hymnwriters exhaust their skill to finds words to express the greatness of the love of God. "O love that will not let me go, I rest my weary soul on thee. I give thee back the life I owe, that in thine ocean depth its flow may richer, fuller be".[8] The great hymns of the church exult repeatedly in the love of God. They conjure for us the glorious declarations of the Scripture, and we hear again the magnificent truth that "God so loved the world, that he gave his only begotten Son, that whosoever believeth in him should not perish, but have everlasting life" (John 3:16).

This is how we might begin to glimpse the love of God, though we cannot measure its extent or grasp its vastness. The day of glory will continue to declare and unfold its meaning. But we begin to see, in the well-known words of the Johannine gospel, that the love of God was so vast in its depth and extent that it was addressed in that remarkable way to people who were perishing. For that is the burden of the familiar text of John 3:16. God set his love upon people who, apart from what his love for them accomplished, were perishing. That is the terrible reality and implication of our sin. Apart from the love of God there is no hope. Had God not set his love upon his people they too, with all those who continue in their rejection of their obligations to God, must finally perish.

That is the terrible burden of John 3:16. Apart from the sovereign and unsolicited love of God we perish. "But God", to quote again the Pauline text to the Ephesians (Eph. 2:4), did something about our condition. He "so" loved us, John declares,

---

[8] George Matheson, 1882.

he "so" loved those whom he had given to his Son to redeem (John 17:6), that he sent his Son to be their Savior. The Scripture that sets the love of God against the propitiatory offering of his Son (1 John 4:10) declares the remarkable fact that God set his love upon people who were the objects of his wrath. That is the fact that evokes our wonder, amazement, and worship.

The same declaration of the heart of the gospel is made in the gospel of John. "He that believeth not the Son ... the wrath of God abideth on him" (John 3:36). The wrath of God remains on those who reject the Son of God. Nothing has been done to remove the wrath of God from them. It remains. It abides. There is no further hope for them. They have what they always wanted. They have "loved darkness rather than light" (John 3:19). They remain the comfortable slaves of Satan and sin. They have no hope beyond this life, and an eternal separation from God awaits them, "the blackness of darkness for ever" (Jude 13).

But much more is involved in the apostolic declaration that God exhibited his love in sending his Son to be the propitiation for our sins. Is it true, we may ask, that God loves the sinner, or that he loves the sinners for whom Christ died, because Christ died for them? Let us approach the answer to that question from another direction. We have seen that Christ as our Redeemer, in the words of the Catechism, executes the offices of a prophet, priest, and king. In the discharge of his priestly office Christ "satisfied divine justice and reconciled us to God".[9] Moreover, in the discharge of his heavenly high priestly office Christ now "makes continual intercession for us".[10] The meaning of the heavenly high priestly office of Christ is spread clearly across the Scriptures. The writer to the Hebrews observed, for example, that Christ, as our "high priest", "is able also to save them to the uttermost that come unto God by him, seeing he ever liveth to make intercession for them" (Heb. 7:25). But what is the nature of Christ's intercession at the Father's right hand on our behalf?

The answer may be put both negatively and positively. Our

---

[9] *Westminster Shorter Catechism*, Question 25.
[10] Ibid.

Lord does not, and cannot, plead with the Father to agree that we have not sinned. The suggestion that he might do so would fly monstruously in the face of all that is implied in the coming of Christ into the world to discharge his priestly office on our behalf. But equally, our Lord does not, and cannot, plead with the Father to agree that we have sinned, but that our sin can be overlooked, or assumed not to be worthy of divine recognition, in the light of the love that was displayed in the dying of the Son for us. Further, Christ does not, and cannot, plead with the Father to look upon us with love and complacence solely or simply because he has died for us, as though in that way he would constrain the love of God toward us. All such claims, which need to be carefully and reflectively examined, would involve errors, some perhaps of seemingly slight importance on the surface of things. But the errors involved are actually of such fundamental importance as to deny the very gospel they would claim to present.

In his eternal intercession before the Father, Christ, who has been made for us "a priest for ever after the order of Melchisedec" (Heb. 7:17), presents the fact and the reality of our sin. He recognizes our just desert because of our sin, and the coverage with his righteousness that is divinely imputed to us by reason of his perfect work for us. But he does not, and by virtue of the eternal construction of the Covenant of Redemption he cannot, plead with the Father to set his love upon us solely or simply because of the work that he has done as our Redeemer. On the contrary, the glory of the gospel is that the precise opposite is true.

It is not true to say that God loves us simply because of the substitutionary work of Christ for us. Rather, the substitutionary work of Christ came to effect and conveyed its benefits to us precisely because God loved us.

This is what we have in view when we speak of the unconstrained love of God. There is, and there can be, no explanation of the love of God beyond and outside of the sovereign declaration of his own will. We find the only explanation of the love of God is his own free and unconstrained determination, in his own eternal counsel, of what he had willed.

In the predeterminate council of the Godhead, God the Father designed and provided a redemption for those whom, from among the fallen offspring of Adam, he freely and sovereignly chose to make up his eternal kingdom. The wonder of the gospel and of the Covenant of Redemption from which it issued is not that God did not, in that eternally free and sovereign deliberation, choose all men for eternal salvation. That he did not do so is clear from abundant Scriptural testimony. And we have already seen in this chapter that on those who do not come to him in Christ, or whom, as John puts it in the sixth chapter of his gospel, the Father does not draw to himself (John 6:44), the wrath of God remains.

The wonder of the gospel of the grace of God is not that God refrained from choosing some to eternal life. All men deserved only to stand under the eternal justice of God and to incur the penalty which, in accordance with God's initial promise, was justly due to them for their sin. The wonder of the gospel is that God should have chosen to redeem any at all. No one could have had any claim on God's love or mercy. All were justly lost. The wonder is that God in his sovereign good pleasure should have set forth a redemption for any at all. In accordance with the eternal counsel that issued in the Covenant of Redemption, Christ the Son undertook to come into the world, to assume the human nature, yet without sin, of the people whom the Father gave to him to redeem, and to offer to God the Father on their behalf the full obedience that accomplished their redemption. The Holy Spirit, the blessed third Person of the divine trinity, undertook to call and to sanctify those whom the Father chose and for whom the Son would die, to apply to them the benefits of the redemption that Christ accomplished, and to bring them to glory.

It follows that it is again not true to say that God loves his people simply or solely because Christ died for them. The contrary is true. Christ came into the world and died for them because God loved them, and because, by reason of that love, he designed such a remarkable redemption for them.

The Pauline epistles are replete with the apostle's declarations to that effect. "God commendeth his love toward us", Paul declares, "in that, while we were yet sinners, Christ died for us" (Rom. 5:8). While we were yet lost in sin God set his love upon us. There was not, and by virtue of our fallenness and the corruption of sin that clung to us there could not have been, any virtue or merit in ourselves that could commend the love of God to us. It was by his free grace, by his sovereign will and unsolicited mercy, that he set his love upon us. The apostle delights in declaring the divine monergism that designed and accomplished our salvation. "By grace are ye saved through faith", he claims to the Ephesians, "and that not of yourselves: it is the gift of God: Not of works, lest any man should boast" (Eph. 2:8-9).

God's eternal, electing love

The apostolic explanation of the love of God is in these ways grounded in an awareness of the determinate counsel of the Godhead, and in a realization of the terms of the Covenant of Redemption and the design of our salvation that issued from it. "God sent his Son", John writes (1 John 4:10). The Son of God who existed with the Father, in consubstantial union with the Father and the Spirit, was "sent" into the world to accomplish the objectives of redemption. God "gave" his Son, it is recorded in the Johannine gospel (John 3:16), that his people might be saved. The eternal pre-existence of the Son is clarified in numerous texts, and the apostolic statements bring into focus the eternity of the love of God.

The text of Paul's epistle to the Ephesians states that "He (God the Father) hath chosen us in him (Christ) before the foundation of the world, that we should be holy and without blame before him in love. Having predestinated us unto the adoption of children by Jesus Christ to himself, according to the good pleasure of his will, to the praise of the glory of his grace, wherein he hath made us accepted in the beloved" (Eph. 1:4-6). We see on the very surface of the text that the entire design and scope and objectives of our redemption are referable, as a primary and originating cause, to "the good pleasure of his will". There is not, and there cannot be, any more ultimate explanation, or any more final causation, of the plan of redemption than the sovereign will of God. No more ultimate explanation or cause of the love of God exists than the sover-

THE FRACTURE OF FAITH

eign dictates of his will.

We may put the doctrine by asking what is to be understood as the primary and originating cause of the design and provision of our redemption? Is it to be found in the love of God? We have spoken at length of the love of God that is so extensively displayed in his sending his Son to be our redeemer. But we are asking now whether the love of God is revealed to us as the final or ultimate cause we are seeking to understand. The Scriptures repeatedly declare that the dictates of the love of God are traceable simply and finally to the deliberation and the ordination of the will of God. No more ultimate access is available to us than a realization of the dictates of the will of God. We are required to bow before the revelation that God "worketh all things after the counsel of his own will" (Eph. 1:11).

But while that is so, we observe in the passage before us (Eph. 1:4-6) that the love of God came prominently into conjunction with his will in that predeterminate council that established the terms of our redemption. God willed to set his love upon us. He willed to send his Son to be, in the discharge of the messianic office that he willed in love to set forth, the Redeemer of his elect. That, the text observes, issued from an election, a "predestination", that was established "before the foundation of the world". The eternal character of that love forces its impress upon us.

The statement of the text (Eph. 1:4-6) is that God has chosen us in order that we should be "holy and without blame before him in love". The text then continues with the explanatory statement: "Having predestinated us ...". A question arises as to whether the apostle's words, "in love", should be attached to the preceding words, or whether they should be read in conjunction with the succeeding statement, "Having predestinated us ...". Further, some textual scholars have questioned whether those important words, "in love", should be taken to refer to the entire process and deliberations of the divine will as referred to at the beginning of the text in the words, "He hath chosen us ...". In that case we should have for our consideration three possible understandings of the Pauline text.

First, it might be said that God the Father has chosen his people "in love". Second, the writer could intend to state that we are to walk before God "in love". Or third, it may be envisaged that God has "predestinated us unto the adoption of children" and has done so "in love".

It is true that well-founded and legitimate rules of translation do not always eliminate room for sound and equally reliable alternatives in our response to the text. By that statement we do not intend to diminish the importance of a strict attention to the words of the text. For our doctrine of the inspiration of the Scriptures requires us to state that the words of the autographs, in all their individuality and plurality, are the very words of God. We hold to the verbal and plenary inspiration of the Scriptures. In the present instance, however, we can take account of the alternatives of translation that have been suggested, and we can ask what considerations of biblical doctrine might assist or determine our understanding of the text.

Some expositors have understood this Ephesian text in a manner that argues for the retention of the translation as it is given, for example, in the King James text.[11] The argument that the "in love" is to be understood as characteristic of what the Christian's life and walk is to be is highly cogent and carries strong conviction.

It might well be thought, nevertheless, that in this case the "in love" can properly, and probably more correctly, be attached to the succeeding statement of the apostle. In that case it is being stated that the "predestination" by which God the Father established our redemption in Christ was a predestination in love. On the basis of such an understanding of this important text, and in the light of our preceding discussion of the love of God, the apostle here presents us with an astounding fact. The love of God was operative in all of his ordination that structured his plan of redemption. It informed all of the processes that put that plan into effect for our benefit and for his glory.

The text, in that case, comes into clear conjunction with the statement we have noted in the first epistle of John. We see again that it was the result of the dictates of the love of God that, as John states, "sent His Son to be the propitiation for our

---

[11] See D. M. Lloyd-Jones, *God's Ultimate Purpose: An Exposition of Ephesians 1:1 to 2:3*, Grand Rapids: Baker Books, 1978, Ch.8.

sins". That love is a love that issued from the divine desire and the sovereign, uncaused will of God. It was settled upon the people of God's choice in the eternal council, "before", as the text has stated, "the foundation of the world". God loved his people, we are required to understand, in that eternity that was, and is, outside of time and beyond all of the temporal processes and structures that God has made.

The eternity of the love of God, or the projection of that love to his people before the foundation of the world, is confirmed in a remarkable and arresting manner in the high priestly prayer of our Lord that is recorded in the seventeenth chapter of the gospel of John. At the conclusion of the supper discourses on the night of his betrayal, Christ prayed to his Father on our behalf. He is there praying, he says to the Father, "not for the world, but for them which thou hast given me" (John 17:9). He had referred to the subjects of his prayer by saying that "thine they were, and thou gavest them me" (John 17:6). Our Lord is there bringing before the Father the interests of those whom, in that predeterminate council of the Godhead, the Father had given to him to redeem. Now he is about to give his life for them. Now the shepherd is about to lay down his life for his sheep. He has a clear knowledge of who they are. The good shepherd, he says, knows his own sheep "by name" (John 10:3). He knows their names because he wrote their names in the book of life before the foundation of the world (Rev. 13:8; 17:8).

But we may ponder the remarkable declaration that our Lord makes in that high priestly prayer, as he brings to the throne of the Father all those for whom he prayed. He acknowledges, he says to the Father, that "thou hast loved them, as thou hast loved me" (John 17:23). How, we may ask, can that have been so? Is not Christ, the Son of God, one with the Father, as he himself declares when he claims that "I and my Father are one" (John 10:30)? Does he not exist eternally with the Father in a consubstantial union, and have we not already confronted the realities inherent in that fact? And can, then, a likeness of love be conferred on the Son himself and on us who, as we have seen, were chosen "in him" in God's predestinating counsel? Can we raise our conceptions to grasp the truth that something of the intra-trinitarian love devolves on us? The declaration of our

Lord in that sacred high priestly prayer astounds us in its import and its meaning. While we cannot compass the intra-trinitarian love, and while we cannot compass in its vastness the love of God to us, we are here brought nearer to the meaning of God's love for us.

We hear our Lord praying on the night of his betrayal and acknowledging to the Father that "thou hast loved them, as thou hast loved me". We pause before the import of that profound declaration. We do not plumb its real extent. But we hear our Lord continue, "thou lovedst me before the foundation of the world" (John 17:24). We know, then, that it is here that a similar conferral of divine love falls upon us who are the objects of his choice. God loved us, too, before the foundation of the world. We know the verity of the declaration of God to his people of old, and we know with a conviction that cannot be erased that we, too, are partakers of the fact and the promises it implies: "I have loved thee with an everlasting love" (Jer. 31:3).

The Christian's response

We can no longer doubt the reality of the love of God for us and the eternal security that it gives us. We know something of the beginning of that love in the eternal counsels of God. We have traced something of its import in that it gave us the very Son of God to be our Redeemer. And we know something of the meaning of the apostle's statement that Christ, "having loved his own which were in the world, he loved them unto the end" (John 13:1). We know that our eternal security is grounded in the eternal love of God for us. The question then presses upon our conscience: What is our response to the love of God? And what does that response mean and imply for our life in this world?

The answer will engage us again when we consider further some relevant aspects of the Christian's life and walk. For the present, let us ask whether we are sensitive to the question that our Lord asked one of old. "Peter", he said, "lovest thou me?" (John 21:15). Or are our ears dulled by the carelessness of sin and the cares of the world? Do we hear our Lord patiently asking again, "Lovest thou me?" How often must he ask before we hear? Do we respond with a sincere and unsullied affection

115

and say with Peter "Lord, thou knowest all things; thou knowest that I love thee". Do we, with the saints of old, offer our hearts sincerely to God who has brought us into an indissoluble union with himself in Christ? God grant that it may be so.

Do we hear, and are we attentive to obey him, when he says to us, "If ye love me, keep my commandments"? (John 14:15). Do we love the law of God, the precepts that he has set forth as a rule for our lives? Have we taken care to grasp the meaning of the apostolic admonition that "whoso keepeth his word, in him verily is the love of God perfected [and] hereby know we that we are in him"? (1 John 2:5). Do we grasp the fact that it is as we learn to know and love and live by the law of God that the love that God has for us is perfected, or brought to the fuller realization and expression of its potential significance? God grant that it may be so.

May we by his grace learn to love him more. May we learn to share something of the passion and the motion of heart of the hymnwriter who declared that "Lord, it is my chief complaint that my love is weak and faint; Yet I love thee and adore; O for grace to love thee more".[12] We know that Christ is our all-sufficient Redeemer. In him alone all our felicity abounds. May he grant, by his grace, that we shall learn to walk before him "in love", bringing to expression and realization in our lives the objective and purpose for which he redeemed us (Eph. 1:4). Doing that, may we realize more perfectly that the objective for which our salvation was designed was that we might be "to the praise of the glory of his grace, wherein he hath made us accepted in the beloved" (Eph. 1:6). God grant that it may be so.

---

[12] William Cowper, "Hark, my soul, it is the Lord ..."

7

The Satisfaction of Christ

When we speak in this chapter of "the satisfaction of Christ" we refer to the satisfaction which, in his life and by his substitutionary death, he provided to the justice and the law of God and to God's wrath against the sinner and his sin. The love of God extends to sinners who have no claim at all on his mercy. The good news of the gospel is that God saves sinners. We come now to consider more closely the means by which the redemption that Christ accomplished provides the grounds of the transition from wrath to grace of the people of God.

In many respects we have already considered that redemptive process at some length. We have seen that in the first epistle of John the apostle has laid down three fundamental propositions or points of doctrine which, taken together, direct us to the heart of the gospel. First, John states at the very beginning of his epistle that "God is light, and in him is no darkness at all" (1 John 1:5). God, that is to say, is a holy God. The reality of God's holy wrath against sin made necessary the propitiation of which John speaks.

Second, God expressed his love for sinners, for the sinners whom he had chosen in Christ to redeem, in that he "sent his Son to be the propitiation for our sins" (1 John 4:10). That fact, the sovereign choice of the grace of God in sending his Son into the world to be our Redeemer, defined for John the very meaning of the love of God. The redemptive work of Christ involved not only the expiation of our guilt, but also the propitiation of God's wrath. The obedience of Christ that gives us our title to heaven encompassed both his keeping of the law on our behalf and his bearing in his death the penalty that was due to us for our breaking of the law.

Third, by virtue of the redemption that God provided in his Son, we stand justified in the presence of God. That redemption exists by virtue of the fact that "the blood of Jesus Christ his Son cleanseth us from all sin" (1 John 1:7). "Christ made peace", Paul argues to the Colossians, "through the blood of his cross" (Col. 1:20). And the apostle makes the same claim to the Ephesians that in Jesus Christ "we have redemption through his blood" (Eph. 1:7). The universal declaration of the Scriptures is that those who are saved are saved by the blood of Christ. At this crux of the gospel statement the Scriptures declare that our Redeemer died for us a real historical death in real historical time. In doing so, he satisfied the demands of the wrath of God against us because of our sin.

The Johannine declaration rings clear in the Christian consciousness. "If we walk in the light, as he is in the light, we have fellowship one with another, and the blood of Jesus Christ his Son cleanseth us from all sin". This is the Christian's highest good, to know God and to have fellowship with him. Until the day of glory dawns and we then know "face to face" (1 Cor. 13:12), we have the "light of the knowledge of the glory of God in the face of Jesus Christ" (2 Cor. 4:6) who came to "declare" God unto us (John 1:18). By his Spirit he comes and dwells with us (John 14:17) and bears witness to us "that we are the children of God" (Rom. 8:16).

If we walk in the light, John says, in the light of the righteous law of God, then we have fellowship "one with another". The reference in that statement is not to the possibility of fellowship with others of the saints of God, though that is a high privilege that the Christian enjoys. The fellowship of which John speaks is a fellowship that exists between God the Father on the one hand and the Christian on the other. Our union with Christ involves and carries along with it union with God in his triune existence. Our union is with the Father, the Son, and the Holy Spirit.

The Johannine statement that the blood of Christ cleanses us from sin has primary reference, in the context in which it occurs, to the character and the development of the Christian life. It has a direct and important reference to the development of the Christian's sanctification. It brings before us clearly, however, the fact that our entire redemption depends on the efficacy of the blood of Christ, or on what was accomplished by and through the shedding of the blood of Christ. The blood of Christ brings us, through the faith that by his Spirit he creates within us, to God the Father. John is here stating that all of our salvation, in all of its parts and in all of its scope and prospect, is what it is because the blood of Christ was shed on our behalf.

Because, as the hymnwriter puts it, of "the fountain filled with blood drawn from Immanuel's veins"[1] we "have access, through him, by one Spirit unto the Father" (Eph. 2:18). The Christian whose conscience is cleared by the astounding facts of redemption shares the apostle's exulting cry, "God forbid that I should glory, save in the cross of our Lord Jesus Christ" (Gal. 6:14). All of our salvation is what it is because Christ shed his blood for his people.

The covenantal structure of redemption

The redemptive offices of Christ were discharged in accordance with the terms of the Covenant of Redemption established in the predeterminate, intra-trinitarian council of the Godhead before the foundation of the world. "God our Father ... hath chosen us in him before the foundation of the world ... having predestinated us unto the adoption of children by Jesus Christ to himself, according to the good pleasure of his will" (Eph. 1:2,4-5). Peter, also, sets the argument of his epistle against the decree that issued from that predeterminate council. He writes, he says, to the "elect according to the foreknowledge of God the Father, through sanctification of the Spirit, unto obedience and sprinkling of the blood of Jesus Christ" (1 Peter 1:2). The separate and distinctive offices of the three persons of the Godhead in effecting our redemption are here clearly displayed.

---

[1] William Cowper, 1771.

119

The covenant that God established not only guarantees the consummation of our redemption. It provides the key to the understanding of the revelation that he has provided. In clarifying the terms of the Covenant of Redemption, the Scriptures underline the eternal security of those whom, in accordance with its provisions, the Holy Spirit of God brings to Christ. Brought into clear perspective are the guarantees that follow from that eternal covenant of grace. The terms of the covenant are spread across the surface of the biblical text. The Covenant of Redemption in Christ provides the key to the Scriptures.

The Old Testament Scriptures insist repeatedly on God's jealousy for the terms of his covenant and for his faithfulness to what he has promised. A final reference to that occurs in the last book of the Old Testament prophets. Malachi spoke at length against the ways in which the priests at that time had turned their backs on their obligations and responsibilities under the covenant of priesthood that God had established with them. That covenant of priesthood was, of course, a part of God's administration of the larger Covenant of Redemption. It was a crucial aspect of the form of administration that the covenant assumed in the Old Testamental and anticipatory dispensation.

The priests, Malachi charged, had "corrupted the covenant of Levi" and they had "profaned the covenant of our fathers" (Mal. 2:8,10). That, a careful reading of the Old Testament text reveals, was God's repeated complaint against his people. In various ways and in varying situations they had denied the obligations of the covenant in terms of which God had called them to be his people. Nothing brings to more sensitive or articulate focus God's charge of infidelity against his people than the complaint that they had denied and rejected the covenantal obligations for which they were liable.

But in the third chapter of his prophecy Malachi exults in the promise that "the Lord ... the messenger of the covenant ... shall come..." (Mal. 3:1); and again, "the Sun of righteousness shall arise with healing in his wings ..." (Mal. 4:2). God will be faithful to his eternal commitment. He will infallibly redeem his people. His anointed One, the promised Messiah, the "messenger of the covenant", the "Sun of righteousness", will discharge his redemptive office and he will "save His people" (Matt. 1:21). The faithfulness of God to the covenant he established conducts us to the meaning of the work of Christ for us. He came in order that, as Daniel repeated the promise, "in the midst of the week" he might "confirm the covenant with many" (Dan. 9:27). In that climactic moment to which all of history pointed he brought in the new kingdom of righteousness.

At an early stage in the history of redemption God established with Abraham a covenant, into the blessings of which the Christian enters by reason of his faith in Christ. Those who believe are thereby the seed of Abraham (Gal. 3:29). The dramatic establishment of the Abrahamic covenant is recorded in the fifteenth chapter of Genesis. Abraham was instructed at that time to divide certain animals into parts (Gen. 15:9) between which God himself passed. That episode points to the deepest meaning of what we shall see as the covenantal malediction on which the fact and the efficacy of Christ's substitutionary work turns.

The establishment of those covenantal arrangements, together with the swearing of the covenantal oath that was integral to it, involved the undertaking of precise and unalterable obligations. The understanding of the terms and the scope of God's covenant requires, therefore, a grasp of the different potential results that may ensue from the development of the covenantal relations. As in the case of the initial Adamic covenant (Gen. 2:17), an obedient fulfillment of its terms and requirements would lead to blessing and benediction. But disobedience, or a repudiation of the obligations inherent in the covenant, would involve the liability to the penalties which in that case were anticipated under the covenant. It would lead, that is, to punishment and malediction.

The promise of blessing on the one hand and the promise of curse on the other have always been, in the very nature of the relations between God and man, inherent in all of God's covenantal dealings. That was clearly so, not only in the initial Covenant of Creation. The parallel promises of blessing in the event of covenantal obedience, and of curse in the event of dereliction from covenantal obligations, have continued throughout the successive administrations of God's relations with his people (See Deut.Chs.27-28). Benediction and blessing in the event of obedience, and malediction and curse in the event of unfaithfulness, structure the covenantal commitments.

At issue now is the implication of the fact that God, in the manifestation referred to in the initial establishment of the Abrahamic covenant, passed between the divided parts of the animals. In that action God swore that he himself would be faithful to his covenantal promises. If he should not be, it is there being announced, then let him not be God. He there swore by his own name, as the letter to the Hebrews clarified and confirmed, that he would be faithful. "For when God made promise to Abraham, because he could swear by no greater, he sware by himself ... wherein God, willing more abundantly to shew unto the heirs of promise the immutability of his counsel, confirmed it by an oath" (Heb. 6:13,17).

The grace and the condescension and mercy of the eternal God deserve the sinner's unending contemplation. The eternal age itself will not exhaust the wonder of it. But now, we should ask, what of Abraham, and what is to be said of his standing under the obligations that the covenant imposed upon him? We know that the sign of the covenant was the circumcision that God introduced at that time and for that purpose (Gen. 17:10; see also Gen. 17:14). At Rom. 4:11 the apostle refers to the circumcision of Abraham as both a "sign" and a "seal" of righteousness. But in submitting to the act of circumcision Abraham was in turn swearing a maledictory oath. That oath was parallel to, and reciprocal with, the maledictory oath that God himself had sworn.

The penalty for unfaithfulness was death. It was for that reason that the sign of the covenant as given to Abraham, the act of circumcision, was itself a blood sign. The shedding of blood that was intrinsic to it anticipated the full penalty of death that would be due for the breaking of the law of the covenant. The acceptance of the conditions of the covenant, and the consequent recognition of the full potential scope of penalty for the repudiation of them, are reflected in the maledictory oath. The promise that was thus suspended on covenantal unfaithfulness implied the total suffering of penalty, the total death of the offender.

We focus, then, on the fact and meaning of the maledictory oaths implicit in the covenant that God made with Abraham. Abraham's position under the terms of the covenant and the outcome that ensued has significance not only for him, but for all those who, through him, were contemplated as the beneficiaries of the covenant. Did Abraham, then, adhere faithfully to the covenantal obligations that were imposed upon him? Was Abraham faithful to God who had called him to such a high position of favor? Or in starker terms, did Abraham sin, and did he thereby warrant the weight of the penalties and the curse implicit in the covenantal promises?

The answer is clear from the testimony of the Scriptures. It is confirmed beyond argument in the Christian's own life history. Abraham and his posterity fell clearly under the "curse of the law" (Gal. 3:13). With all the progeny of Adam, they were exposed to the wrath and condemnation of God. That is clearly displayed in the opening chapters of Paul's epistle to the Romans and in his letter to the Galatians. The *Westminster Catechism* responds with reference to Adam's sin, that "all mankind, descending from him by ordinary generation, sinned in him, and fell with him, in his first transgression".[2] Neither the obligations of fidelity imposed upon man at the establishment of the earliest creation covenant, nor the obligations sustained by God's people by virtue of their standing under the terms of the Covenant of Grace, were honored by those who were the subjects of them. The sorry facts of the case are that all were exposed to the wrath and the curse of God.

All were thus exposed to the liabilities and the penalties which, as it was clearly articulated in the Abrahamic covenant, their maledictory oath anticipated. This, it can now be seen, has extensive implications for the significance of the satisfaction that Christ provided for us. It is necessary, therefore, to confront and consider the full weight of the maledictory implications that are thus incurred. For at this point we see again the significance of the propitiation that John in his first epistle has referred to so eloquently and meaningfully. But in that same Johannine declaration the remarkable good news of the gospel is an-

---

[2] *Westminster Shorter Catechism*, Question 16.

nounced. God himself, recognizing the plight and condition of those whom he chose to redeem, took action to meet and satisfy the terms necessary for the accomplishment of their redemption. That comes to prominence in the light of the malediction inherent in covenantal repudiation or disobedience.

At that earliest covenantal inauguration God swore his own faithfulness. He did not incur any liability and he did not, and could not, become subject to any disapprobation for non-fulfillment of the terms of the covenant. God must be God. He is the same in his righteousness and immutability "yesterday, and today, and for ever" (Heb. 13:8). But the remarkable fact of our redemption is that God took upon himself in Christ the malediction that was due to us. Christ bore the maledictory curse for us (Gal. 3:13). In that remarkable fact the reality of the penal, substitutionary sacrifice of Christ comes to its most poignant significance. Not for himself, but for us, Christ subjected himself to the humiliation of his incarnation and bore the wrath of God the Father on the cross. There "the church of God [was] purchased with his own blood" (Acts 20:28).

The prophets, who spoke repeatedly of Christ (John 5:39), spread their testimony lavishly across the pages of the sacred text. "Surely he hath borne our griefs, and carried our sorrows ... He was wounded for our transgressions, he was bruised for our iniquities, the chastisement of our peace was upon him; and with his stripes we are healed ... the Lord hath laid upon him the iniquity of us all ... it pleased the Lord to bruise him [and] make his soul an offering for sin ... he hath poured out his soul unto death, and he was numbered with the transgressors, and he bare the sin of many ..." (Is. 53:4-6,10-12). Here we come face to face with the heart of the gospel. God, who is eternally faithful to his oath and promise, has himself borne in Christ the penalties, the curse of malediction, that justly accrued to us. They accrued to us as we stood before him in all of the disintegrity and dereliction from obligation of which we were culpable.[3] The heart of

---

[3] The covenantal structure of redemption has been widely discussed in the theological literature. The following quite incomplete references provide a partial history: L. Berkhof, *Systematic Theology*, Grand Rapids: Eerdmans, 1941, "Man in the covenant of grace", 262ff.; Herman Witsius, *The Economy of the Covenants between God and Man*, Escondido: The den Dulk Christian

the gospel comes to clear expression in the fact that he "who knew no sin was made to be sin for us ... that we might be made the righteousness of God in him" (2 Cor. 5:21).

The satisfaction provided by Christ

Against the realization of the holiness of God, and in the light of the need for propitiation and the malediction that was entailed in it, we look now at what we have referred to as the satisfaction of Christ. By that we mean the satisfaction that Christ provided to the demands of God's law and his wrath against sin. The use of the term includes not only the penal, substitutionary atonement of Christ, but the entire work that Christ accomplished for us, in that he was our substitute in all of the relations that we sustained to the law of God. The satisfaction he provided was a satisfaction of the demands of divine justice in all of its expressions and dimensions. Those demands encompassed the need, consistent with the divine righteousness, that the penalty for the breaking of the law must be paid, and that the law itself must be kept. The satisfaction of Christ was addressed to the fullest scope of that dual necessity.

The satisfaction of Christ is referable to his obedience as broadly and comprehensively constituted. It has reference to all that was involved in the completion of his mediatorial, messianic assignment that lies at the heart of the gospel. Paul, in his letter to the Romans, outlines the gospel definitively in that respect. In an important and closely reasoned paragraph in the fifth chapter he sets in juxtaposition the sinner's union and solidarity with Adam and the union and solidarity with Christ of those whom he redeemed. "As by one man's disobedience", Paul

---

Foundation, Reprint, 2 vols. [1822] 1990. (This work is a *locus classicus* treatment of the subject.); Francis Turretin, *Institutes of Elenctic Theology*, Phillipsburg: P&R Publishing, 1994, Trans. G.M. Giger, Ed. J.T. Dennison, Jr., "The Covenant of Grace and its twofold economy in the Old and the New Testaments", Vol. 2, 169ff.; John Calvin, *Institutes of the Christian Religion* Philadelphia: The Westminster Press, Trans. F.L. Battles, Ed. J.T. McNeill, 2 Vols. [1536, 1559] 1960, passim; Robert L. Dabney, *Lectures in Systematic Theology*, Grand Rapids: Zondervan, [1878] 1972, Lecture 36, "The Covenant of Grace", 429ff.

argues, "many were made sinners, so by the obedience of one shall many be made righteous" (Rom. 5:19). Here we see the solidarity in Adam that connotes the sinner's position on the one hand, and the solidarity in Christ that the redeemed sinner enjoys on the other. Moreover, the effects and implications of the solidarity in the respective cases are probed and elucidated in such a way as to conduct us to the heart of the gospel.

The "disobedience" by which many were constituted sinners was the initial Adamic sin. That entailed the sinful, fallen condition of all his posterity. The guilt of Adam's sin, the Scriptures explain, was imputed to all those of whom he was, by God's appointment, the federal head. When Adam sinned, "death passed upon all men, for that all have sinned" (Rom. 5:12). When Adam sinned, we sinned. By virtue of the relations that God had established, Adam's sin, and the guilt and the liabilities to penalty inherent in that sin, were imputed to us. That imputation was an immediate imputation. By Adam's sin all men were constituted sinners. Henceforth, all men exist in a fallen condition, the compliant slaves of the Devil, "the strong man armed [that] keepeth his goods in peace" (Luke 11:21).

But the obedience of Christ that Paul sets against the disobedience of Adam stands in the place of the liability of the sinners for whom, in accordance with the terms of the Covenant of Redemption, Christ came as a substitute. That obedience encompasses Christ's active obedience and his passive obedience. By Christ's active obedience is meant his actual keeping of the law of God on the sinner's behalf. His passive obedience refers to his actual dying on behalf of sinners, the shedding of his blood and the offering of an atonement for sin.

In his active obedience Christ satisfied the demands of the law in that he actually and actively fulfilled its requirements. That, as our condition in sin attested, we had failed to do. By reason of our fallen condition we were without ability to keep the law. We need only inspect the demands of the law in its moral aspect, or the moral law, to observe that we have failed at every turn to honor our obligations under it. We have not loved the Lord our God with all our heart and soul and mind and strength. Responsible to God under the clear terms of the Covenant of Creation, we know that we have failed to honor the obligations that our creaturehood entailed. We are therefore guilty before God our Maker and Judge, and we are liable to the penalty that our dereliction from those obligations incurs. We know that our guilt leaves us without excuse.

But the gospel invites us to grasp the astounding fact that Christ has kept the law for us. Because he has done so, and because an obedience to the requirements of the law has been provided, our title to heaven is secure. For that reason, and not alone for the reason that the penalty for our breaking of the law has been paid, "there is therefore now no condemnation to them which are in Christ Jesus" (Rom. 8:1). At that important point at the beginning of the eighth chapter of his letter to the Romans, Paul, after his explanatory digressions in the sixth and seventh chapters of that letter, is taking up the implications of the point he had reached at the end of the fifth chapter. For at that latter point the apostle had set out the implications of the substitutionary obedience of Christ.

"Where sin abounded", he had said there, "grace did much more abound" (Rom. 5:20). By placing together the "sin abounding" and the grace "more abounding", the apostle points to the twofold fact that sums up his great argument. Sin abounded in that we too fell into the state and condition of sin when Adam sinned. But by stating that grace "more abounded", the apostle is saying that by the grace of God set forth in Christ we are raised, not simply to the state that Adam enjoyed before he fell. Rather, grace more abounded. We are raised in Christ to a state far higher than that from which we had fallen. We are raised to a state far higher than Adam had enjoyed. That higher state, that "more abounding" of grace, exists in the fact that now we are joined to Christ in a vital, organic, spiritual, and indissoluble union. That is the glory of the gospel. The sinner who is redeemed is now joined to Christ.

Of course it cannot be said that there was no passive aspect or element in the active obedience of Christ. We know that he willingly subjected himself to the rigors and demands of the law because of his love for us. The Scriptures are eloquent on the point. Nor can we say that there was no active aspect or element in the passive obedience that Christ offered in his dying in the place of sinners. In his explanation of his office as the shepherd who gives his life for his sheep, he made it clear that "No man taketh it from me, but I lay it down of myself" (John 10:18). The apostolic statement is addressed poignantly to the point: "Christ Jesus ... made himself of no reputation, and took upon him the form of a servant ... and being found in fashion as a man, he humbled himself, and became obedient unto death, even the death of the cross" (Phil. 2:5-6).

In all of the work of Christ as our substitute there was a deliberateness, a steadfastness by which he discharged impeccably the obligations that he had assumed as our Redeemer. His dedication to those obligations was noted at a highly climactic point in his earthly career. At the conclusion of his Galilean ministry Christ "stedfastly set his face to go to Jerusalem" (Luke 9:51). He must needs go to Jerusalem. He must needs pursue to the end the objectives for which he had come into the world. He must give his life for his people. At that climactic moment he deliberately chose the way of the cross.

But let us look more closely at the active obedience of Christ on our behalf. By that, we have said, our responsibility for the keeping of the law, in the important sense in which we had failed in that obligation, was discharged. But two further and important implications follow. First, not only the fact, but also the necessity, of Christ's active obedience must be allowed to impact our thought. For if it were imagined that the substitutionary work of Christ extended only to his dying on our behalf, or to his paying the penalty for our having broken the law of God, then our position would still have been rendered precarious. For even though the penalty for disobedience on our part had been paid, the righteousness of God still required that his holy law must be honored and kept. Even though the penalty for broken law had been paid, the law would still, beyond and after that, have to be kept. But that is something that we could not do. If we were left again to provide an impeccable obedience to the law of God, we must of necessity fail.

But the gospel declares that Christ has kept the law for us. By reason of his twofold obedience, our title to heaven is secure. Beyond that remarkable fact of substitution, however, a second and important point is to be noted. The Christian person is not thereby released from the obligation of obedience to the law as a rule of life. The law in its moral aspect, or the moral law encapsuled in the Ten Commandments, remains the rule of life for the Christian.

In our reference to the passive obedience of Christ we have in view his death on our behalf. The necessity and significance of that death is already implicit in the malediction inherent in our failure to honor the obligations of God's covenant. Peter has again summarized the gospel at this point. We are redeemed, he says, not with "corruptible things ... but with the precious blood of Christ ... who verily was foreordained before the foundation of the world" (1 Peter 1:18-20). In his recapitulation of the prophecy from the fifty-third chapter of Isaiah, Peter presents us with the gospel by stating that Christ "his own self bore our sins in his own body on the tree, that we, being dead to sins, should live unto righteousness, by whose stripes ye were healed" (1 Peter 2:24).

The atonement that Christ provided was an actual historical atonement that was offered in actual historical time. The death that he suffered in his human nature was an actual death in which he sustained "the sorrows of death" and "the pains of hell" (Ps. 116:3) on the sinner's behalf. It was after his cry of dereliction on the cross that he could say "It is finished", and our redemption was accomplished. As our high priest, the antitype of the priestly administrations in the earlier and anticipatory dispensation, he "once offered up himself" (Heb. 7:27), and "by his own blood he entered in once into the holy place, having obtained eternal redemption for us" (Heb. 9:12). Unlike the repetitive offerings of the anticipatory priestly administrations, Christ "now once in the end of the world ... appeared to put away sin by the sacrifice of himself". He was "once offered to bear the sins of many" (Heb. 9:26,28). And Peter states that "Christ also hath once suffered for sins, the just for the unjust, that he might bring us to God" (1 Peter 3:18).[4]

---

[4] The doctrine of the atonement is discussed in masterful terms by John Murray, *Redemption: Accomplished and Applied*, Grand Rapids Eerdmans, 1955, 13ff. A valuable discussion is contained also in A.W. Pink, *The Satisfaction of Christ*, Grand Rapids: Zondervan, 1955, though Pink errs in his argument that the atonement that Christ offered is to be understood as only hypothetically necessary, rather than being (as John Murray explains) an

The oblation of Christ

The satisfaction of Christ, in relation, particularly, to his passive obedience and the atonement that he made for our sin, can now be considered in three important aspects. Together they throw their light on the meaning of his redemptive and messianic work. We refer to these as, first, the nature of the transaction, or the relation that occurred between the Father and the Son when, on the cross, our Redeemer died and accomplished our redemption; second, the scope or extent of the atonement that he thus provided; and third, the office of intercession, or his heavenly high priestly office that, following the completion of his sacrificial work, he performs on our behalf.

We shall speak in this section of what we refer to as the oblation of Christ. That term refers to the offering that Christ provided to God as the atonement for sin. What, we ask, was the substance of that atonement, or the characteristics of its accomplishment, that provides its effectiveness in achieving the ends that were contemplated? We know that the objective of Christ's coming had been made clear from the beginning. "Thou shalt call his name Jesus", the angel announced, "for he shall save his people from their sins" (Matt. 1:21). The scope of the atonement that Christ provided is inherent in that earliest announcement. He came to save "his people". But our interest at present is in asking the simple and straightforward question, did he in fact succeed in what he came to do? If, as was projected, he came to save his people, then did he in fact do so, and did he in fact succeed in accomplishing what he was sent into the world to do?

The answer is clear. We see from the sacred record that in

---

absolute necessity. The difference in terms is important, in that the argument for a hypothetical necessity claims that God could have chosen to redeem in any way he might have wished, but that it was by the giving of his Son that the redemptive plan was actually effected. Murray, on the other hand and more correctly, argues that the atonement of Christ was absolutely necessary, or, that it was a "consequent absolute necessity" (loc. cit, 16), consequent on God's having chosen to redeem. As the hymnwriter, Cecil Frances Alexander (1848) has put it, "There was no other good enough to pay the price of sin; He only could unlock the gate of heaven and let us in".

his death Christ actually saved his people. That is the glory of the gospel. But we consider at this point the manner of his accomplishment of that remarkable objective. The Scriptural data are extensive. Let us confine our attention for the moment to the statement that Paul makes by way of his summary of the gospel in his letter to the Galatians. In the course of his doxological introduction to that letter Paul refers to "our Lord Jesus Christ who gave himself for our sins, that he might deliver us from this present evil world, according to the will of God" (Gal. 1:3-4). Paul there emphasizes the fact that the supreme act of atonement was that our Redeemer "gave himself".

The apostle returns to the same definitive statement when he says in the following chapter of the letter that "the Son of God ... loved me, and gave himself for me" (Gal. 2:20). In the moment and the act of atonement our Lord "gave himself" for us. In the human nature that he had assumed for us he died an actual historical death in actual historical time. He actually died. His death was placed to our account. He died that we might live. John Owen, in his masterful treatment of this subject, could therefore speak of "the death of death in the death of Christ".[5]

The writer of the letter to the Hebrews presents the meaning of the atonement in the very same terms. In the discharge of his priestly office, he says, Christ "offered up himself" (Heb. 7:27). The "blood of bulls and goats" sufficed for the discharge of the typical offerings under the arrangements of the old and anticipatory dispensation. By virtue of those offerings the people of God acquired a ceremonial holiness that permitted them to come before God in their acts of repentance and worship. But Christ, "through the eternal Spirit offered himself" (Heb. 9:13-14). Christ has "put away sin", the same author states, "by the sacrifice of himself" (Heb. 9:26).

But what was there effected, and what is it in which the efficacy of the death of Christ inheres? In his death, Christ submitted to the full and complete and total liabilities and penalty that were due to us because of our sin. Those liabilities accrued to us because of our dereliction from the obligations of

---

[5] John Owen, *The Works of John Owen,* London: Banner of Truth, 1967, Vol. 10, 139-428.

God's gracious covenant. Christ suffered and bore in his death the full rigors of the wrath of God that was properly addressed to us, the curse of malediction that we had sustained by our failure to honor our covenant obligations. In that moment of atonement, the great eschatological moment to which all of history and God's promises and purpose had pointed, our Redeemer satisfied the demands of God's justice. The penalty for our sin was paid to the full extent of the rigor that God's righteousness and justice demanded. In the death of our substitute Redeemer who paid a substitute penalty for us, we whom he redeemed were freed completely from the condemnatory rigors of the law of God.

"The Lord hath laid on him", the prophet has claimed, "the iniquity of us all" (Is. 53:6). In that moment of atonement, Christ was made to be sin for us (2 Cor. 5:21). He was not made a sinner. But he was made sin. It was our sin that was laid upon him. God the Father looked upon his Son and in the moment of dereliction he saw our sin upon him, and on that sin he poured out the full extent of his holy wrath. The Father, who cannot look with complacence upon sin, turned his face from his own Son. In that terrible moment of agony the Redeemer's cry of dereliction, *"Eli, Eli, lama sabachthani",* "My God, my God, why hast thou forsaken me?" (Matt. 27:46), evinced his bearing the full weight of the curse for us. At that moment he suffered "the pains of hell" (Ps. 116:3) on our behalf. At that moment of penal, substitutionary suffering our redemption was secured. There was only one way in which that redemption could be accomplished. It was accomplished because, as the apostle has crystallized the gospel for us, Christ "gave himself".

The Scriptural record is replete with declarations to that effect. But what are the results and effects of that supreme redemptive act? In fulfilling the objective of the propitiation that he offered, Christ did in fact "obtain eternal redemption" for us (Heb. 9:12). In that propitiatory and expiatory act, Christ "purged our sins" (Heb. 1:3), and "by his stripes we are healed" (Is. 53:5). Now we have "peace with God" (Rom. 5:1). God our Father, who loved us from the beginning with a love that moved him to send his Son into the world for that propitiatory objective, has satisfied his own demands. He has fulfilled his objective "that we might receive the adoption of sons" (Gal. 4:5). That was his purpose, that we might be brought into the grace of adoption, that we who were "not a people" might become "the people of God" (1 Peter 2:10). Now he has given to us "the Spirit of adoption" (Rom. 8:15). Now, by the application to us of the benefits of the redemption that he provided in his Son, we are in fact "delivered from the power of darkness and translated into the kingdom of his dear Son" (Col. 1:13). Now "in Christ Jesus our Lord we have access with confidence" to God our Father (Eph. 3:11-12). "Through him (Christ) we have access by one Spirit unto the Father" (Eph. 2:18).

The extent of the atonement

We see, then, why the answer to our previous question is in the affirmative. Christ did, in fact, realize the objective that the angel announced. He actually saved his people for whom he died. As to all of the rigors of the demands of his law against them, God, by virtue of the atonement that Christ his Son provided, is satisfied. He has saved his people.

At this point, however, a misrepresentation of the gospel has frequently occurred. Too frequently, it has been claimed that Christ in his death offered an atonement for all men indiscriminately and that he bore, in a sense that is not always clearly specified, "the sins of humanity". The truth is that the biblical doctrine refers the atonement of Christ not to "humanity" in an abstract sense, whatever the denotation of such an abstract term might be. The atonement of Christ, the Scriptures declare, was directed concretely, not abstractly, to the specific case and condition of specific people who were the subjects of God's eternal Covenant of Redemption.

John Owen, who wrote at the height of the flowering of Reformed theology in the mid-seventeenth century, addressed the question of what we are to understand as the Scriptural statement on the point. His work stands as the classic discussion of these issues and has not been surpassed or answered by the claimants of the doctrinal positions from which we are dissenting. In the fashion that was current in his time, Owen gives his work a long explanatory title which, because of its relevance to the questions we have raised in this chapter, is worthy of note. He describes it as *"A Treatise of the redemption and reconcilia-tion that is in the blood of Christ, with the merit thereof, and the satisfaction wrought thereby, wherein ... the whole controversy about universal redemption [is[fully discussed"*. Owen asks, in effect, for whom did Christ die? That is the question that has divided the historic confession that the church inherited from the Reformation, or what we shall refer to as the doctrine of *particular atonement,* from what has been known historically as Arminianism, or the theory of a general or universal or indiscriminate atonement. Owen observes that "God imposed his wrath due unto, and Christ underwent the pains of hell for, either all the sins of all men, or all the sins of some men, or some sins of all men".[6]

If the first of these possibilities were true, then all men must of necessity be saved. For Christ, the Scriptures eloquently declare, did not die in vain. In our Lord's high priestly prayer he summed up the results of his redemptive mission by claiming to the Father that "those that thou gavest me I have kept, and none of them is lost" (John 17:12). The possibility we have just inspected is therefore inadmissible, given the clear fact that not all men are saved. On the testimony of Scripture we know that such a universal redemption was neither intended nor achieved.

If the third possibility were true and Christ bore some of the sins of all men, then it is clear that all men are still lost. For in that case sin remains for all men, and the penalty of that sin remains and must still be borne by the subjects of the curse themselves. Christ, in that terrible case, died completely in vain.

But if, as the Scriptures declare, the second of the possibili-ties is true and Christ bore all of the sins of some men, then those men are, definitively and completely, saved. The penalty in their case has been completely paid. Christ did not die in vain. He actually accomplished what he was sent into the world to do. He died for his people, and in dying for them he actually

---

[6] John Owen, *The Works of John Owen*, London: Banner of Truth, 1967, Vol. 10, 173. See the Banner of Truth edition of this work, 1959, 61-62 and 137. This latter edition contains a valuable "Introductory Essay" by J.I. Packer, which has also become a classic discussion of the subject.

and definitively saved them.

It has frequently been claimed that Christ, in providing a general or universal atonement, has done all that was necessary to make salvation possible. In the light of that, it is then said, those will be saved who now take advantage of the offer of redemption that is thereby provided and turn to Christ in faith. But the vacuity of such a claim lies on its very surface. For it fails completely to understand the state and condition of man in sin. It fails completely to comprehend the biblical meaning of the results and the effects of Adam's Fall. It fails to grasp the fact of the terrible inabilities that characterize the soul in its fallen condition. It mistakenly supposes that man in sin possesses an ability to turn to God, an ability to believe that the Scriptures know nothing about. It denies the biblical claim that man in sin is the captive, compliant, God-hating slave of the devil.

Such a claim as we now have in view presents what we may call a possibility theory of salvation. It claims that Christ died simply to make salvation possible. It implies that in the last analysis, therefore, man, if he is saved, saves himself. He does so by virtue of the exercise of his supposedly sovereign ability to believe. But that, we have seen at adequate length, is the precise opposite of the gospel.

Man is saved, if he is saved, not by any such autosoterism or by his own autonomous sovereignty and sovereign decision. Nor is he saved by a synergism, a mixture of effort in which, supposedly, God having done his part, man now does his part. The consistent declaration of the Scriptures is that man is saved, if he is saved, by a divine monergism. Salvation is due, in all of its parts and dimensions, to the grace of God. It is by the grace of God that we are saved (Eph. 2:8), and salvation in all its parts is by grace. It is by the grace of God that Christ is made unto us wisdom, and righteousness, and sanctification, and redemption (1 Cor. 1:30). He is made that unto us, by the sovereign grace of God, against the ignorance, guilt, pollution, and misery in which sin, by Adam's Fall, had bound us.

The possibility theorizing in the matter of redemption founders irreparably on two further points. First, it completely confuses the proper relation between faith as the instrumental cause of justification and the status of regeneration and justification to which, by the grace of God, the repentant sinner is brought. It must be asked whether, in his sinful condition, a person does in fact possess an ability to exercise faith in Christ in order that he might be born again. The answer is clear from the very form of the question. It is not the case, if we are attentive to Scriptural categories at that point, that a man will be born again if and when he exercises faith in Christ. Man possesses no innate ability to do so. Rather, the declaration of the gospel is that when an individual has been born again, or when, by the sovereign and unsolicited ministry of the Holy Spirit he has been made the beneficiary of that new creation in the soul, without which, our Lord has said, no man can see the kingdom of God (John 3:3), then inevitably he will come in faith to Christ.

The Scriptures know nothing of a possibility theory of salvation that claims, in other words, that faith precedes regeneration, or the new birth that the Spirit of God imparts. The Scriptures are everywhere eloquent in claiming to the contrary. Regeneration is prior to faith. Those come to faith in Christ in whom, by the sovereign work of his Holy Spirit, God himself has created the faith to believe. "By grace are ye saved through faith", the apostle states, "and that not of yourselves, it is the gift of God" (Eph. 2:8). A man believes because he has been born again. It is not the case that he is born again because he believes.

But secondly, the possibility theory founders in its misunderstanding of the relation between the atonement of Christ and the reality and the scope of the sin for which he atoned. The Scriptures have declared that Christ bore all the sins of some men. We focus now on the fact that for those for whom he bore their sins, he did in fact bear all of their sins. The possibility theory, to the contrary, claims that Christ bore the sins of men in general, or, to use the familiar formula, that he bore the sins of all men indiscriminately. It then goes on to claim that if men do not now come to faith in Christ it is simply their unbelief that remains and damns them.

But surely, unbelief is itself the final and irreparable sin. If that sin remains, then Christ did not bear all of the sins of men at all. There remains a sin, the most terrible sin of unbelief, for which Christ's atonement has no efficacy or efficiency. The conclusion then follows that Christ died in vain. In that unhappy event his death did not, as the proponents of the possibility theory claim, cover the sins of all men indiscriminately at all.

The Scriptural doctrine of the atonement presents us with the fact that Christ died, and that in his death he bore the penalty of the sins of particular people. It presents, that is, the doctrine of particular atonement. That biblical doctrine has, of course, been caricatured by its opponents in numerous ways. It has been said that a doctrine of particular atonement, notwithstanding the extensive Scriptural evidence on which it stands, diminishes the grace and the efficiency of the atonement itself. By restricting or limiting the scope and extent of the atonement to certain people, it is said, the grace of God is diminished rather than honored as it should be.

But a moment's reflection will make it clear that any so-called limitation of the atonement is being made, not by those who insist on the particularity of the atonement, but by those who claim a generality of scope for it. For while it might be claimed that the biblical doctrine limits or restricts the atonement as to its extent, the opponents of that doctrine clearly limit the atonement as to its efficiency. For the general atonement theory, or the possibility theory as we have referred to it, claims, in effect, that Christ in his death did not really and actually save any person at all. He died simply and only to make salvation possible. The Scripture states, to the contrary, that in his death Christ actually accomplished the purpose and objective for which he came. In his death he actually and definitively saved those for whom he died.

Our Lord himself entertained precisely that awareness as to the scope and objectives of his death. When, in his extensive discourse on his mission and objective as the good shepherd who gives his life for his sheep, he said that "I lay down my life for the sheep" (John 10:15), he clarified the definitiveness of his atonement. "I give unto them eternal life", he said, "and they shall never perish" (John 10:28). When we read those words, our minds hark back to our Lord's nocturnal encounter with Nicodemus, following which he gave us what is no doubt the best known statement of the gospel. "God so loved the world, that he gave his only begotten Son, that whosoever believeth in him should not perish, but have everlasting life" (John 3:16). Those for whom he came to die, we are told in that gracious statement, will not perish. Some will perish, those who remain in their sin. But in his own statement of his task and office as the good shepherd, Christ explains again that those for whom he is about to die "shall never perish".

The conception that our Lord entertained as to the scope and objective of his death is confirmed in an arresting way in his continuation of that discourse on his office as the good shepherd. Certain of the Jews, who were still incredulous and who protested uncertainty as to his identity, came to him and asked him to clarify still further whether he was in fact the Christ who should come. "Tell us plainly", they said (John 10:24). Our Lord's response was startling in its import and depth. "Ye believe not", he said, "because ye are not of my sheep" (John 10:26).

The terrible reality, Christ is saying, is that he did not come to die a death that would atone for the sins of all men. He came to die for his people. The reality is, as he observed to the Jews on that occasion, that there are some who, in the eternal mystery and purpose of God, were not given to him to redeem. The scope of the Covenant of Redemption identified those who were the subjects of it. On them God set his love, and for them he sent his Son to be the propitiation for their sins.

That is clarified finally in our Lord's high priestly prayer. In the climactic moments that preceded his crucifixion, Christ prayed to the Father on behalf of those for whom he was about to die. He identified them in precise particularity in his statement to the Father that "thine they were, and thou gavest them me" (John 17:6). Moreover, "I pray for them", Christ says, "I pray not for the world" (John 17:9), and in that priestly prayer the discriminatory particularity of the eternal counsel of God and of the Covenant of Redemption is clearly expressed.

The apostle Paul insists upon precisely that strain in his own clarification of the gospel. In his charge to the elders of the church at Ephesus, he enjoined them to "feed the church of God", which he referred to as the church "which he [Christ] hath purchased with his own blood" (Acts 20:28). By that the apostle referred to those whom God the Father gave to the Son to redeem. The same apostle wrote to the Ephesians that "Christ loved the church, and gave himself for it" (Eph. 5:25). The Christian's security rests in that particularity and in the definitiveness and the complete fulfillment of the objectives of the atonement.

In that, moreover, lies the richness of the declarative message of the gospel. The apostle, in his address to the Athenians on Mars' hill, made it clear that "God commandeth all men everywhere to repent" (Acts 17:30). All men are under obligation to God by virtue of the terms of the covenant of creation and the law of God that it set forth. The people of God whom he had called out from the nations of the world and to whom he had given his inscripturated law were under a special obligation; and the repudiation of that obligation implied the curse which, in due course, Christ was to bear.

All men everywhere, as the apostle has said, are guilty by reason of their repudiation of covenantal obligations, and all men are called upon to repent. But the state and condition of man in sin is such that he does not possess the ability to repent unless, in the mercy of God, that very gift of repentance is given by the Spirit of God himself. We should not, at this vital point, evade the Scriptural message of the free offer of the gospel. But we must see that in the gospel of redemption God calls upon men to do what in fact they have no ability to do. The Scriptures have nowhere told us that responsibility is suspended on ability. Such a claim is a most serious and unfortunate error of supposedly autonomous thought.

Any lower statement than the general call to repentance would diminish the gospel of grace beyond recognition. "Whosoever believeth", the Scripture says (John 3:16), has everlasting life. And the canon closes on the very same note of urgency: "Let him that is athirst come. And whosoever will, let him take the water of life freely" (Rev. 22:17). There can be no diminution of the gracious invitation of the gospel. It is a gospel for "whosoever". But sadly, in view of the state of sin that we have explored, we have to ask quite simply "who will?". And the answer is that only those will come in whom the grace of God does its ordained and renewing work.

Sinner, the word of grace says, see your lost condition in sin, and seeing that, see the mercy of God set forth for sinners. Do you want to know where the rescue and relief from sin is to be found? It is only in Christ. He alone is the sufficient substitute for sinners. You are commanded, in peril of your eternal soul, to repent and turn to God. But you must know that you have no ability in yourself to do that. You must see that you have no strength or merit because of your sin. You can only cry to God for mercy. But have you at last begun to see that in your sin you have outraged the holiness of the God with whom you have to do? Have you at last begun to know the terrors of lostness, the "bondage" and blindness in which your sin has kept you these many years (Rom. 8:15)? If that is so, then know that it is only by the grace and mercy of God that the awareness of those terrible realities has dawned on your soul. Turn to God in thankfulness and repentance and adoration for his grace.

You may know with a certainty that the good news of the gospel is that in Christ God saves sinners. He has saved sinners such as you. You may know that he waits to receive you, because he has said not only that "all that the Father giveth me shall come to me", but also that "him that cometh to me I will in no wise cast out" (John 6:37). There is cleansing for you in the blood of Christ. If you have become conscious of your sin and your need of him, you may come. You may come because you can know, from the very condition of sin and of need of which you are now aware, that God is working in you to bring you to himself. That is the measure of his unfathomable grace. He waits to receive you in Christ his Son whom, as the apostle has made perfectly clear, he sent "to be the propitiation for our sins" (1 John 4:10).

The intercession of Christ

The good news of the gospel is that God sent his Son to be the propitiation for our sins. We know that in his human nature Christ died for sinners, and that in that human nature he rose again from the dead. The glory of the gospel is that in Christ we see, as John Owen so long ago put it, "the death of death". But we know also that in the totality of his person he ascended into heaven, and as the angels announced to the disciples of old, "This same Jesus, which is taken up from you into heaven, shall so come in like manner" (Acts 1:11). We know that in his human nature our Redeemer now sits at the right hand of the Father and intercedes on our behalf. He was made for us "a priest for ever" (Heb. 7:17). And in his human nature Christ now exercises a heavenly high priestly office on behalf of the church that he has redeemed.

The promise of Isaiah is fulfilled, that "He shall see of the travail of his soul and shall be satisfied" (Is. 53:11). Christ, who has joined us to himself by virtue of his substitutionary work for us, now intercedes for us and presents our case to the Father. The terms of that intercession and the effectiveness of it depend upon and follow from the propitiatory offering that Christ made to the Father in the discharge of his redemptive office. The Scriptures present the fact of Christ's heavenly priestly and intercessory office in the context of their presentation of the propitiation that he made for us.

In the seventh chapter of the letter to the Hebrews Christ is said, in the fulfillment of his propitiatory commitment, to have offered up himself. But in that same context it is said that "he ever liveth to make intercession for them" whom he has redeemed (Heb. 7:25-27). The Scriptures thus join together the propitiatory and the intercessory offices of Christ. It is impossible to envisage the intercessory office and activity of Christ separately from his atonement and propitiation. In his human nature he fulfilled and discharged the one, and now in his human nature he is engaged in the other.

The same interdependence of the offices of Christ is exhibited in the argument of the letter to the Romans. In his lyrical response to the question, "Who shall lay anything to the charge of God's elect" (Rom. 8:33f.), Paul claims that any condemnation of God's redeemed people is precluded by the work of Christ and its plenary effectiveness. But in describing the extent and the scope of that work, Paul joins together the facts that "Christ hath died", and that he has "risen again", and that, moreover, he "maketh intercession for us". The death, the resurrection, and the intercession of Christ cohere in their effects and significance. They are congruent in their relevance to our eternal salvation and security.

The epistle of John similarly joins together the propitiatory and the intercessory work of our Lord. "If any man sin", John has argued, "we have an advocate with the Father, Jesus Christ the righteous" (1 John 2:1). And in that context he states that Christ's intercession has been endowed with the status and effectiveness it possesses because of the prior completion of his propitiation. John states immediately there, "And he is the propitiation for our sins".

A clear conjunction between Christ's propitiation and his intercession is presented also at the beginning of the letter to the Hebrews, in which the priestly office and responsibilities of Christ come especially to the fore. Christ became, the writer says, "a merciful and faithful high priest in things pertaining to God, to make reconciliation for the sins of the people" (Heb. 2:17). In the text as we have quoted it from the familiar King James version, the word that has been translated as "reconciliation" is precisely that which at other places is properly translated as "propitiation". Here the priestly office and function of Christ extends explicitly to his propitiation, and it is related directly also to his intercession.

That is clear from a minimal statement of what is involved in Christ's discharge of his intercessory priestly office. The writer to the Hebrews goes on in that same context to add: "For in that he himself hath suffered being tempted, he is able to succour them that are tempted". The high priestly office of Christ is, in one of its aspects, directed to God the Father. In another aspect, it is directed to those whom he has redeemed. The latter is in view in the statement of the writer to the Hebrews that we have just inspected. The church that Christ redeemed he now sees as the "travail of his soul" (Is. 53:11), and he takes satisfaction in the salvation of his church. Christ did not redeem the church and then leave her to herself without his continual succour and sustenance and comfort and support. To imagine that he did is to fail to understand that by virtue of his completed work his church is now indissolubly joined to him. He is her very life. By his Spirit he works in her and for her to bring her to himself, "a glorious church, not having spot, or wrinkle, or any such thing; but that it should be holy and without blemish" (Eph. 5:27).

The heavenly high priestly work of Christ, then, presents itself to us in its twofold nature. It is, on the one hand, his sympathy with, and his identification in suffering with, his people, knowing and understanding their trials and temptations and delivering them out of them all. His priestly work involves, on the other hand, his intercession with the Father on behalf of his church. As to the former, the writer to the Hebrews has again concluded that "We have an high priest [who is] touched with the feeling of our infirmities; [who] was in all points tempted like as we are, yet without sin". On that basis we may "come boldly unto the throne of grace, that we may obtain mercy, and find grace to help in time of need" (Heb. 4:15-16).

We forget to our peril that our Redeemer did in fact face the tempter in all respects as we do, and that he conquered on our behalf. In all of the faculties and capacities of his human soul, Christ suffered the strain and the pressure of temptation to sin. Are we to say now that we are subject to stresses of temptation that Christ knew or knows nothing about? Are we to say, as a result, that he does not and cannot understand our position and the strains and agonies that it imposes upon us? Are we to say that the holy and sinless Son of God could not and did not realize the temptations to sin that press so excruciatingly upon us? And are we to say, then, that he cannot in fact be the help in time of need that the writer to the Hebrews has just claimed him to be? Perish all such groundless imaginations. Our comfort, for life and for eternity, is in Christ, it is in him alone, and it is completely in him.

As to the second of the aspects of Christ's heavenly high priestly work, his intercession on our behalf, we know that the Father did not set his love upon us simply or solely because Christ died for us. To the contrary, Christ came into the world and died for us because God the Father had set his love upon us before the foundation of the world. God the Father is not, therefore, constrained to love us because of the work that Christ has done and does. But while that is so, and while the love of God brought into being the entire plan of salvation, our case is nevertheless presented by Christ to the Father. It is a case that rests simply on the fact that Christ did discharge meticulously on our behalf all that was necessary, in the eternal counsels of God, to satisfy divine justice and to reconcile us to God. God now looks on the finished and efficacious work of his Son, and he sees us now, as Christ presents us to him, enrobed in his Son's perfect righteousness. He has made us, in every sense, "accepted in the beloved" (Eph. 1:6).

In that great eschatological moment, that moment of dereliction when Christ bore the sins of his people on the cross, God the Father looked upon his Son and saw their sin, their total sin, and he poured out to its full extent the rigors of his wrath upon it. Now, in a profound action of reciprocal imputation (2 Cor. 5:21), God looks again upon his Son and sees us who are redeemed in him, not any longer in our filthiness and sin, but clothed in the robe of Christ's perfect and spotless righteousness (Is. 61:10). In that, God has brought us to himself. We now have fellowship with him. Let us "walk in the light", as John the apostle has enjoined us, that our fellowship may be "with the Father, and with his Son Jesus Christ" (1 John 1:7,3). Let us be about the business, as Paul said to the Corinthian church, of "perfecting holiness in the fear of God" (2 Cor. 7:1).

In the chapters that follow we shall examine further the implications, and the relevance and meaning for the Christian life and walk, of the issues we have now inspected. In doing so, we shall need to bring into perspective the significance for the Christian life of the scope of the gospel as we have now contemplated it. The holiness of God that made the propitiatory offering of his Son necessary, the love of God unfathomably set forth in Christ, the complete satisfaction that Christ accomplished, and his continual high priestly work on our behalf, will cast their light and display their significance for the Christian life and walk.

The Christian saint, upon whom his sainthood devolves by reason of his separation unto holiness in Christ, is also a sinner. We shall need to understand the high meaning of the ministry to us, notwithstanding our failings and our sin, of Christ by his Holy Spirit, by whom he has committed himself to conduct us to glory.

8

The Disarray of Faith

The stance and testimony of the church, and its relevance to the culture and the moral dissolution of the age, have been tarnished by the devaluation of its doctrine and the uncertainty that clouds its statement of the evangel. For that reason, our focus in the preceding chapters has been on a positive statement of Christian doctrine that explored the salvific significance of the biblical revelation and the divine redemptive purpose. We have been concerned with a positive statement of what the church, if it wishes to stand on its doctrinal heritage and its historical mission, can be expected to say by way of guidance to its members and to society at large. Our discussion has been determined by the categories of Creation, Sin and the Fall, and Redemption, as we had contemplated them under the heading of our "Triad 1".

Ahead of us now lie important questions regarding the application of that biblical doctrine to the individual Christian life. We are interested, in a more precisely personal sense, in what is involved in one's coming to faith in Christ, in the meaning and scope of the Spirit's work of regeneration that makes saving faith possible, and in the development of the new life in Christ that follows. We shall turn to those questions in our concluding two chapters below.

Meanwhile, in this and the following chapter, which may be regarded as somewhat of a parenthesis in our doctrinal studies, we shall consider in a preliminary fashion some of the issues and questions that fall within the important area of Christian Apologetics. We indicated the general content of that aspect of Christian thought in what we referred to as our "Triad 2".

As we do so, we are conscious of what we refer to as the *Disarray of Faith*, or the condition of the contemporary church that disturbs the careful observer and that provides the standpoint against which an adequate apologetic is to be assessed. The perspective we command will be clarified by a brief and deliberately incomplete review of the historical developments that have brought the church to the position in which it stands.

The question at issue

The twentieth century promised the eclipse of the problems of ordinary life. It was to be the century of the common man. Inheriting the hopes of nineteenth century optimism that was fathered by evolutionary hypotheses, by an ambitious scientific positivism, and by the pushing back of economic frontiers, the journey upwards seemed to be assured. But as the century waned, its aspirations were falsified. The irony of what was billed as the century of the common man is that, at its end, man and his culture are mired in a moral and social collapse. Scientific progress of unimaginable scope has occurred. Technology has kept pace, and the culture of crass commercialism has tried, but failed, to fill the void in the human soul.

The indictment could be expanded. But our concern is with the implications that it has had for the life and thought and testimony of the church. We have observed at several points in the preceding chapters the trends in thought and belief that have impacted and troubled the church. A fairly generalized subjectivism, that followed from the bequest of nineteenth century theology and a neo-Pietistic reaction that it fostered, took the church substantially away from an engagement with social and cultural concerns. The earlier positivism turned in the twentieth century to an existentialism that degenerated to a philosophy of despair.[1] An earlier tradition of system building

---

[1] See Chapter 1, n. 4,5.

in thought gave way to linguistics and arguments about the meaning of words in philosophy. Intellectual life itself seemed diminished.

In Christian thought, a rescue was proposed in Karl Barth's attempted retrieval of a Reformed theology.[2] But there is reason to doubt that his neo-universalism, that destroyed the possibility of a genuine transition from wrath to grace, did more than change the form in which a latter day modernism had scuttled the church's earlier belief. Tillich's conception of God as the ground of being diminished the reality of a personal God who was both transcendent and immanent in the world that he had made.[3] Macquarrie's theological existentialism, brave in its agenda that fascinated the pulpit, has failed to make meaningful contact with the evangelical pew.[4] At mid-century, theology

---

[2] In addition to the sources cited in chapter 1, notably the works of Cornelius Van Til, see also the same author's *The Reformed Pastor and Modern Thought*, Phillipsburg: Presbyterian and Reformed Publishing, 1971. See also G.C.Berkouwer, *The Triumph of Grace in the Theology of Karl Barth*, Grand Rapids: Eerdmans, 1956.

[3] Tillich's position in the development of twentieth century theology, though it is distanced from the Reformed distinctives that have influenced our own study in this book, warrants inspection because of the considerable impact and influence he has had on the preaching of the church. For his doctrine of God, see his *Systematic Theology*, Chicago: The University of Chicago Press, 1951, Vol. 1, 235ff. For Tillich, "It is as atheistic to affirm the existence of God as it is to deny it. God is being-itself, not *a* being", 237. The same conception appears in Tillich's *The Protestant Era*, Trans. J. L Adams, Chicago: The University of Chicago Press, Abridged edition, 1957, 63. For examples of Tillich's sermons see his *The Shaking of the Foundations*, New York: Scribner's Sons, 1948. Tillich's theological system and its place in twentieth century theology has been evaluated in Cornelius Van Til, *The Reformed Pastor and Modern Thought*, 154-85. Note particularly Van Til's comments on Tillich's conception of God as "the ground of being" on 170, and his argument that Tillich's embrace of the concept of the "analogy of being", a somewhat different position from that taken by Barth, identifies him with traditional Roman Catholic theology. A condensation of Tillich's theology that illustrates its influence on the mid-century church can be inspected in John A. T. Robinson, *Honest to God*, Philadelphia: Westminster Press, 1963.

[4] John Macquarrie, *Principles of Christian Theology*, New York: Scribner's Sons, 1966. Macquarrie gives a provocative review of trends and traditions in philosophic theology and acknowledges his own debt to the "philosophic

was emboldened to make the astounding pronouncement that God was dead.[5]

Reformed theological thought did not soon recover from the malaise into which it had fallen at the turn of the century.[6] But reaction in the life and teaching of the church did emerge. On the one hand, a so-called social gospel was promoted, that was as much concerned with the potentialities of social engineering as it was with traditional beliefs.[7] A fundamentalism followed, whose apparent commitment to an earlier and traditional Reformed agenda was slender.[8] And against the distancing of itself from socio-cultural issues that then set in, a neo-

---

categories of [the existentialist] Martin Heidegger [and] such Protestant giants as Barth, Brunner, and Tillich", ix.

[5] An evaluation of what was for a time the influential "God is dead" theology is available in Cornelius Van Til, *Is God Dead?*, Phillipsburg: Presbyterian and Reformed Publishing, 1966.

[6] See David B. Calhoun, *Princeton Seminary: Vol. 2, The Majestic Testimony 1869-1929*, Edinburgh: Banner of Truth, 1996, 329-429. The developments that account for the unfortunate reduction of the influence of Reformed theology are reflected in an interesting fashion in John W. Stewart's "Charles Hodge Revisited", *The Princeton Bulletin*, XVIII:3, 1997. Charles Hodge was a distinguished professor of systematic theology at Princeton Theological Seminary in the mid-nineteenth century, and Stewart's essay was in celebration of the 200th anniversary of Hodge's birth. Stewart's summing up is to the effect that "he [Hodge] should be placed and interpreted within his historical context - both theological and cultural. His nineteenth-century ethos will make it apparent that his assumptions, worldview, *and theological agenda* are significantly different from our own" 279, emphasis added. David F. Wells has contributed a relevant and insightful essay ,"Charles Hodge", in David F. Wells, Ed., *Reformed Theology in America: A History of Its Modern Development*, Grand Rapids; Baker, 1997, 37-62.

[7] This movement is prominently associated with the name of Walter Rauschenbusch, who became professor of church history at Rochester Seminary in 1897 "and through his writings and lectures promoted the political and economic transformation of America until his death in 1918". Stanley J. Grenz and Roger E. Olson, *20th Century Theology: God and the World in a Transitional Age*, Downers Grove: InterVarsity Press, 1992, 61.

[8] A very effective critique of this movement, and particularly of the relation to it of J. Gresham Machen, whose *Christianity and Liberalism*, Grand Rapids: Eerdmans, 1923, had presented a dissent from the then emerging liberalism and a defense of Reformed theological distinctives, is contained in D. G. Hart, *Defending the Faith: J. Gresham Machen and the Crisis of Conservative Protestantism in Modern America*, Grand Rapids: Baker Books, 1994.

evangelicalism developed.[9]

That movement, it was thought, would propel the evangelical church to a new level of visibility and influence. But it would do so on the basis of a new conception of the importance of reason and reasoning ability in both theological and human affairs. Its agenda, that continues its influence at the present time, gives every appearance of having failed to grasp in a clear sense the implications for the human condition of the noetic effects of Adam's Fall. The intellectual and theological program that the movement fostered has influenced the preaching and teaching of the church to a marked degree.[10] It has, to a large

---

[9] The most prominent theologian of the neo-evangelical movement is Carl F. H. Henry, the founding editor of the journal, *Christianity Today*, which gained high intellectual respectability under his editorship. See C.F.H. Henry, *God, Revelation and Authority*, Waco: Word Books, 6 Vols., 1976-1983. See also the same author's *Confessions of a Theologian: An Autobiography*, Waco: Word Books, 1986. On the level of evangelism, the neo-evangelical movement is represented by Billy Graham, in whose thought system the theology of the movement takes on a pronounced Arminian emphasis. A partial critique of aspects of the movement is contained in David F. Wells, *No Place for Truth*. See chapter 1 above, n.5.

[10] On the level of theological apologetics and apologetic method, R.C. Sproul, John Gerstner, and Arthur Lindsley, in their *Classical Apologetics: A Rational Defense of the Christian Faith and a Critique of Presuppositional Apologetics* (see chapter 1 above, n.12), though they write from a purportedly Reformed theological perspective, have taken a position that is more closely consistent with the apologetic predilections of neo-evangelicalism. Those authors have dissented strongly from the apologetic of Cornelius Van Til who has argued, in a manner similar to the emphases we have adopted in the preceding chapters, that Christian reasoning must necessarily begin with God as one's basic presupposition. Valuable light is thrown on the alternative approaches to apologetic reasoning by Thom Notaro, *Van Til and the Use of Evidence*, Phillipsburg: P&R Publishing, 1980, and the attempted rebuttal of Notaro by Sproul et al., in their *Classical Apologetics*, 304-309. Overriding all debates on this level is the question of a Scripturally correct understanding of the status and capacity of human reasoning ability after, and as a result of, Adam's fall. The point at issue can be put by saying that differences of understanding exist as to the nature and scope of the unregenerate sinner's knowledge. In an earlier chapter (ch. 5) we have taken precise account of what it is that the sinner can and does know. In that context we brought to emphasis also the reality of the bias against, and the hatred of, God that exists in the natural human soul. That bias, we have seen, leads to a natural tendency for the sinner to suppress every awareness of God (as Rom. 1:18 advises us) and to argue, as a result, that the explanation of reality is the

149

degree also, captured the seminaries. And its influence in theological apologetics has diminished a sounder understanding of the reality of God as the presupposition of Christian thought.

The disarray of faith to which these developments have led has heavily impacted both the Christian testimony and the Christian life. Christian ethics is in comparable disarray. The church is in the world, though its witness rings only uncertainly, and the world is very much in the church. What, in the light of the cultural and intellectual forces that have brought us to our present position, is to be said, not only of Christian belief in general and of Christian ethics in particular, but of the manner in which the voice of the church can command a hearing in the arena of opinion at this time? It is to that question of apologetic import that we now turn.

When we referred to the questions of Christian apologetics under the heading of "Triad 2", we indicated the threefold areas on which the content of the evangel casts its light. We referred to "Being and reality", "Knowledge", and "Behavior". In the discussions that followed we have effectively addressed what needs to be said under the first of those headings. The Christian explanation of being and reality is, we have seen, a two-layer explanation. First, God exists in his uncaused eternal being, in both communicable and incommunicable attributes; and second, all of reality external to the Godhead exists by virtue of God's having called it into existence.[11] Man himself, created in the

---

opposite of what God has stated it to be. It is that bias in the soul, that is born of its fallenness and hatred of God, that neo-evangelicalism has been reluctant to take fully into account. The sinner who is unregenerate knows that God is, but by virtue of his deliberate suppression of God's witness to him he does not know who God is. He has a bare cognition of reality, but no true knowledge or understanding of reality. He has no ultimate principle of predication or interpretation of meaning that permits him to understand reality correctly as God has established it. In terms that are reflected in our discussion in the preceding chapter of the effects of regeneration on the faculties of the soul, the difference of apologetic starting point and method turns on alternative conceptions of the epistemic status and capacities of the regenerate, as opposed to the unregenerate, mind.

[11] See Cornelius Van Til, *The Defense of the Faith* and *A Christian Theory of Knowledge*, Phillipsburg: P&R Publishing, 1967 and 1969. On the subject of this and the following chapter see also John Frame, *Cornelius Van Til: An Analysis of His Thought*, Phillipsburg: P&R Publishing, 1995, and the same

image of God, is, in his being, an analogy of God. As a result he is, in his very constitution, revelatory of God. God has revealed himself to man in his created environment that eloquently speaks of God, and in the sense and awareness of God, the *sensus deitatis*, that is inherent in the human consciousness.

Time itself is a created entity. All of created reality exists within a temporal complex. Differences exist, therefore, not only between the being of God and the being of man, but between, also, the knowledge of God and the knowledge of man. Our knowledge and our capacities for knowing and understanding, temporally bounded as they are, are necessarily sequential. We can and we do know different things at different times. We perceive and learn and we organize the conceptions that constitute our knowledge. But the knowledge that God possesses, both his knowledge of himself and his knowledge of reality external to himself, is not temporally bounded and sequential. God knows sequences, but he does not know sequences sequentially.[12] God knows all things in one eternal act of knowing. All the facts of reality are God's facts, and they and their histories exist in the arrangements and constellations that they do because God has thought all of the facts before the foundation of the world.

The manner in which these questions of being and knowledge have been addressed in the preceding chapters makes a further extensive discussion unnecessary. The third element of our "Triad 2", that brings into focus the question of behavior, will be addressed again in our concluding chapters. It will be possible to place the question of behavior in the context of what the evangel implies for the Christian life. At this point only one preliminary statement might be made. Its relevance will become clearer as we proceed. It has to do with the relations that necessarily exist between being, knowledge, and behavior, the elements that "Triad 2" has contemplated.

The Christian explanation of being and knowledge con-

---

author's *The Doctrine of the Knowledge of God*, and *Apologetics to the Glory of God: An Introduction*, Phillipsburg: P&R Publishing, 1987 and 1994.
[12] We recall the statement to that effect by Robert L. Dabney in his *Discussions: Evangelical and Theological*, London: Banner of Truth, 2 Vols. [1890, 1891] 1967. See Vol. 1, 294. See also Chapter 4 above, n.2.

cludes that being is prior to knowing. That is to say, the question of what there is to be known needs to be addressed before the question of how the knowledge of it can be attained. In other words, the *what* of knowledge necessarily precedes the *how* of knowledge. That follows from what has already been said. For if we understand that all that exists is what it is because it has been spoken into existence by the word and the will of the sovereign God, then the manner of knowing must necessarily be dependent on the capacities for knowing that creation in the image of God has planted in the human constitution. The created person is, in his being and constitution, an analogue of God. The constitution of the person itself reveals God. Similarly, it now has to be said that the person's knowledge is an analogue of God's knowledge. Because of our boundedness in time, we do not know in the manner in which God knows. Our knowledge ability and our knowledge processes are themselves derivative. They exist and we experience them because they are created within us.

In the same way as being is prior to knowing, it has to be said also that being and knowing are prior to behavior. That is so in two respects. First, the nature of the person and the knowledge that he or she possesses determine the nature and the quality of that individual's behavior. The Scriptures claim repeatedly that the nature of the individual is such that "as he thinketh in his heart, so is he" (Prov. 23:7). And we have already seen that the meaning of sin is such that one's behavior is determined by the character that qualifies him either as the slave of Satan or as committed to Christ.

Secondly, the fact that being and knowledge are prior to behavior determines the criteria that do, or should, guide behavior and human action. At the Fall, man made his false assertion of autonomy. As to his being, he falsely asserted that he was not the creature of a Creator-God. He was not, therefore, under responsible obligation to God. He was in himself autonomous. As to his knowledge and his capacity for knowing, he asserted that he could discover for himself the meaning of reality, without reference to the explanation that God provided for him. And now, as to his behavior, he asserted that he could discover within himself, or within the reality that surrounded him or in a social and cultural consensus, all necessary criteria of behavior.

But the Christian explanation requires the contrary statement. God in his being and sovereignty is prior to human existence and to all possibilities of human knowledge. And the processes and criteria of truth in knowledge depend on the criteria that God has established. In the same way now, the criteria of behavior and action are those that God has provided. That follows from the reality that it is "in him [God] we live, and move, and have our being" (Acts 17:28). As Van Til has put it, God is our ultimate environment.[13] In all of the possibilities of knowing and reasoning and behavior, God is the Christian's presupposition.

In the light of what we have said to this point, it will not be necessary to repeat our earlier discussion of the nature of being and reality. And we can set aside for the moment any further discussion of behavior, as that will occupy us again in our examination of the Christian life. It will be sufficient to expand, in this and the following chapter, on the question of knowledge, or the question of the manner in which the evangel throws its light on the true origin and processes of knowledge, and on the reasons why we can know that what we know is true.

The status of faith

The historic Christian position on the matter of knowledge has always been clear. It can be put briefly in contrast to the opinions of non-Christian thought.

The Christian's highest good, his *summum bonum*, is to know God, to glorify and enjoy him, and at last to see him as he is. The prophets and apostles, martyrs and saints, have heralded through the ages that God has made himself known to his people. The Christian confession has rung clear, that life and light and immortality have come in the Son of God. "This is life eternal", he prayed on the night on which he was betrayed, "that they might know thee, the only true God, and Jesus Christ,

---

[13] Cf. Cornelius Van Til, op. cit., notably his *Defense of the Faith* and *A Christian Theory of Knowledge*.

whom thou hast sent" (John 17:3). But there is reason to fear that the church's declaration is dulled, and that the message of life is compromised. The faith the church offers to the world is a paled and a lessened image of what it once had been. Christian belief and Christian life have been diminished.

Christianity, it is almost a commonplace to say, is in disarray. That, no doubt, has in many respects always been true, particularly, to use Schleiermacher's phrase, in the eyes of its cultured despisers.[14] For it is to a "little flock" that the secrets of the kingdom of God have been entrusted (Luke 12:32). And we are told that not many wise, not many noble are called. As the Lord of Heaven was "despised and rejected of men" (Is. 53:3) when he was in this world, so a similar honor has devolved on those who have followed him. The thought systems, the behavior norms, and the culture of the world have substantially evaded the imperatives of the Christian faith.

But the disarray is, at this point of history, clear on even the shallowest of perception. It comes to expression on a number of levels that have been the subject of scrutiny both within and outside of the church. They have to do, at a minimum, with four aspects of the faith and the interface of Christianity and the world, and with their significance for the testimony of the church to the world.

First, an accommodation of theological doctrine to alien thought systems has muted the clarity of the testimony of the gospel. The church's doctrine is as much philosophically, culturally, and socially, as it is Scripturally, informed.

Second, the thought systems of the world have themselves moved from at least a modest recognition of God, of his existence and the proof of his being, to the assumption, if he exists at all, of his irrelevance. We shall therefore have something to say in the following chapter of the ways in which the question of knowledge and truth has occupied the minds of prominent opinion-formers in the history of thought. An

---

[14] F. Schleiermacher, *On Religion: Speeches to its Cultured Despisers*, Trans. John Oman, Introduction R. Otto, New York: Harper & Row, 1958. See also Stanley J. Grenz and Roger E. Olson, *20th Century Theology: God and the World in a Transitional Age*, Downers Grove: InterVarsity Press, 1992, 39ff.

antithesis has resulted between Christianity and confessedly autonomous thought, and that will be addressed in a minimal and non-technical fashion.

Third, attempted alliances of Christian confession and elements of non-Christian thought have occurred, with a further important result. The church no longer provides a clear and uncluttered guidance to what the confessing Christian is to believe and to do. The muted and misleading testimonies of the pulpit have served to confuse rather than enlighten the pew. There is abroad, as an all too clear result, a theological-doctrinal indifference. Christian profession has become preoccupied with individual self-interest, self-indulgence and personal gratification. The church is relied upon to cater to personal and socio-cultural needs, and increasingly to psychological mollification. An earlier concern for worship in its pristine meaning and objectives has been sabotaged by many congregations in the interest of extra-Scriptural procedures.

Fourth, a clearly observable and important result has followed from the capitulation of Christian confession to secular criteria of belief and practice. It has led to a generalized cultural accommodation of the members of the church to the life and behavior patterns of the world. Belief and behavior have been jointly tarnished, if it can be said that their distinctive vitalities have not been substantially destroyed. For belief and behavior are inevitably joined. What one believes is projected onto, and it influences and determines, what it is that one does.

That relation had in itself determined the course of social and cultural history in earlier times. It determined, as can be seen on only a minimal inspection, the bequest that in large part the late nineteenth gave to the twentieth century. For it is a shallow superficiality to imagine, as occurred at that time, that a distinctively Christian ethic is, or can be, supportable without the Christian doctrine. When the latter has been effectively scuttled and sounder moorings have been discarded, the former, or what were once supportable canons of Christian behavior, no longer have meaning or foundational justification.

In the fifth place, an issue of vital relevance and concern follows from what has been said. The professing church, or the church as an institutional entity, has increasingly absorbed the management and organizational norms of the enterprise culture in which it is set to bear witness. In both the mega-church and the village assembly, the management cultures, the organizational ways of doing things, and the assumed criteria of achievement and success, have substituted newer conceptions for older paths and Scriptural priorities.

But our principal concern is with the four primary issues that we have raised: first, the accommodation of theological doctrine to alien thought systems; second, the evaporation from influential thought systems of a theocentric orientation and the embrace of the pervasive assumption of the human autonomy; third, the absence of clear directives as to belief and practice from the pulpit to the pew and the fracture of faith that results; and fourth, the cultural accommodation of Christian life-patterns to the systems and schemes of the world.

Some historical influences

In these several respects the face of faith is markedly changed from what it was in earlier times. Theological doctrine once had a closer relevance to life. But the face of faith is fractured virtually beyond recognition. In their contribution to that condition, the first two of our concerns are very clearly interrelated. The most pressing question that can engage us is whether it is possible, and if so how is it possible, to know God. It is the statement of the evangel that the Christian knows God because God makes himself known. God has said through the prophet Jeremiah that "I will give them an heart to know me" (Jer. 24:7). But in the light of that, we need to look briefly at what has been thought and said in the past on the question of the possibility of that knowledge. Because of the influence of changing opinion on the message of the confessing church, we need to look at the reaction of thought in general to the question of truth.

The continuing, sometimes close and sometimes shaky, relation between Jerusalem and Athens, or between, that is, the church and the secular academy, has attracted the close attention of scholars in the sacred and the secular disciplines. Between Tertullian's "What has Jerusalem to do with Athens" in the early church centuries, and the twentieth century capitulation to existentialist theology and forms of latter day postmodernism, challenging and absorbing patterns of relations can be traced.[15] From the birth of so-called modern theology at the hands of Schleiermacher in the early nineteenth century, through the fashions of subjectivism that followed, to Barth's attempt at a new reformation theology in the twentieth century and to a new hermeneutic that essentially accommodates contemporary postmodernism, theology has variously wandered from its erstwhile Scriptural foundations.[16]

When Descartes gave impetus to modern thought in the seventeenth century with his *"cogito ergo sum"*, "I think, therefore I am", the thinker's imagination was set on its anthropocentric course. It was not that Descartes had no place for God. God was there, and it was even inconceivable for Descartes that God could deceive the thinker in the construction of his thought schemes. But in the Cartesian system, man himself was effectively at the center of things. In place of his "I think, therefore I am", Descartes might more profitably have said, "I think, therefore God is". But in modern thought as it has developed, man was soon at the center of reality and God was consigned to the periphery.

That in itself, however, exists in tension with what developed as a result of the influence of modern science. In earlier times, Ptolemy and his conceptions of a geocentric universe had set the pattern of thought. Man and his planet earth was in a very definite sense at the center of reality. But the Copernican

---

[15] Tertullian, *The Prescription Against Heretics*, VII. See E.R. Geehan, Ed., *Jerusalem and Athens: Critical Discussions on the Theology and Apologetics of Cornelius Van Til*, Phillipsburg: P&R Publishing, 1971, vi.

[16] See F. Schleiermacher, *The Christian Faith*, Ed. H.R. Mackintosh and J.S. Stewart, Edinburgh: T. and T. Clark, [1830] 1928; H.R. Mackintosh, *Types of Modern Theology: Schleiermacher to Barth*, New York: Charles Scribner's Sons, 1937; Cornelius Van Til, *Christianity and Barthianism*, Phillipsburg: P&R Publishing, 1962; James M. Robinson and John B. Cobb, Jr. Eds., *The New Hermeneutic* (in *New Frontiers in Theology: Discussions among Continental and American Theologians*), New York: Harper & Row, 1964; Antony Flew and Alasdair Macintyre, Eds., *New Essays in Philosophical Theology*, New York: Macmillan, [1955] 1964; Cornelius Van Til, *The New Hermeneutic*, Phillipsburg: P&R Publishing, 1974.

revolution changed that. It has not always been clearly appreciated how that very change turned opinion in general on its head. When a heliocentric conception of the universe replaced the earlier geocentric scheme, or when it was realized that the earth revolved around the sun and not the sun around the earth, not only was the planet earth dislodged from the center of thought, but so was man as he existed on his planet. A tension in thought thereby developed.[17]

By virtue of that scientific tension, the place of man was diminished. And yet, at the same time, philosophic thought became markedly and more articulately anthropocentric. The impetus in that direction that Descartes established pursued its course through the eighteenth century Enlightenment. It led, first, to a culmination in the skepticism of David Hume, and then, in reaction from that, to the philosophy and epistemology of Immanuel Kant at the end of the eighteenth century.

It is properly said, so far as the development of extra-biblical thought is concerned, that all roads lead to Kant. And so influential did Kant's thought system become throughout the next two centuries, that he has been called the philosopher of Protestantism. That, no doubt, sets him apart from Thomas Aquinas, whose attempted marriage of Aristotle and the Scriptures makes him the philosopher of Catholicism.[18] But to say that Kant was the philosopher of Protestantism is only to mark the decline of Protestantism itself. For above all else, Kantianism stands for the all-pervasive assumption of the autonomy of man.[19] That, of course, is what we have already suggested has come to characterize in a perverse sense the culture of contemporary confessional Christianity.

At the same time, Christian thought has itself been ambivalent as to the significance and place of man. A theological

---

[17] A useful survey is contained in Richard Tarnas, *The Passion of the Western Mind*, New York: Ballantine Books, 1991. Tarnas' work, though it is not informed by an enlightened understanding of the Christian faith, in spite of the relatively large space given to the early and medieval developments and influence of Christianity, is a valuable survey of the main currents of Western thought.

[18] Thomas Aquinas, 1225-1274.

[19] The place and significance of Kant will be considered further in chapter 9 below.

Arminianism has held tenaciously to the assumption of the autonomy of man. That is so in the assumptions it makes regarding man's competence as to knowledge and the possibility of his salvation. The same ambivalence has characterized more basic assumptions. Quite apart from what might be termed the theology of despair that effectively abolished the possibility of knowledge in its capitulation earlier in the twentieth century to existentialism, theology developed in tension with secular thought on another and important level.

The development of positivism in the later nineteenth century led to the philosophic doctrine that only that is knowable that is subject to verification, or, in later forms, to falsification, by empirical test. What could be known existed in the world of things that could be handled and touched and measured. Here we have the development of Kant's so-called phenomenal realm to which, as he saw it, the possibility of knowledge was confined. What existed beyond the phenomenal realm, or what might exist in the so-called noumenal realm, was unknowable. It thus became the positivist fashion to conclude that the God-question, the question of the existence or otherwise of God, was not itself an admissible question. Philosophic thought ceased to be troubled by questions regarding the knowability and character of God, and the existence of God was regarded as a nonsense question. It was non-sense in that the asking of the question did not make any sense. For the question itself was not subject to empirical test. Only that could be known, it was claimed, that existed in the realm of possible sense reaction and the tests of verification or falsifiability that logically followed.

God was thus effectively banished from men's thought and imagination. To the extent, therefore, that theology continued to have anything to say about God, man, and the relations between God and man, it was in uneasy tension with thought in general. It is understandable, against those forces of intellectual development, that more modern offsprings of secular thought should have been born. At an earlier time, as we have seen, God was banished from his world and set well outside of it on the periphery of reality. It was to be expected that in due course a more advanced position would be taken, and that it would be taken in such a way as to invade theological thought. That developed as what had to be called the death of God. God having been banished from his world, he was in due course himself taken to be dead. But that has itself produced further intellectual reaction and developments.

The central motif that characterizes contemporary thought has come to be called postmodernism. Modernism is now the name that is given to the thought system that descended from Descartes through the various channels we have indicated and it stood, in one way or another, for the competence of human reason in the discovery of knowledge and truth. In that imagined process, man and his reasoning or epistemic capacity was autonomous. He did not have any real need of God and his categories of interpretation, meaning, and behavior. We have already indicated that theological Arminianism, among contemporary theological systems, has continued to stand firmly and articulately for the autonomy of man.

But postmodernism has in very significant respects turned the earlier modernism on its head. Not only in the social sciences, the humanities, and the law, where postmodernism early made its influence felt, but in theology also the same developments have occurred. Postmodernism, so far as its relevance to our present study is concerned, stands for the proposition that no longer is any objective truth attainable. One man's truth is as good as another man's truth. In theology the point of entrance is through theology's hermeneutical principle. Hermeneutics refers, in general terms, to the science of interpretation. Now, in theology as in the secular disciplines, the assumption that objective principles and criteria of interpretation existed and were serviceable in the search for truth has been surrendered. Now there is not truth. There are only truths.

That has a very significant meaning so far as theology's approach to the Scriptures is concerned. It means that there are, it is imagined, new levels and possibilities of interaction between text and interpreter. The reader or interpreter is what he is by virtue of all of the determining forces that have formed him throughout his life history. The individual brings a uniquely determined self to the text and its interpretation. What the individual sees in the text is determined by who, at the time, he or she is. That individuality may, of course, be changed by his or her exposure to the text. The next time the text is approached by that person it is effectively approached by a different individual. In that manner a dialectical relation between the text and its reader is established. Truth, as a result, is no longer objectively existent and able to be grasped for what it is. Truth is now what it is to the individual at any one particular instance in time and in any particular situation.[20]

In the language of the postmodernist enterprise, the reader "deconstructs" the text. That is to say, he is free to take the words and sentences of the text and to import into them the meaning they have to him, as that is determined by his own experience, ideas, and social and cultural conditioning. The complex of meaning that is thereby achieved is then reimported into the text, in disregard of what might otherwise have been the initial and objective intention of the author. Thus we have the deconstructivist-postmodernist "hermeneutical circle".

It is important to observe the implications of all such post-modern developments. We saw a moment ago a significant devolution of modern thought. First, God was abolished from, or excluded from, his world. Second, that led in due course to the death of God. Now, in contemporary postmodernism thought has progressed, in what might have been anticipated as a natural momentum, beyond the death of God to the death of man. For postmodernism, in many of its clearest expressions, stands on the assumption that there does not exist a continuous human nature. That important point can be made more fully.

There exists in the human self what we can refer to as an epistemological discontinuity. The individual knows different things at different times. But while we say that in those respects the individual is characterized by an *epistemological discontinuity*, we may insist on the individual's *ontological continuity*.

The individual, that is, continues to be the same person, with the same ethical responsibilities and the same obligations under the law of God, in both his unregenerate and his regenerate states. But postmodernism has effectively abolished the person in its claim that there is not a continuous human nature. The

---

[20] See the brilliant discussion of contemporary hermeneutics in D.A. Carson, *The Gagging of God: Christianity Confronts Pluralism*, Grand Rapids: Zondervan, 1996.

death of God has led, with inexorable logic, to the death of man. It is an ironic result of the marriage of theology and the postmodernist hermeneutic that man, whose standing and prospects in relation to God it might have been the province of theology to investigate, has effectively ceased to exist. At least, he has ceased to exist in any theologically meaningful sense.

The fracture of faith

We have spoken of the status of faith and the disarray in which the faith expressed by the church appears to stand. A larger examination of the causes and results of the theological malaise and the doctrinal indifference that abounds would confirm the effects that have followed from the church's capitulation to the thought forms and the behavior norms of the world. The church is in the world, primarily, one would hope, to herald forth the good news of the evangel, the gospel of life in Christ. But it is true, also, that the world is in the church. The invasion that has occurred has produced its results in both belief and life.

There is cause for alarm at the fracture of faith, to the extent that the faith the church presents to its members has, on the face of it, been altered virtually beyond recognition. At least that is so when it is seen against the doctrinal deposit of the Scriptures and what the church has historically confessed. What has followed is that the Christian in the pew has, from the preaching and the teaching of the church, only a seriously diminished body of truth at his or her disposal. The individual Christian's faith is a diminished image of what, on the grounds of the Scriptures, he or she might be expected and encouraged to assent to. The content of the faith that the church presents to the world is fractured beyond comparison with the deposit of truth that came down to us through the Reformers and their successors.

Before we turn to a more direct discussion of the relevance of the evangel for the Christian life, we shall consider in the next chapter what Christian thought and doctrine hold regarding the relation between knowledge and truth. That will complete, for our present purposes, what was envisaged in chapter 1 under the heading of "Triad 2", the questions of Christian apologetics.

9

Knowledge and Truth

To hold to the possibility and the validity of the knowledge of God is to stand aside from modern opinion. It is to stand aside from much of what, following Descartes at the beginning of modern philosophy in the seventeenth century and down to recent times, has been referred to as modernism, and also from what has come to be known as postmodernism in contemporary thought.

The possibility and processes of knowledge, and the possibility of knowing God, have raised a number of questions and issues in the long history of non-Christian thought. We shall look in this chapter at two such basic questions, against which a Christian apologetic position can be established. We are concerned with, first, the basic question of *what* is to be known; and second, the nature of the knowledge process, or, in short, *how* we know.

The *what* and the *how* of knowledge

We may put those questions in slightly different terms. We are interested, first, in what the history of thought has understood to be the nature of reality, or what exists as potentially knowable. What, in other words, is the "real", the potential object of knowledge, as that may exist both in and beyond the phenomenal realm or the world of men and things? Second, we shall ask what are to be understood as the processes by which knowledge is achievable, what is the knowledge or epistemic capacity of the knowing individual, and whether, as a result, access to real or "true" truth is possible. Our interest is in what is to be known, how it can be known, and what is the source or guarantee of truth in relation to it.

Christian thought has given distinctive answers to these questions, though the answers have exhibited somewhat different emphases and starting points at the hands of different Christian thinkers. In the history of the church and its theological formulation, there have been different understandings of the capacity and competence of human reason and reasoning ability. There have been, for example, different understandings of the manner in which, and the extent to which, the capacity and competence of human reason has been affected by Adam's Fall. That, we have seen, dragged the race down into a state of captivity to sin, and theologians have discussed, as a result, what is to be understood as the noetic effects of the Fall. By that is meant the effects of the Fall on the mind of unregenerate man as he exists after, and as a result of, the Fall.

The position we shall take in what follows can be simply stated at the beginning. It is that what exists as the object of knowledge exists because of God's establishment and ordination of it. All of the facts, we shall say, are God's facts. And knowledge is possible because of the accordance that God has creatively established between the facts and the capacities of the knowing individual. Moreover, the Christian knows God because God has made himself known. God, we shall say, is the Christian's presupposition. "In him we live, and move, and have our being" (Acts 17:28). God is not discoverable as the result of autonomous human investigation. The Christian knows that "God is, and that he is a rewarder of them that diligently seek him" (Heb. 11:6).

The answers to the questions that arise on all of these levels must be Christologically understood. In Christ, "all the treasures of wisdom and knowledge" reside (Col. 2:3). He came to declare God the Father to us (John 1:18), and in doing so he declared that he is "the way, the truth, and the life" (John 14:6). In the light of that, we are entitled and required to insist that every fact, on every level of human awareness, must be interpreted and understood Christologically. Every fact, that is to say, is to be understood in relation to the reign of Christ and the significance for the human condition of what it was that he accomplished. Every fact is what it is because it is God's fact. Or to put that in another way, there do not exist any, as we might refer to them, "brute" facts that constitute a basis or foundation for human knowledge. Philosophically, there do not exist any brute facts that constitute ultimate epistemological data. We refer in that to "epistemological data" because the branch of philosophy that has investigated the question of the origin and processes and validity of knowledge has traditionally been viewed under the heading of epistemology. It is that branch of thought and opinion that we are now bringing to brief focus from the perspectives of the Christian processes of knowledge.

All of the facts of the universe are what they are because of the place they occupy and the function they perform in the eternal plan of God. In other words, all of the facts are preinterpreted facts, preinterpreted by virtue of their place in God's comprehensive preordination. The task of human investigation and of the knowledge process, therefore, is to seek to reinterpret the facts that are assessable in the light of the preinterpretation that God has already established. In short, the existence of every fact cannot be separated from the meaning of the fact. It is the meaning that gives the fact its factness. And in relation to every fact we are required to endeavor to think God's thoughts after him.

For the Christian, the significance of that statement is clear on the basis of even the briefest reflection. For consider, to go for a moment to the heart of the Christian faith, the atonement that Christ accomplished. The Scriptures set forth in clear and unmistakeable terms the fact of the death of Christ. But the Scriptures do not, in doing so, set forth a bare fact. The Scriptures expose and explain the meaning of the fact, the purpose and intention and meaning of the death of Christ. It is therefore the declaration of that meaning that gives the fact of the death of Christ the factness that it possesses. Meaning, it will become clearer, inheres in the structures of reality that God has established. It is precisely their relation to that elemental

165

truth that distinguishes all forms of non-Christian and apostate thought from that of the Christian faith.

The question of the knowledge process, or of the availability and the acquisition of truth, can be considered in the light of God's initial creation mandate. When God created man he entered into a covenant with him in terms of which he established him as his vicegerent, or as a prophet, priest, and king. He was to discharge those offices in his relation to the universe in which he came to his self-awareness. He was to be a prophet in that he was to interpret and to understand the meaning of the universe he inherited, and he was to work out all of the potentialities of meaning inherent in that created reality. He was to be a priest in that it was his task and responsibility to dedicate that reality and its meaning structure back to God. He was to understand it and to develop and to use it to, and for, the glory of God. He was to be a king in that he was to rule over his inherited universe to the glory of God. The earliest biblical record establishes that pristine function and office in what has been referred to as the creation mandate. "God created man in His own image ... male and female ... And God blessed them, and God said unto them, Be fruitful, and multiply, and replenish the earth, and subdue it, and have dominion over ... every living thing" (Gen. 1:27-28).

The earliest record also makes it clear that God communicated to Adam a clearly articulated special revelation. That had reference not only to the terms of Adams's probation and the prohibition of his eating the forbidden fruit. It included also what may be referred to as certain creation ordinances. They related to work, marriage, family and social relations, the sabbath, worship, and the structures of righteous morality. It is precisely those mandates and ordinances that were reexpressed and rearticulated in the Ten Commandments given to Moses. At that later time they were promulgated in an inscripturated form that was adapted to man's fallen condition. For though Adam's probation was terminated in his lapse from the obligations of the covenant that God had established with him, the responsibilities inherent in the creation mandate remained. The disregard of that covenantal obligation delineates the sinful condition that now exists, and the recognition of its sanctity and perpetuity informs the Christian's perceptions.

The dialecticism of modern thought

Let us digress for a moment to look briefly at an aspect of non-Christian thought that will illustrate the points that have just been made. To adapt the language of the distinguished mid-twentieth century Christian apologist and philosopher, Cornelius Van Til,[1] we may refer to what has been labeled the dialecticism of modern thought. By "dialecticism" we mean the shifting back and forth, a swinging to and fro, between one type or character of explanatory principle and another, the latter being in essence the opposite or contradiction of the former. The dialecticism of modern thought can be characterized by referring to the non-Christian principle of continuity on the one hand, and a corresponding principle of discontinuity on the other.

The former principle implies that on the metaphysical level, or on the level of what can be said and concluded regarding the nature of being, there exists the notion of being-in-general in which man and God, if he exists at all, both participate. On the epistemological level, or in relation to the possibility and the truth of knowledge, the non-Christian principle of continuity implies that there exists a universal or generalized reason. We may say, from the point of view of that thought scheme, that the notion of reason-in-general on the epistemological level is correlative to that of being-in-general on the metaphysical level. That generalized reason is assumed to be essentially penetrable to the human mind, and it is assumed also that God, if he exists, and man both participate in it. Modern thought, therefore, has suppressed the essential postulate of Christian thought, namely the fact of the Creator-creature distinction on the levels of both being and knowing. The modern assumption implies that what is knowable to man is, given only time and resources, knowable completely. Raised at the beginning of the knowledge and explanatory process, therefore, is the vision of completeness or

---

[1] Cornelius Van Til, *A Christian Theory of Knowledge*, Phillipsburg P&R Publishing, 1969, 318, 338.

comprehensiveness in knowledge. Man is said to know truly only when he has known comprehensively and exhaustively.

But over against the principle of continuity is the alternative postulate, equally present and pervasive, the non-Christian principle of discontinuity. That principle involves the assumption of the non-createdness of the universe. It assumes that underlying all things is the operation of chance, randomness, and stochastic or probabilistic laws. The principle of discontinuity therefore involves the assumption of the ultimacy of chance. Anything can happen.

The important point is that in this basic dialecticism, the first assumption we raised, that of continuity and reason-in-general, stamps modern thought with its aspect of rationalism. The second assumption, that of discontinuity or the ultimacy of chance, stamps it with its aspect of irrationalism. Modern thought is thus engaged in a rationalist-irrationalist dialectic. It implies that against the earlier assumption of exhaustiveness or comprehensiveness of knowledge we must place the equally pervasive assumption that at the end of all his investigations man can know nothing at all. All is chance. Man knows everything or he knows nothing.

That dialectical characteristic of non-Christian thought has forced the conclusion that there is, in fact, no singular objective truth. There exists only a plurality of truths. That is the essence of what has been reached in contemporary postmodernism. Leaving aside for the moment the stark contradiction of Christian thought that such a conclusion implies, we may illustrate the nature of contemporary thought by looking briefly at a couple of examples of the way in which it has come to expression. Because of the pervasive influence of the newer systems of thought, instances are observable in all intellectual disciplines and implications follow on many levels of human behavior. We observe, first, an expression of it in the work of an influential thinker in the social science disciplines. G.L.S. Shackle, in his erudite book, *Epistemics & Economics*, has observed that "It has been the posture of science that there is truth to be found. Truth is unique. But to be unique it must be complete, since otherwise there will be freedom to complete it in any number of different ways. ... What presumption is there that the 'objective' truth, and a truth that can be humanly conceived, can be matched and identified with each other?"[2] Shackle continues: "If the unique and complete truth must therefore eternally elude us, there is reason and necessity to accept other insights into the nature of science ... Truth must then be seen as plural, choosable, capable of being invented. Its ultimate and essential purpose ... is to console the human mind."

That pessimistic stance in relation to the possibility that truth is attainable again exhibits the dialectical dilemma of modern thought. Again man either knows everything or he knows nothing at all. The stance that is taken has evaded the Christian distinction between true knowledge and comprehensive knowledge. In Shackle's conception of science, the function of any one of the available plurality of truths is to console the mind. And for that purpose, it appears, any one construction of truth is as good as any other. Here, on the level of the possibility of knowledge, subjectivism is pushed to its radical extreme. The awareness of truth has, in that conception, no significance for, or relation to, the glory of God.

The Christian's escape from this modern dialecticism results from his acknowledgment that the reference point in all of his predication of meaning is found in God and his plan, mediated and declared in Jesus Christ his Son. But against that Christian view, let us take an example that bears again on the nature of modern thought. The eminent Cambridge economist, D.G. Champernowne, at the beginning of his *Uncertainty and Estimation in Economics*, in the course of laying down the conceptual and philosophic foundations of his subject, discusses the notion of "irrelevance" between independent events. He refers to that as "about the most fundamental concept in the whole theory of probability". In that context he illustrates his point in a startling fashion by stating that "whether Christ ascended into heaven is irrelevant to whether this fair coin will come down heads or tails".[3]

Now in the context of our present discussion, this statement

---

[2] G.L.S. Shackle, *Epistemics & Economics*, Cambridge: Cambridge University Press, 1972, 353.
[3] D.G. Champernowne, *Uncertainty and Estimation in Economics*, Edinburgh: Oliver and Boyd, 1969, Vol. I, 18.

may appear minute and trivial, and hardly adequate to bear the weight that we might place upon it. But on the contrary, the very appearance of triviality brings into focus the important and underlying postulates we are concerned with. For if, as has been argued, every fact in the universe must be Christologically interpreted, the question now before us is rescued from the frivolous by the enormity of its potential relevance. Is, or is not, we can ask, the fact of Christ's ascension, and therefore his finished work in the world, relevant to Champernowne's problem? To press the issue, is it of any significance to say that the apparently random outcome of tossing a coin can have any conceivable relation to the work of Christ?

Before we answer this question in the affirmative, let us acknowledge what would be the implication if it were to be answered in the negative. This would mean that, contrary to the underlying postulate of Christian thought, we had actually discovered one fact situation to which the work of Christ had no relevance. Our basic postulate regarding the possibility of knowledge would then have been punctured. And if there is one point in the phenomenal universe at which the work of Christ is acknowledged not to have relevance, then conceivably any number of other such points are discoverable. The question is then presented of where in fact the so-called cosmic significance of Christ does begin to take effect. If the work of Christ is irrelevant to any fact, it is conceivably irrelevant to all.

The question before us in this seemingly inconsequential case demands an affirmative answer, therefore, for a threefold reason. First, God, the Christian has posited, is the author of possibility, and the outcome of all things and events is dependent upon his sovereign plan and his sovereign ordering.

Second, to argue to the contrary would imply that there existed, or potentially could exist in the universe, a fact situation, seemingly inconsequential though it may be, which God had not ordered and of which he accordingly had no anterior awareness. In that case God would have to wait to discover the outcome of an intra-mundane event. That, it will be clear, is to introduce a temporal successiveness into the knowledge of God. But that, in turn, is tantamount to the introduction of temporal succession into the being of God, or into his knowledge of himself. God is in that case no longer the God of the Scriptures, self-existent beyond the temporal process that he has created. On the contrary, God's knowledge of the facts exists by virtue of his having thought all the facts and ordered them in their apparently contingent relations.

Third, it is in Christ and by virtue of his work that God accomplishes his plan and his ordering of all of the affairs that he has made. It would therefore be taxing credulity to imagine that the work of Christ, who himself has said "Are not two sparrows sold for a farthing? And one of them shall not fall on the ground without your Father. But the very hairs of your head are all numbered" (Matt. 10:29), should be irrelevant to the outcome of Champernowne's toss of a coin. For who is to say, in the interdependent and causal nexus of events, what issues of larger enormity might follow from the tossing of the coin?

The meaning and the attainability of truth

In the light of what has been said, it is important for the Christian thinker to be aware of a number of relevant questions that non-Christian thought has investigated. They can be condensed for our present purposes to the two principal concerns that we have already anticipated. First, what is the nature of the "real" or of reality, and what, in relation to it, is the source of meaning and truth? Or, in other words, does "truth" exist, and if so, what is to be understood as its locus or its source or genesis? Second, what, then, is knowable, how is it to be known, and what degree of certitude, if any, can be held in relation to knowledge?

Those questions take up, with greater or lesser directness, issues we have already raised from the perspective of Christian belief. We have observed that the "real" is that which God has established by his creative decree. Because we have insisted, in the light of the Scriptural data, on the Creator-creature distinction, we have already referred to a two-layer theory of being or reality.[4] First, God exists, in eternal independence of any thing

---

[4] Cornelius Van Til, *The Defense of the Faith*, Phillipsburg: P&R Publishing, second edition., 1963, 23ff.

or cause external to himself. He is self-existent in his being and self-referential in his knowledge. Second, all that exists external to the Godhead exists by virtue of its having been called into existence, created *ex nihilo*, by God's creative will and decree. From this it follows that all interpretation of meaning is to be theocentric, or, in the terms in which that was earlier stated, all content of knowledge derives from a Christologically inter-preted understanding of every fact situation.

The question we are asking is that with which Francis Ba-con, the philosopher, lawyer, and scientist who flourished at the turn of the seventeenth century, began his Essays. "What is truth? said jesting Pilate, and would not stay for an answer".[5] Bacon observed that "Certainly, it is heaven upon earth, to have a man's mind move in charity, rest in providence, and turn upon the poles of truth".[6] Bacon's "poles of truth" may be read as having a primarily ethical reference or, alternatively, a reference to the possibility of knowing, the point at which his Essay, with its invoking of Pilate's question, began. Bacon spoke of "the true God" and of "religion being the chief band of human society",[7] and his essay on the impossibility of atheism raises issues that will concern us again. "It is true, that a little philosophy inclineth man's mind to atheism; but depth in philosophy bringeth men's minds about to religion. For while the mind of man looketh upon second causes scattered, it may sometimes rest in them, and go no further; but when it be-holdeth the chain of them, confederate and linked together, it must needs fly to Providence and Deity".[8] Here, of course, is the notion of what has become known as the cosmological proof of the existence of God, the tracing of observed reality to its first cause.

In the seventeenth century there was a great deal of talk about God. Educated thought was at that time still at a stage at which the question of God, his existence and providence and his knowability, was reckoned to be a legitimate part of serious

---

[5] Francis Bacon, *The Essays or Counsels, Civil and Moral*, Mount Vernon, N.Y.: The Peter Pauper Press, n.d., 9.
[6] Ibid., 11.
[7] "Of Unity in Religion", in *Essays*, 15.
[8] "Of Atheism", in *Essays*, 65-66.

enquiry. God was not yet dead, as he was to become in the nineteenth century at the hands of Nietzsche, the continental "death of God" philosopher, and as was the case in the later neo-Nietzschean tradition in the mid-twentieth century. The feature of seventeenth century thought that still addressed the question of the existence of God ran alongside a rich flowering of Christian thought in the tradition of Reformed theology. The English Puritans at that time produced the richest concentration of biblically informed theology that has emerged in the English language since the Reformation.

But at the same time, a great deal of speculation occurred in the seventeenth century on the relation between reason and religion. It occurred simultaneously with what has been referred to as the beginning of modern philosophy. That came to birth at the hands of the continental philosopher and rationalist, Descartes, and was further developed by the English empiricists, beginning with John Locke in the latter half of the seventeenth century. It was Locke who, in anticipation of the deism that followed in the next century, published *The Reasonableness of Christianity*. In that work, while he presented an apologia for the Christian faith and its understanding of the restoration of fallen humanity in Christ, he nevertheless envisaged a connected system of beliefs which, in the light of their reasonableness, could be grasped by all persons.[9]

The relation between reason and religion was in these ways variously treated in the seventeenth and eighteenth centuries, in the continental rationalism of Descartes, Spinoza, and Leibniz, and the British empiricism of Locke, Berkeley, and Hume. Those movements of thought coalesced in Kant at the culmination of what became known as the Enlightenment at the end of the eighteenth century. In Kant the problem of knowledge was solved in a unique way which, he said, abolished knowledge in order to make room for faith. For Kant, knowledge was confined to what he called the phenomenal realm. We shall return to his very influential system of thought.

---

[9] These movements of thought are discussed elegantly and informatively in Colin Brown, *Christianity and Western Thought: A History of Philosophers, Ideas & Movements*, Downers Grove, Ill,: InterVarsity Press, 1990.

Earlier anticipations of the problem of the "Real" and of knowledge

But let us look behind these relatively modern movements for a moment. We have recognized varying relationships and fashions of thought that we are intentionally not pausing to discuss in anything like adequate detail. They cast us back, however, to the beginning of systematic inquiry. The "birth of philosophy"[10] has generally been stated to have occurred with the Greek thinkers, for example Thales, Anaximander, and Anaximenes who flourished in the sixth century before Christ. Concerned as they were to answer the question as to what constituted the "real", or what formed the substantial reality lying beyond all things, Thales concluded that the primary substance from which all was derived was water, because of what he perceived as the water content of all things and the necessity of water to sustain life. But the details of his answer are not as important as the fact that he raised the question of the ultimate nature of reality. His successors did the same, though their answers were different. Anaximenes again understood all things to derive from a single substance, but that he took to be air. It is significant that in this search for the meaning of reality Thales, for example, stated that "all things are full of gods".[11] The supposed relation between men and the gods occupied a large part of the classic Greek thought and imagination.

If, as is usual, we take the beginning of extra-biblical sys-tematic thought to have occurred at about the year 600 B.C. (though the epics of Homer had been composed probably two centuries earlier) historical perspective is gained by recalling that at approximately the same time Jerusalem had been captured by Nebuchadnezzer and the Jews carried into captivity in Babylon. The subsequent flowering of Greek thought, that in many respects provided the cradle of Western civilization, surrounded the time of the Peloponnesian War in which Sparta defeated Athens, concluding in 404 B.C., the death of Socrates

---

[10] Richard Tarnas, *The Passion of the Western Mind*, New York: Ballantine Books, 1991, 446.
[11] Colin Brown, op. cit., 21.

in 399 B.C., and the founding of Plato's famous Academy in Athens in 387 B.C. That highly significant period in the history of thought therefore coincided with the close of the Old Testament writings. Greek thought flourished in the interregnum between the last of the canonical Old Testament prophets, Malachi, and the coming of Christ. Malachi's work, though the dating of it is uncertain, can probably be placed in the last quarter of the fifth century before Christ, at, say, 425 B.C. It is in that space of time that highly significant questions relating to our twofold concerns of reality and knowledge were raised.

Between the early thinkers we have referred to and Plato there had arisen the school of the Eleatics, Parmenides and Zeno for example, who were much concerned with logical puzzles and paradoxes. But in that concern they exhibited a new conception of the independence and capacity and individuality of the human mind. Inquiry was more firmly set to work to "differentiate between the real and the apparent, between rational truth and sensory perception, and between being and becoming".[12] In doing that, these early thinkers advanced the notion that human reason was to serve as the judge of reality.

We have traced those early developments of thought because coming to expression at that early stage is the postulate of the sovereignty of human intellection in the knowledge process. This was the articulated beginning of the anthropocentric, or man-centered, structure of thought and explanation. In the interregnum between Malachi and Christ, there could not be a Christological interpretation of things, as there could not be, in the darkness that prevailed, a recognition of the God-created reality to which the literature of God's early theocratic people had given testimony. Thought and imagination were anthropocentric in a sense that influenced and characterized its development throughout the next two millenia.

But the early reliance on the competence of reason was accompanied by a generalized skepticism regarding the possibility of knowledge and its conception of the real. That skeptical rationalism was furthered by the school that became known as the atomists, Democritus and Leucippus for example,

---

[12] Richard Tarnas, op. cit., 20.

whose particular doctrine regarding the atomic structure of things anticipated subsequent developments of materialism. But in the swirling, changing, and dialectical nature of early thought, tensions existed. Parmenides of Elea, for example, who wrote a poem, the two parts of which were titled the "Way of Truth" and the "Way of Seeming", reflected in a severely rational way on the meaning of existence and of being. He concluded that reality consisted of one single unchanging substance. Heraclitus, to the contrary, who was influenced by the Pythagoreans, a school of philosophy that flourished in Italy, had emphasized the fact and reality of change. For him the fundamental thing to be said about reality was that it was in a state of continual flux. His statement that "You cannot step into the same river twice" is frequently referred to in the histories of philosophy.

Though the earliest Greek thinkers had spoken extensively of the pantheon of gods, a new emphasis emerged in the last of the movements that anticipated the schools of Plato and Aristotle. In the fifth century B.C. the Sophists, who were mainly a school of wandering teachers, were more interested in practical affairs. They set aside the earlier speculations regarding the gods and introduced a pronounced secular humanism. They made themselves available to teach on virtually any subject that, it was thought, would be useful in mastering the art of living successfully. The flavor of their attitudes is best illustrated by the representative Sophist, Protagoras, who has become famous for his dictum that "Man is the measure of all things". At that point skeptical humanism had degenerated to an explicit anthropocentric, or a blatantly man-centered, orientation.

To anticipate what was to follow at a later time, that anthropocentric or man-centered vision of reality was furthered and in a sense systematized by the work in the second century A.D. of the astronomer Ptolemy, who argued for a geocentric explanation of the universe. But it was not simply that the earth was the center of the universe. The implication also, carrying over the principal notion of the earlier Greek thought, was that man was the center of things. That conception was, of course, dislodged in the fifteenth century, when the heliocentric theory was embraced. The work of Copernicus and Kepler, and following them Galileo and Newton, ushered in a new scientific revolution in which the status of man in relation to the universe was diminished. But as that scientific revolution projected not only its human benefits but also its philosophic implications to the centuries that followed, the diminution of the significance of man, the loss of his sense of importance, carried with it a heightened skepticism that implied a loss of God also. For it soon became apparent, from the new scientific perspectives and in spite of the attempts of the early scientists to retain a place for God, that if God had, in fact, initially established the universe, there was no reason why he was needed to keep it running.

To return to the beginning of things, a more extensive systematization of thought occurred at the hands of Plato, who established his Academy at Athens in the year 387 B.C. Turning away from the preoccupation with material things that the Sophists had emphasized, Plato redirected men's thought to the world of ideas. Reality for him existed in what became referred to as the "forms" lying beyond the world that could be touched and handled and seen. The forms were the real, lying beyond the flux of the empirical world and its changing appearances that had engaged the mind of Heraclitus. But the problem that Plato faced was that of clarifying precisely how, if at all, the forms could be known. It could only be said that wisdom came through contemplation of such forms as that of the Good. Plato's forms set a fashion of thought that recurred throughout the centuries that followed and have been reincarnated in later times in varying forms of idealism.

It is significant that Aristotle, who had been a pupil in Plato's Academy, but who in due course founded his own school, the Lyceum, in Athens in 335 B.C., did, in a sense, bring Plato "down to earth".[13] For he considerably modified the Platonic philosophy and rejected the earlier notion that the basis of reality existed in a transcendent world of ideas. For Aristotle, reality was there and observable in the world of actual concrete things of which actual sensory perceptions existed. He said

---

[13] Richard Tarnas, op. cit., 55.

much about the logical relations in terms of which reality was to be understood and by which the knowledge of the real was to be established. He spoke extensively of causation and what he referred to as the material, efficient, formal, and final causes of things, and he turned thought back to the world of men and things.

But in doing so, in his interest in sensory perception and the experience of things, Aristotle nevertheless emphasized that the understanding of empirical reality depended on, and derived from, rational reflection and critical thinking about experience. In this we see the twofold cleavage in classical thought that has influenced succeeding centuries in the matter of reality and knowledge. For Plato the real existed beyond the world of sense. For Aristotle the real existed to be seen and handled. For Plato knowledge came by rational contemplation. For Aristotle, while, as has been seen, he remains a rationalist of a high order, knowledge comes from a more clearly recognizable intra-mundane source, from the actual world that exists, and from the reactions of sensory experiences to it.

Implications for modern and postmodern thought

The structures of early thought need not be taken further. We now have before us the foundations of two clearly differentiated theories of knowledge that have ever since competed for intellectual allegiance. Plato's interest in his world of forms and ideas stands at the foundation and origin of rationalism. And Aristotle's concern for the world of things stands at the beginning of empiricism. The pendulum of the theory of knowledge has since swung between rationalism and empiricism, and the dialectical cleavage has come to frequent expression: In the same way as Aristotle turned Plato on his head, a similar divergence of view emerged between the continental rationalism in the centuries following the Reformation and the empiricism that flourished from Locke to Kant in the seventeenth and eighteenth centuries. The distinguishing separation of viewpoint occurred again when Marx in the nineteenth century turned Hegel on his head and spoke of a dialectical materialism rather than the dialectical idealism for which Hegel had argued. The nineteenth century idealism gave way in turn to what became known as positivism, as that was developed initially by the philosopher and sociologist Comte. New and highly developed forms of scientism appeared, and the assumption was advanced that all that was knowable existed in the world of phenomenal things.

Kant, as we have anticipated, stands at a watershed in the history of Western thought. At the culmination of the so-called eighteenth century Enlightenment he argued that knowledge comes from reflection on the sensory experiences of the actual world, but that the formation of knowledge was contributed to by the existence within the human mind of what Kant referred to as categories of knowing. He referred to such categories as those of space and time, "*a priori* forms of human sensibility", which were presupposed as existent in the mind and in terms of which sensory experiences were structured into knowledge. The problem that Kant faced, following the earlier development of skepticism, notably at the hands of David Hume, was that of reconciling the fact and the necessity of belief in God with the knowledge of empirical reality that Hume, for example, had addressed. For Kant the solution came, not only or simply in his argument regarding the categories of knowing inherent in the mind, but in what has been thought to be a master stroke in the history of thought. That was Kant's separation between what he would henceforth refer to as the phenomenal realm, or the world of men and things, and the noumenal realm, or the world as it really exists apart from our experience.[14]

That so-called master stroke in the history of philosophy led to the important Kantian conclusion that knowledge was restricted to the phenomenal realm. The noumenal realm existed, but what might exist within it could not be known, except by an act or a leap of faith. It is for that reason that Kant is said to have abolished knowledge in order to make room for faith. In the history of theology Kant, given his emphasis in this way on faith, has been called the philosopher of Protestantism. But such a designation, of course, does not accord with a

---

[14] See John M. Frame, *Cornelius Van Til: An Analysis of His Thought*, Phillipsburg: P&R Publishing, 1995, 165.

sounder understanding of the meaning of faith as that came with and from the Protestant Reformation, and as it informed the subsequent development of systematic theology. For Kant, his so-called faith had no basis or grounding in true knowledge at all, certainly not in a prior revelation of God to man.

What the Kantian achievement in philosophy stands for, given the restrictions on knowledge that he claimed and his understanding of the process of knowledge, is that in Kant we see the final elevation of the human reasoning capacity and processes to the point of prominence and preeminence. In Kant, and in what followed from his work, we have the final establishment of the autonomy of the human mind in the possibility and the discovery of knowledge. Kant stands for the autonomy of man. He stands for the essential creativity of human thought, in contradistinction from the fact that human knowledge is what it is because it is derivative from, and is analogical of, the absolute knowledge that resides in God. Post-Kantian thought has worked out the implications of that fundamental stance. That can be seen by looking a little more fully at some conclusions we observed in the preceding chapter.

As positivism developed in the nineteenth century following Kant, the restriction of knowledge to the phenomenal world was paramount. An optimistic humanism emerged. In the deism that had flourished in the eighteenth century God had been effectively excluded from his world, which could now, it was imagined, continue to run without any intervention from him. Of course, the God-question continued to be asked. Descartes at the beginning of modern philosophy had given considerable attention to the problem of proving the existence of God. The argument he presented was a form of the so-called ontological proof, taking up a line of argument that Anselm had advanced in the eleventh century. It claimed that God's existence was established by reason of the fact that it was possible for the human mind to think of a being, than which no more perfect being could be contemplated. When, then, it was further argued that existence is a necessary attribute of perfection, that most perfect being necessarily existed and was recognizable as God. But while such questions as that of the existence of God did continue to engage the philosophers, and while Kant at the end of the Enlightenment retained the notion of God's existence (though Kant rejected the classic "proofs" of the existence of God, and God was for him, though unknowable, a postulate of practical reason), subsequent thought diminished the status of God in a remarkable sense.

For the positivism that developed, answers to the question of the existence of God ceased to be meaningful. It was not only that discussion could no longer meaningfully proceed on the possibility of different answers on that point. Rather, the question of God's existence was itself taken not to be meaningful. Meaning now attached only to questions that could be answered, in one way or another, by experimentation and testing in the phenomenal world. God was finally excluded from men's thought. If he existed, he could not be known, and if he could not be known there was no point in asking any question about his existence. Previously God had been excluded from his own world, or, that is, from the providential supervision and direction of it. Now God was excluded completely from men's imaginations. That marked the death of God.

That achievement of modern thought was a mature implication of the effects of Adam's Fall. For at the Fall Adam effectively made the assertion of autonomy, spurious though it was, on all of the levels we have already noted. On the level of being or ontology, he asserted that he was not the creature of a Creator-God, and in doing so he effectively denied his creaturehood and the covenantal obligations that his creation by God imposed upon him. On the level of the possibility and the discovery of knowledge, he asserted his autonomy in his claim that he could competently discover in himself, or in the intramundane world around him, all necessary criteria of knowledge. On the level of ethics, he asserted that he could excogitate from within himself all necessary criteria of behavior and conduct. The assertion in that way of metaphysical, epistemological, and ethical autonomy has come to full flower in the age of modern and the latter-day postmodern thought. The collapse of social and cultural cohesion that has followed from the relativism that has resulted from these developments is clearly observable.

What we have seen in the foregoing as the inception and the flowering of modern thought has given way, as was observed at the beginning, to new forms of "postmodernism". This has marked the final collapse of any pretense that absolute truth exists. There is no truth. There are only truths.

As we have noted, in postmodernism we have, effectively, the death of man. It is understandable that the death of man should follow, in philosophic, cultural, and social thought, the earlier death of God. The death of man now comes to expression in the claim that there does not exist a continuous identifiable human nature. For human nature, it is argued, is a product of what are referred to as the overdetermined and overdetermining forces and features and phenomena of human existence. We are what we are because our histories and our cultures and climates and environments have been what they were. But a more basic issue lies at the heart of the postmodernist agenda.

That is the fact that postmodernism has failed to realize that in order to understand the human condition it is necessary to bear in mind two fundamental aspects of it: first, the nature of the human creature as he came from the hands of his Creator; and second, the psychological and the epistemological status that he now enjoys. For as we have seen from the Scriptural data, man is what he now is as a result of Adam's Fall. The pessimism and the nihilism of postmodern thought has turned its back on the rather superficial optimism of the late nineteenth and the early twentieth centuries. Then it was thought, in the heyday of evolutionary hypotheses, that while man may have come from the mud, his journey was to the stars. But two world wars in the twentieth century, the distress of economic depressions, and the disillusionment that came with them, have deadened the optimistic appeal. The optimism of the nineteenth century Victorian culture in England and the pushing back of the economic and cultural frontiers in the new world have given way to a soberness in which, all too sadly, man has not only lost his way but has denied his own being and continuity.

From the perspectives of Christian thought, and against the postmodernist enterprise, it can be recognized that there is an epistemological discontinuity in the human experience. That is, we know different things at different times, and because the possibility of knowledge is bounded by the movement of time we cannot know today what we shall know tomorrow. It is not possible for us to know at any one point in time what our knowledge status, or our epistemic status or capacity, will be at some future time. For we have no way of knowing what the intervening history will be or disclose. But while we may thus acknowledge what we may call an epistemological discontinuity, we hold, on the other hand, to an ontological continuity. We hold, that is, to a continuity of being. That standpoint necessarily follows, not only from our createdness and our identity as God has established it, but it follows also from, and it reenforces, the ethical responsibilities which, as creatures of our Creator-God, we possess. In short, continuity of being, ontological continuity, is the grounding of ethical responsibility, the explanation of the awareness that we shall in due time confront our Creator-judge in a day of accounting.

The knowledge of God and of things

The foregoing discussion has raised at several points the Christian reaction to the streams that have emerged in the development of Western thought. A number of concluding observations can be made and their implications noted.

Our primary concern is with the knowledge of God. That takes up in various ways the question of knowledge more broadly considered, the discovery and the formation and certitude of knowledge. We have been concerned with the twofold questions of reality on the one hand and knowledge on the other. We have seen that in the history of thought a difference of view has turned on the question of whether the "real" exists in an unknowable world, the realm of ideas or forms for Plato and the noumenal realm for Kant, or whether reality inheres in the world of our sensory perceptions, the actual world of men and things. The question has arisen as to whether we can have knowledge of things and relations beyond the empirically sensible world. As to the methods of knowing and the possibility of certitude in knowing, differences of view have been observed between rationalism on the one hand and empiricism on the other.

These issues and questions are brought into relationship by the recognition of what the Scriptures have revealed as the nature of reality. We have already inspected the point, in taking note, for example, of Van Til's two-layer theory of reality or being. God is, we have said, and he exists in his eternal aseity, or in his self-existence that is not dependent on or caused by anything external to himself. God's knowledge is similarly self-referential and again it cannot depend on any thing or event external to himself. All of the events and occurrences and phenomena of the history of the universe that God called into existence are what they are because God thought them before the foundation of the world.

The Christian knows that God is, because God has revealed himself in the consciousness of every creature that he made in his own image. Notwithstanding the Fall and its implications for all those for whom Adam was the federal representative, God has not left himself without witness to the hearts of men. Every man knows that God is. The sense and awareness of God, the *sensus deitatis*, leaves all men without excuse, as the apostle elaborated at length in the first chapter of his epistle to the Romans. It is God in whom "we live, and move, and have our being" (Acts 17:28).

The Christian knows what he knows because God is the presupposition of all his knowing. The existence and being of God are not discoverable for the Christian as the outcome of an investigative process. In that sense the Christian's stance is not determined by the difference of view between rationalism and empiricism of non-Christian thought. Rather, God is the Christian's presupposition, because God has revealed himself. He has revealed himself in his inscripturated Word and in the created universe and in history. He has revealed himself in his Son who came to be the redeemer of his people. And in giving his Scriptural revelation he has provided the reliable source of authentication of knowledge and belief.

As to the meaning of reality, then, and the possibility of knowledge of it, the Christian knows, first, that the real is what God has called into created existence and committed to Adam as his inheritance at the beginning. Second, the Christian knows and has access to knowledge, because God has established a correspondence or an accordance between the objects of knowledge as thus conceived, on the one hand, and the subject of knowledge, or the knowing person and his knowledge capacities, on the other. That follows from the initially established creation mandate that required man to interpret and understand the substance and potential of created reality in order that, as we observed earlier, he might dedicate it back to God and might rule over it to the glory of God. Because God has established the structure of reality and thereby ordained that the creatures he made in his own image might come into an understanding as well as an experience of it, the Christian possesses an answer to the questions both of the nature of reality and the possibility of knowledge of it.

We have said that God is the Christian's presupposition. The Christian theory of knowledge may be said to be a presuppositional theory. But it is not the case that one set of presuppositions might well be as good as any other set of presuppositions. To the contrary, the Christian's presuppositions are those that God has revealed in his Word as determining every thought and knowledge claim and conclusion. The Christian, as the apostle stated it to the Corinthian church, brings "into captivity every thought to the obedience of Christ" (2 Cor. 10:5). It is for that reason that we observed at an earlier point that every fact that comes potentially within the scope of human knowledge must be Christologically interpreted. All of the facts are God's facts, and the Christian knows them truly only as he knows God truly.

It is true, of course, that remnants of rationalism remain within the apologetic literature of the church.[15] But the

---

[15] See, as a recent example, R.C. Sproul, John Gerstner, and Arthur Lindsley, *Classical Apologetics: A Rational Defense of the Christian Faith and a Critique of Presuppositional Apologetics*, Grand Rapids: Zondervan, 1984. See the discussion in chapter 8, above, n.10. When we say, as above, that God is the Christian's presupposition, we have drawn attention to the starting-point of a genuinely Reformed theological apologetic. God is not discoverable at the end of a chain of logical reasoning and investigation. *God is*, is our initial postulate. The awareness of God is indelibly embedded in the human consciousness. The fact that absolute being, absolute personhood, and absolute meaning and knowledge exist in God establishes meaning and the discoverability of meaning in the external reality that God has spoken into existence. We hold to the impossibility of the contrary, meaning that any contrary assumption implies that the universe is a universe of randomness and chance, without a principle of coherence, without meaning, and without the possibility of explanation. We do not lay open our apologetic method, that is,

Christian's acknowledgment is that of Jeremiah of old, "O Lord, I know that the way of man is not in himself: it is not in man that walketh to direct his steps" (Jer. 10:22). He knows that the source of knowledge is to "follow on to know the Lord" (Hosea 6:3). The Christian has reflected carefully on the Pauline injunction, "Let no man deceive himself. If any man among you seemeth to be wise in this world, let him become a fool, that he may be wise. For the wisdom of this world is foolishness with God. For it is written, He taketh the wise in their own craftiness". And again, "The Lord knoweth the thoughts of the wise, that they are vain. Therefore let no man glory in men" (1 Cor. 3:18-21).

The Christian knows, in the last analysis, because the promise that God has given through the prophet Jeremiah has been, and is progressively being, fulfilled: "I will give them a heart to know me ... and they shall be my people, and I will be their God" (Jer. 24:7). The Christian's knowledge and interpretation of all of the reality in the phenomenal realm depends on his perception of what God has already established and interpreted as the fact situations. But the question persists as to what the Christian may know of reality beyond that realm. The answer follows from all that has been said to this point. The Christian knows, by the testimony of the Spirit of Truth whom Christ and the Father send to him, that he has been adopted into the family and the kingdom of God in Christ (Gal. 4:5, Rom. 8:15). He knows, on the basis of the assurance of his High Priest, the Son of God who has ascended again to the right hand of the Father, that knowing God, he has eternal life.

---

to the danger of capitulation to the supposed efficiency of autonomous human reason (rationalism) such as is implicit in the statement that "the right approach to the subject of the existence of God is to assemble and assess all of the data we can and then come to a conclusion based on what we consider satisfying evidence or reasonable probabilities", John Blanchard, *Does God believe in atheists*? Darlington, UK: Evangelical Press, 2000, 194. We do not bring the question of the knowledge of God under the dominion of the proposition that "The attempt to establish primary truths on which we can build absolute knowledge has proved to be futile ... All our knowledge about anything that really matters is a matter of probability" (idem, loc. cit). See also, however, the contrary statement as to the certain (not probabilistic), inevitable, and inescapable knowledge of God in Blanchard, idem, 481-82.

10

Knowing God

At the heart of the evangel lies the declaration that to know God is to know life eternal. There is a transition from wrath to grace for those who are the beneficiaries of the redemption purchased by Christ. That transition moves the sinner whom the love of God has sought from the state of sin, condemnation, and death to that of righteousness, justification, and life. The Pauline claim evokes the confirming conviction of the Christian heart, "God ... hath delivered us from the power of darkness, and hath translated us into the kingdom of his dear Son" (Col. 1:13). "There is therefore now no condemnation", the same apostle concludes, "to them which are in Christ Jesus" (Rom. 8:1).

The realities involved in that summary statement have been explored in the preceding chapters. God, existing in eternal separateness and holiness, transcendent above all reality external to himself, has entered into time for man's redemption, as man in the Person of his Son. By his works of providence and redemption he is immanent in all of the histories and events of the world of men and things that he has made. The love of God, the expression of his holiness coordinate with his wrath against sin, has provided a rescue and relief for the sinner he calls to himself. God has set his love on those who were the objects of his wrath.

The problem of knowledge is solved by the light that the evangel throws upon it. The real, or what exists to be known, is what it is because God thought it in his one eternal act of knowing before the foundation of the world. In creating man in his image and in placing him in his reality environment as the analogue of his own being, God has established an accordance between what there is to be known and the human capacity for knowledge by which it is perceived and understood. The knowledge of God himself exists in the human soul because God, notwithstanding the entrance of sin and the darkness and ignorance to which it led, has kept open the channels of communication to man. The *sensus deitatis*, the sense of God, is ineradicable in the human heart.

In the preceding chapters we have traversed much of the areas that were contemplated in the first two of the "Triads" under which, in chapter 1, we summarized the ground to be covered. "Triad 1", that referred to Creation, Sin and the Fall, and Redemption, has to this point been spanned by our discussion of the call of the evangel and the holiness of God at one end, and the satisfaction of Christ at the other. But there is much more to be said in those respects. The subject areas contemplated under "Triad 2" were anticipated in our discussion of Christian doctrine and have been explored in the preceding chapters on "The Disarray of Faith" and "Knowledge and Truth". In this and the following chapter we shall complete our study of the relevance for the Christian life of all that has been said to this point.

The discussion of Christian doctrine, and of the respects in which we can know that our understanding of Christian doctrine is true, remains barren and meaningless unless we grasp its significance for life and Christian behavior. When the early Christians met, following the coming of the Holy Spirit on the day of Pentecost, it was said of them that "they continued stedfastly in the apostles' doctrine and fellowship, and in breaking of bread, and in prayers" (Acts 2:42). The priority at that time of the apostolic doctrine, the working out of the substance and meaning of what it was they were to believe, has been spread across the pages of the New Testament. We need only recall the injunction of Peter at which we looked in an earlier context, "Be ready always to give an answer to every man that asketh you a reason of the hope that is in you" (1 Peter

3:15). In any real apprehension of Christian truth, there can be no cleavage or disjunction between doctrine and life. Our concern at this point is with the fact that nothing is more practical in the progress of the Christian life than properly conceived and properly applied Christian doctrine.

We have spoken, under the heading of "Triad 3" of the beginning of the Christian life in God's effectual calling and the regenerating work of his Holy Spirit in the soul. And then, on the basis of that, we envisaged the application to those for whom Christ died of the benefits and graces of the redemption that he accomplished. Those benefits include the gifts of repentance and faith, the realities of justification, adoption, and sanctification, and the Christian's eschatological hope.

We begin our final discussion of these important questions by considering in this chapter two preliminary areas: first, the meaning in actual fact of the Christian's knowledge of God; and second, the respect in which the salvific implications of that knowledge are dependent on the effectual call of God and the regenerating work of the Spirit of God in the soul. We shall take note also of certain misconceptions and misstatements of doctrine that have gained currency in connection with the latter question. We shall ask, in particular, what it means to say that as a result of regeneration the individual is a "new person", or that he or she is characterized by a "new nature". What, it will then have to be asked, is the meaning of sin in the life of the Christian?

The knowledge of God

In the first chapter of his letter to the Romans, Paul argues convincingly that every individual knows that God is. By virtue of the *sensus deitatis* inherent in the human consciousness, in the very act of self-awareness man is aware of God. Calvin begins his *Institutes* with the statement that "no one can look upon himself without immediately turning his thoughts to the contemplation of God".[1] There are, to repeat the manner in

---

[1] John Calvin, *Institutes of the Christian Religion*, Trans. F.L. Battles, Ed., John T. McNeill, Philadelphia: Press [1559] 1960, Book 1, Ch. 1, 35.

which we previously addressed the point, no psychological atheists. By virtue of that fact, every individual knows that he is the creature of a Creator-God higher than himself; that he is therefore under obligation to God; that he has failed to honor that obligation in obedience to the law of God; and that he is, as a result, liable to the penalty for his dereliction from that law. Paul has put the case in his letter to the Romans by saying that all individuals, because of the darkness of sin to which they have been reduced, are God-haters (Rom. 1:30), and that the natural proclivities of the soul are such that they suppress every wakening awareness of God (Rom. 1:18).

But when we say that every person knows that God is, by virtue of the inherent communication of God to him, we do not say that God does, or is under any obligation to, maintain a continuous conviction of those realities within the human soul. Many people do, with greater or lesser degrees of success and apparent comfort, live as though there were no God. They are living as practical atheists. In the state of sin to which we were reduced by Adam's Fall, the natural impulse is to live the lie that hides behind the pretense that God does not exist. Because the individual in the state of sin wants nothing to do with God or with the things of God, he naturally suppresses the conviction of God.

But we are concerned at this point not with the fact that every individual knows *that* God is, but with the Christian realization of *who* God is. That realization comes by virtue of God's sovereign initiative of grace in his renewing, re-creating approach to the soul. Then the person knows something of the glory and the holiness of God, the grace and the mercy of God as he has set forth his purpose of redemption, and the benefits of reconciliation and peace with God.

We reflect on the prayer of our Lord on the night on which he was betrayed. On that occasion, the supper ended, the discourse that climaxed his ministry to his disciples now brought to its close, our Lord prayed for those for whom he was about to die. At that poignant moment he prayed "not for the world, but for them which thou hast given me" (John 17:9). The Son of God and the Son of man who would be made sin for us had now, he prayed to the Father, "finished the work which thou gavest me to do... I have manifested thy name unto the men which thou gavest me out of the world: thine they were, and thou gavest them me" (John 17:4,6). The cross lay ahead. Judas had gone, and his perfidious pecuniary plot would soon work out its design. But our Savior paused, that in that climactic hour he might bring to the Father those whom he loved, whom he loved to the end. The piercing simplicity of his words, and the profundity of the divine intention they encapsule, burn their import on the consciousness of those he came to redeem. They were his sheep whom he knew "by name" and for whom he would soon lay down his life (John 10:3,15). "This is life eternal", he prays, "that they might know thee, the only true God..." (John 17:3).

To know God is the Christian's highest good. The immediacy of that follows from the fact that the Christian does not belong to this world. Christ "gave himself for our sins, that he might deliver us from this present evil world" (Gal. 1:4). Now, for the one who is joined to Christ, old things have passed away and all things have become new (2 Cor. 5:17). Then in the light of that, and because his identity and his existence are now what they are, the Christian is an eschatological person. He looks to the end and objective that his union with Christ implies. A *telos*, a prospect, engages the Christian's redeemed imagination. He looks, with a perception and an acuity that the world cannot begin to understand, to what God has promised as the summing up of "all things in Christ" (Eph. 1:10). The Christian lives in the determining context of a hope that is fixed on Christ.

The knowledge of God is the uniquely defining characteristic of the Christian's life. That knowledge of God, moreover, is ethical. That means that to know God is to love God. It is to live in such a manner as to keep his commandments and to conform the conduct and pattern of life to the requirements of his holy law. The behavioral implications of that determine the course of the Christian life.

But the importance of knowing God rests in the reality that we have, thereby, as we have heard the Savior declare, the entrance to life eternal. Conferred in the implications of that knowledge is the restoration of the Creator-creature relation from which, in Adam, we fell. It was possible, the Scriptures

THE FRACTURE OF FAITH

make clear, for Adam not to fall. The tree of life had been placed in the center of the garden in order that, subject only to the satisfactory termination of his probation, Adam might have eaten of it and been confirmed in righteous moral state. Now the tree of life, from which our first parents were excluded by the angel's sword (Gen. 3:24), is again prepared for the people who know God. In the new Jerusalem there is again the tree of life and "Blessed are they that do his commandments, that they may have right to the tree of life, and may enter in through the gates into the city" (Rev. 22:2,14). It was possible for our first parents not to fall. But the sequel of their probation is all too clear. Now it is not possible for the one who is joined to Christ to fall. Now the *posse non peccare* (the "possible not to fall") of Adam is replaced by the eternal security, the *non posse peccare* (the "not possible to fall"), of those who know God, who are joined to him in Christ.

A heart to know God

We recall a highly significant vision and prophecy of Jeremiah. Approximately six hundred years before the birth of Christ, at roughly the same time as the earliest of the classical Greek philosophers flourished, Jeremiah prophesied the imminent captivity of Judah. In the twentyfourth chapter of his prophecy it is recorded that "Nebuchadnezzar king of Babylon had carried away captive Jeconiah the son of Jehoiakim king of Judah, and the princes of Judah, with the carpenters and smiths, from Jerusalem, and had brought them to Babylon ..." (Jer. 24:1). The history of the surrounding events, along with that of the earlier captivity of the northern kingdom of Israel by the Assyrians and the adventures of the Assyrian kings in their relations with Israel, Tiglath-Pileser, Shalmaneser, and Sennacherib, is related in the Second Book of Kings, from the fifteenth chapter onwards. Of immediate interest is the prophecy of Jeremiah and, in particular, his vision at the time of the southern kingdom's captivity.

In that vision Jeremiah saw two baskets of figs. "One basket had very good figs, even like the figs that are first ripe: and the other basket had very bad figs, which could not be eaten, they were so bad" (Jer. 24:2). God explained to Jeremiah that the bad figs were understood to presage God's abandonment of Zedekiah, king of Judah, and his officials, and the judgment of God upon them for their sin and corruption. Our interest at present, however, is in the interpretation that God gave of the basket of good figs. We have in it a remarkable statement of God's purpose with relation to those whom, in his eternal decree, he chose to redeem to himself, the remnant that would make up his true and eternal kingdom.

"Thus says the Lord, the God of Israel" Jeremiah reports, "like these good figs, so I will acknowledge them that are carried away captive of Judah, whom I have sent out of this place into the land of the Chaldeans for their good. For I will set mine eyes upon them for good, and I will bring them again to this land; and I will build them, and not pull them down; and I will plant them, and not pluck them up. And I will give them an heart to know me, that I am the Lord; and they shall be my people, and I will be their God, for they shall return unto me with their whole heart" (Jer. 24:5-7).

The sovereignty and the love of God are here set against his justice and righteousness. It is God who casts down and who binds up, who deals with his people in discipline and chastisement, and who returns to them in love and compassion. It was he who "sent out of this place into the land of the Chaldeans" the very people upon whom, from among the nations of the world, he had set his love. But now, he states, he will redeem his people, he will bring them again to the land that he had prepared for them, and, to sum up the statement of his purpose, "I will be" he says, "their God".

But our attention is arrested by the explanation of his relation to his chosen people that God gave to Jeremiah. *"I will give them"*, he says, *"a heart to know me"*. We look now, not only to the sovereignty of God in his action and purpose, but to the blessing that he thereby confers upon those whom he has redeemed. They enter into the benediction and the blessing that God has reserved for them because, in his sovereign love, he gives his people a heart to know him.

But how does that all come about? What is the foundation and source and origin of the Christian's knowing God? What are the fuller and expansive implications of that high prerogative? And what, more precisely, are the responsibilities and obligations imposed upon one who thus knows God?

Effectual calling and regeneration

We had occasion, in our discussion in chapter 2 of "The Call of the Evangel", to look in preliminary fashion at the call of God by which, by the operation of his Holy Spirit, he brings the sinner to newness of life in Christ. We saw then that a close relation exists between what has been referred to historically as effectual calling and regeneration. We recall the statement of the Catechism: "Effectual calling is the work of God's Spirit, whereby, convincing us of our sin and misery, enlightening our minds in the knowledge of Christ, and renewing our wills, he doth persuade and enable us to embrace Jesus Christ, freely offered to us in the gospel".[2] As a result of the operation of the Spirit of God that is involved in that calling, an individual is brought by a divine intervention to a knowledge of God that once was foreign and unimaginable.

We remarked in an earlier context that differences of view have existed among evangelical and Reformed theologians as to whether a logical priority should be understood to exist between effectual calling and regeneration. We observed then that any discussion of such a priority is substantially beside the point. For in understanding and referring to what is involved in the sovereign work of God in this connection, regeneration is to be viewed as a constituent element in the total work of effectual calling whereby the sinner is brought to a state of repentance and saving faith.

If the calling of God is effectual, that calling is not complete until, by the intervening grace of God, the individual is brought to a point of repentance and saving faith in commitment to Christ. There is, then, a beginning and an end to the entire or overall process that we are now describing as effectual calling. The end result or the outcome of that process is the exercise of repentance and faith on the part of the awakened individual. The

---

[2] *Westminster Shorter Catechism*, Question 31.

beginning of the process is the sovereign, gracious, and unsolicited work of renewing and re-creation in the soul by the Holy Spirit. To the latter work we give the designation of regeneration.

In that remarkable work, the Holy Spirit speaks his word of calling to the recesses of the soul. To appreciate the objectives and the intention of it a little more fully, let us contemplate the state of the faculties of the soul to which the new-creating work of the Spirit is addressed. In his initially created condition, Adam was established in a state of "knowledge, righteousness, and holiness".[3] Our first parents' original righteousness was not a characteristic or a feature of their original condition that was in some sense added on after their creation. Such a mistaken understanding has been held in the history of theology, and the "added on" gift of righteousness that was thus attributed to Adam was referred to as a *donum superadditum*. But the Scriptural data dissent from that proposition. Adam enjoyed an original righteousness that was intrinsic or inherent to his constitution as a rational creature made in God's own image.

In our discussion in an earlier chapter of the meaning of sin, and in particular of what we referred to as the self-direction of sin in the life of the unregenerate person, we had occasion to refer at some length to the condition of the faculties of the soul as they existed in man's initial and prelapsarian state. We have seen also that in his established state as God's vicegerent, Adam stood under covenantal obligations to discharge the offices of prophet, priest, and king. As he remained in that relation to his Creator, a harmony existed among the faculties of the soul, and the mind, or the intellectual faculty, functioned as the prince of the faculties. But we saw that the harmony of the faculties was shattered by the Fall and that, in the condition that ensued, the heart, or the emotional faculty, usurped the hegemony of the mind.

Our immediate concern is not to repeat the arguments we have already adduced in those earlier contexts. Our interest at this stage is in the regenerating work of the Holy Spirit by which the soul is renewed and is, in fact, raised to a higher

---

[3] See *Westminster Shorter Catechism*, Question 10, and Col. 3:10, Eph. 4:24.

condition than Adam had originally enjoyed. "Where sin abounded", the apostle explained in his letter to the Romans, "grace did much more abound" (Rom. 5:20). Now the soul that is born again by the sovereign work of the Spirit of God is, by virtue of that reality, joined to Christ in what we have seen as an indissoluble union. Now Adam's *posse non peccare* (possible not to fall) has been replaced by the Christian's *non posse peccare* (not possible to fall). It is not possible for the Christian to fall, that is, from his or her union with Christ, and therefore from eternal security.

But what, then, is to be characterized as the work of regeneration that turns the soul to seek Christ? We adduce from the statements of the Catechism as already noted[4] that the work of the Holy Spirit can be inspected under a fivefold heading. It is a work of convincing, enlightening, renewing, persuading, and enabling. That work implies effects produced on and within the faculties of the soul. The regenerating work of the Spirit in the soul can be seen directly against the condition to which the faculties had been reduced. Regeneration is a sovereign work of the Holy Spirit that turns the individual to seek Christ in a whole-souled repentance and faith. In regeneration, and in the effects that it produces that lead to eternal life, the whole person is engaged.

In the first place, regeneration does not involve the creation of any new faculties that the individual did not previously possess. Rather, it involves the endowment of the faculties with new abilities and capacities, and it implants within the soul a new righteous disposition and principle of action. Because, by the work of regeneration, one is brought by a divine intervention to a knowledge of God that once was foreign and unimaginable, his mind and heart and will are engaged in the movement of all of the faculties of his soul to love and to respond to God. With a new awareness, that before could not have been contemplated or understood, the mind that was once blinded by the god of this world is enlightened. "For God, who commanded the light to shine out of darkness, hath shined in our hearts, to give the light of the knowledge of the glory of

---

[4] *Westminster Shorter Catechism*, Question 31.

God in the face of Jesus Christ" (2 Cor. 4:6). The heart that was once consumed by a hatred of God now turns with a new desire for God and a seeking after him. The will is renewed and the soul that hated God and that fled from every suggestion and thought and imagination of God and his law is now his willing servant. "Thy people shall be willing in the day of thy power", the Psalmist has observed (Ps. 110:3), or as another translation has it, "Thy people will volunteer freely in the day of Thy power".

The heart, the mind, and the will are freely engaged in the sinner's turning to Christ. The apostle has summarized the meaning of that in his statement to the Roman Christians. "Ye were the servants of sin" he says "but ye have obeyed from the heart that form of doctrine which was delivered you. Being made free from sin, ye became the servants of righteousness" (Rom. 6:17-18). The mind is engaged in its grasp of what Paul here refers to as the "form of doctrine" to which the people to whom he wrote were exposed and which they had embraced. The heart was engaged in that their obedience was "from the heart". The heart that once loved and moved with a naturalness to the things that were evil now reached with a new urgency for God and his righteousness. And the will was now engaged in the very action of obedience that culminated in their response and their engagement with Christ and their commitment to him.[5]

---

[5] The understanding of regeneration in relation to its significance for its effects on the faculties of the soul, or what we might refer to as a faculty psychology, has a long history in classic Reformed theology. A.A. Hodge addresses the matter by observing "that there are in the soul, besides its several faculties, habits, or dispositions, of which some are innate and others are acquired, which lay the foundation for the soul's exercising its faculties in some particular way... [and] in the new creation God recreates the governing disposition of the regenerated man's heart holy". Hodge cites the discussion of Jonathan Edwards, who refers to "a principle of nature [as] the foundation which is laid in nature, either old or new, for any particular kind or manner of exercise of the faculties of the soul. So this new 'spiritual sense' is not a new faculty of understanding, but it is a new foundation laid in the nature of the soul for a new kind of exercise of the same faculty of understanding. So that new holy disposition of heart that attends this new sense is not a new faculty of will, but a foundation laid in the nature of the soul for a new kind of exercise of the same faculty of will", A.A. Hodge, *Outlines of Theology*, Edinburgh: Banner of Truth [1860] 1972, 458. Regeneration is discussed in

Because God has said that "I will give them a heart to know me", the response of the whole person to God's gracious work in the soul is assured. The benefits of Christ's redemption, mediated to the sinner by the ministry of the Holy Spirit, encompass the evangelical gifts of faith, repentance, obedience, joy, and love for God. The sovereign work of God in the soul takes up the process of the Christian's sanctification, his conformity to the pattern of God's holiness, and, as the *Westminster Catechism* puts it, his progressive dying to sin and living unto righteousness.[6]

A heart that knows God is a heart that is alertly awake to the Savior's plea, "I stand at the door, and knock; if any man hear my voice, and open the door, I will come in to him, and will sup with him, and he with me" (Rev. 3:20). The heart that knows God is the heart of one to whom the Redeemer Christ, his company and his companionship, are dearer than life.

The Christian's joy exists in his knowing God, in his place in the church that God has called out of the world for himself. It is the church that the Savior loved and for which he gave himself (Eph. 5:25). The Christian now participates in the benefits and the blessings that the redemption that Christ accomplished has guaranteed to him. That redemption has been accomplished in fulfillment of God's eternal purpose, and in itself it fulfills every dimension of the covenantal promises that God has made. It confirms to the Christian the assurance of eternal life.

Regeneration and the nature of the Christian person

We have said that the work of regeneration that the Holy Spirit effects in the soul involves the endowment of the faculties with new abilities and capacities and the creation in the soul of a new disposition and principle of action. Such a radical change takes place in the person that the only way to describe the one to whom it has happened is to say that he is a "new creation" (2 Cor. 5:17). The change that the Holy Spirit effects in the soul is so radical, so completely transforming, that when the New

similar terms in L. Berkhof, *Systematic Theology*, Grand Rapids: Eerdmans, 1941, 468.

[6] *Westminster Shorter Catechism*, Question 35.

Testament writers search for words to describe it they can only fall back on what our Lord himself said. The only way to describe what has happened is to say that the individual has been "born again". He is now something completely and radically different from what he was before. John's gospel refers to such people as being "born of the will of God" (John 1:13). Peter puts it by saying that they are "born again by the word of God" (1 Peter 1:23), and John refers to the one who loves as being "born of God" (1 John 4:7).

But now, in the light of that, we must ask a question that has troubled the church's understanding of what is involved, and that has given rise to a variety of doctrinal formulations. Should we say that the "born again" person still possesses his old nature, but that he now has also a new nature? Does he possess both an "old" and sinful nature and a "new" or regenerate nature? That, we shall see in what follows, is the very thing we can not say. As a result of regeneration, the individual is a new person who can now be described only by saying that he is characterized by a new nature. His capacities of soul are now what they were not before. They have been renewed. They are not different faculties, but they have been so transformed in their abilities that their nature is completely different.

The focus of our thought in relation to regeneration falls, in that way, on the new nature that describes the person who is thereby the beneficiary of the Spirit's sovereign, re-creating work. But care should be exercised in speaking of the regenerate person and the regenerate nature that describes the person. To clarify what is involved, let us consider what must be understood in all such doctrinal formulation as individual person-hood, and in particular what is to be said of the individual person as he exists in the image of God.

We are interested in the fact that man as created is both body and soul. We want to bring to emphasis now the fact that we do not say that man *has* a body and that he *has* a soul. Consider what would be involved if we said that. We would then be speaking of three entities. We would have, first, the man who possesses the body and the soul. Then secondly, we would have the body that he possesses. And then we would have the soul that he is said to have. There would be those three entities, the man, the body, and the soul.

But we don't say that. We say, rather, not that man *has* a body and a soul, but that man *is* body and soul. We shall see in a moment why we make that point. As we do so, we shall have occasion to refer to the manner in which the nineteenth-century theologian, Robert Dabney, has looked at these same questions. As Dabney observes, the individual "has one consciousness, he knows that he is one indivisible personality".[7] The focus of our thought must fall at this point on the one indivisible personality that the individual is. John Murray has held the same view when he says that "The body is an integral part of personality ...".[8] In the same way, we hold in mind in our discussion of regeneration the same oneness of the integral personality of the individual.

We shall speak, in various ways and on various levels in what follows, of the nature of the individual. So far, we have focused our thought not on what man *has*, but on what man *is*. We have said, not that man *has* a body and a soul, but that he *is* body and soul. Now in a similar way we shall say not that man *has* a certain nature, but that what he *is* is characterized by a certain nature. In other words, the so-called "nature" is simply what describes the man. The man is what his nature is.

We can look ahead at this point to anticipate what we shall say by way of further implication about the individual when he has been made regenerate. We shall say, consistent with our analogy, not that he has a new nature, but that he himself is "new" by virtue of the characteristics of nature that now describe him. But because of the integral nature of the individual in his personhood, and because the characteristics of nature that now describe him are what they are because the Holy Spirit has endowed him with them, it is not a matter of his possessing both an "old" nature and a "new" nature. The new person in Christ is what he is simply because the characteristics of nature that now describe him are what they are. Again the man is what his nature is. The "nature" is what describes the man.

This is a point of doctrine that has been sadly and badly

---

[7] Robert L. Dabney, *Discussions: Evangelical and Theological*, London: Banner of Truth [1890] 1967, Vol. 1, 196.

[8] John Murray, *The Epistle to the Romans*, Grand Rapids: Eerdmans, 1959, Vol. 1, 221.

misunderstood in the evangelical church. The erroneous doctrine that there is in the regenerate Christian both an old nature and a new nature is traceable to a teaching that was prominent in Plymouth Brethren circles in the mid-nineteenth century, and which was given further prominence in the Scofield Bible. It has found its way, unfortunately, into the New International Version translation of the Scriptures, where that version repeatedly translates the word "flesh" as "sinful nature". It thereby preserves the false doctrine of two natures in the regenerate man.[9] Implicit in the doctrine is a serious danger on a very practical level. For many who hold the "two natures" doctrine do, nevertheless, acknowledge the reality of sin in the Christian person. But then sin is easily explained by saying that it is the old nature that sins and not the new nature.

In response to such a claim, two things can be said. First, sin in the regenerate person is very real. There can be no confusion about that. We who are regenerate are, in spite of our regenerate status, guilty of sin every day. But second, when we sin, it is not a matter of one of our natures sinning. It is we who sin. And we in our persons are guilty of sin. We must not confuse in our doctrine two things that are quite distinct. The fact that the regenerate person is a "new" individual who is described by the characteristics of a "new" nature, must be kept quite distinct from the fact that that new person is still capable of sin.

Before we proceed any further, let us ask again what it is that regeneration involves. We say, to use the words of Dabney, that "it reverses the moral *habitus* [i.e. disposition] prevalently, [that is, that a new disposition is prevalent, or prevails, in the soul] but not at first absolutely, and that the work of progressive sanctification carries on this change... In the *carnal state*, the habitus [or disposition] of the sinner's will is absolutely and exclusively godless. In the *regenerate state* it is prevalently but not completely godly. In the *glorified state* it is absolutely godly".[10] But the important fact is that the Christian is "one indivisible personality", and it is that one person who, by virtue of his regeneration, is now disposed, but not yet absolutely, to

---

[9] See the discussion in Robert P. Martin, *Accuracy of Translation and the New International Version*, Edinburgh: Banner of Truth, 1989, 32ff.

[10] R.L. Dabney, *Discussions*, Vol. 1, 196ff.

reflect in his life and actions the perfect holiness of God. And, as Dabney correctly has it, "the Bible is still further from saying that the renewed man has two *'natures'*".[11] The two-natures theory, Dabney says, "flies flatly in the face of the Scriptures".[12]

Referring to those who hold the "two natures" theory, Dabney says, "We challenge them to produce a text from the New Testament where it is said that regeneration is the implantation of a 'new nature' beside the old; or that the renewed man has two hostile 'natures', or any such language. ... Paul ... teaches that the renewed man (one man and one nature still) is imperfect, having two principles of volition mixed in the motives even of the same act; but he does not teach that he has become 'two men', or has 'two natures' in him. Paul's idea is, that man's one nature, originally wholly sinful, is by regeneration made imperfectly holy, but progressively so...".[13] "[The doctrine of the two natures in man] contradicts the consciousness of every Christian, even the most unlearned; for just as surely as he has one consciousness, he knows that he is one indivisible personality, and that he is one agent and has *only one will*, swayed indeed by mixed and diverse motives".[14]

John Murray, again recognizing the integral personality of the individual, puts the same point by saying that "the old man is the unregenerate man; the new man is the regenerate man created in Christ Jesus unto good works. It is no more feasible to call the believer a new man and an old man, than it is to call him a regenerate man and an unregenerate. And neither is it warranted to speak of the believer as having in him the old man and the new man".[15]

Sin in the life of the Christian

Regeneration, and the fact that the Spirit of God brings the individual person to a new condition of union with Christ, can

---

[11] Ibid., 194.
[12] Idem.
[13] op. cit., 192-93.
[14] Ibid., 196.
[15] John Murray, *Principles of Conduct: Aspects of Biblical Ethics*, Grand Rapids: Eerdmans, 1957, 218.

in no sense be taken to mean that henceforth, and by that reason, the person is free from sin. For sin is most decidedly the action of the person, and it cannot be dismissed as the sin of an "old" nature as distinct from the "new". At this point, therefore, we confront the reality of sin.

When we say that the regenerate person is a new person, characterized by a wholly different nature from what previously described him, we nevertheless acknowledge that that person sins. How, then, are we to explain that? Because it is the person who sins, it is the person who is responsible for the sin. So our doctrine does not in any way minimize the reality or the seriousness of sin. Rather, it emphasizes it.

The real situation has been explained by John Murray when he says that "the believer is a new man, a new creature, but he is a new man not yet made perfect. Sin dwells in him still, and he still commits sin. He is necessarily the subject of progressive renewal ... but this progressive renewal ... is not to be conceived of as the progressive crucifixion of the old man".[16] We are to say, then, that the Christian is a new person, characterized and described by a new nature, but that his faculties of soul, while they have been renewed with new endowments in the manner we have seen, have not yet been made perfect. They are still capable of being deceived by sin, by the allurements of the world, and by the subtleties of the Devil and his angels. That ability to be led into sin by old habits and old imaginations remains by virtue of the still-existing principle of "indwelling sin". It is what Paul wrote about so eloquently in the seventh chapter of his letter to the Romans. Sin dwells with the Christian, because, while his faculties have been renewed in principle, their transformation to the image of the holiness of God has not yet been perfected.

We can put that differently in the language of the seventeenth century Puritan theologian, John Owen. In his treatise, *A Discourse Concerning the Holy Spirit*, Owen addresses the reality of sin in the life of the truly regenerate person. "In those who are constantly inclined and disposed unto all the acts of a heavenly, spiritual life, there are yet remaining contrary

---

[16] Ibid., 219.

dispositions and inclinations also".[17] Here we see the same understanding of sin as is reflected in the argument of Dabney that we have just considered. Owen goes on to say that "There are yet in them [regenerate Christian individuals] inclinations and dispositions to sin, proceeding from the *remainders* of a contrary habitual principle".[18] What Owen refers to as the "contrary habitual principle" is again a reference to what is described in the Scriptures as indwelling sin. It is against that sinful principle, and with the objective of the destruction of it, that the Christian is directed to the duty of the mortification of sin (Rom. 8:13). For there can be no progress in sanctification, as we shall observe again in the following chapter, unless there is progress in the mortification of sin.

At this point, as Christians whose thought is captive to the Word of God, we must be prepared to acknowledge that we confront a mystery. That, of course, has to be said of all of the doctrines of the Christian faith. All of our doctrines terminate in mystery. And our task as Christian thinkers is to endeavor to see, and to understand by the light of the Word of God, where it is that the mystery exists. We must not at any point allow the mystery associated with the fact and the doctrine to rob us of the truth and reality of the fact and the doctrine. The mystery we confront at present is that the new man in Christ, the person who is now described by a new nature, is capable of sin and that he does, in fact, sin. Why, we have to ask again, is that so?

The reality is that God in his eternal wisdom, while he has implanted within us the new abilities of soul, and while he has so renewed the faculties of our souls with new abilities and capacities that can only be described by saying that our nature is "new", has not yet transformed us to the state of perfection of holiness that we shall one day attain. We are still in the body. The body, we have seen, is an integral part of our personality. We say the same in connection with it as we say of the faculties of the soul; namely, that it is no longer conditioned and

---

[17] John Owen, *Discourse Concerning the Holy Spirit*, in *The Works of John Owen*, ed. William H. Goold, 1850-1853, Republished by Banner of Truth, 1965, Vol. 3, 488. See also the valuable discussion in Sinclair B. Ferguson, *John Owen on the Christian Life*, Edinburgh: Banner of Truth, 1987, 64.

[18] Idem. Italics in original.

controlled by sin. But the body is capable of actions that are sinful, and our faculties can still be confused and led astray by Satan and sin.

We are new people, and one day we shall be perfect. But that day is not yet. God in his wisdom has left us in this world to live through the experience of seeing our own selves progressively transformed to become at last fully consistent with the new persons in Christ that he has already made us to be. We can fall into sin, and we are responsible for sin. But sin can no longer reign over us. And as John has said in his first epistle, when we realize who we are, then by reason of that reality we cannot consent to continue in sin (1 John 3:6,9).

We turn in the following chapter to the vital question of the meaning for the conduct of the Christian life of the issues and questions we have now raised. What are the implications for life of the reality that one can, and that the one who is regenerate by the sovereign and gracious ministry of the Holy Spirit does, know God? What is the meaning of the progressive sanctification of the life that is lived in union with Christ? And what, finally, is the nature of the hope that the Christian holds? When he who is our Savior appears "we shall be like him; for we shall see him as he is" (1 John 3:2) and we shall live and reign with him, "our great high priest" (Heb. 4:14) forever.

11

The Life and Walk of Faith

The Christian's salvation, in all of its parts and dimensions and processes, is what it is because of the sovereign, unsolicited, and unmerited grace of God. At the heart of Reformed theology is the Pauline statement to the Ephesians, "By grace are ye saved, through faith; and that not of yourselves, it is the gift of God" (Eph. 2:8). The individual who was once "dead in sin" (Eph. 2:1) is not saved and brought to his new condition by an autosoterism. He does not save himself. Nor is he saved by a synergism, or by a process of work in which God does his part and the individual does his part. For if that were the case, if the individual were to reserve to himself any residual sovereignty in the process of salvation, then God would be robbed completely of the sovereignty that is his alone. One is saved, if he is saved, not by an autosoterism or a synergism, but by a divine monergism. God alone saves, and to him all glory in the redemption of sinners is due.

When we speak of the process of salvation we have in view not only the accomplishment of redemption by the obedience of Christ, as that is considered in its comprehensive aspects of his active and his passive obedience, but also the application of redemption. We are speaking of what is referred to in doctrinal terms as the *ordo salutis*, or the order of salvation.[1] That takes

---

[1] See the excellent treatment of this subject in John Murray, *Redemption: Accomplished and Applied*, Grand Rapids: Eerdmans,1955.

up the Holy Spirit's work of effectual calling and regeneration and the sinner's justification, adoption into the family of God, sanctification, and perseverance to the end. What that involves is summed up in the title of Henry Scougal's book, *The Life of God in the Soul of Man*, that had a large influence in the revival of the eighteenth century.[2]

The meaning and scope of the evangel remains incomplete, therefore, until we have considered its relevance for behavior in the ordinary affairs and conduct of life. The Christian person remains, as Paul explained to the Romans, in a "body of sin" (Rom. 6:6). While that is so, the transition in status that Christian regeneration involves comes to expression in new behavior patterns and norms. And the Christian's responsibility is to understand the meaning and mandates of the law of God in such a way that a conformity to it will become, progressively, the determining passion of his life. The Christian develops, by virtue of the ministry of the Spirit of God in the soul, a new habitual spontaneity and stability of obedience to the righteous law of God.

The justification of the sinner

The call of the evangel is clear. "Believe on the Lord Jesus Christ", the apostles explained to the Philippian jailer, "and thou shalt be saved" (Acts 16:31). And the gospel of John states clearly that "He that believeth on the Son hath everlasting life" (John 3:36). The gospel declaration is replete with the invitation to life in Christ Jesus. The prophetic invitation of Isaiah is confirmed, "Ho, every one that thirsteth, come ye to the waters, and he that hath no money; come ye..." (Is. 55:1). And the repetition of the invitation from the lips of our Lord himself is so extensive in the gospel record as not to call for statement in detail. It is he alone who is "the way, the truth, and the life" (John 14:6).

But the problem of the sinner's transition from wrath to grace turns on the fact that he is himself enslaved to sin and

---

[2] Henry Scougal, *The Life of God in the Soul of Man*, Harrisonburg, VA: Sprinkle Publications [1739] 1986.

cannot of his own volition turn to God. The sovereign, re-creating work of God in the soul necessarily precedes the sinner's turning in faith and trust to Christ. It is by faith in Christ, the Scripture makes clear, that one is saved. That is clarified beyond all doubt in the theological treatise of Paul in his letter to the Romans. "By the deeds of the law there shall no flesh be justified in his sight ... [But] being justified freely by his grace through the redemption that is in Christ Jesus ... we conclude that a man is justified by faith without the deeds of the law" (Rom. 3:20,24,28). And again Paul says to the Galatians, "no man is justified by the law in the sight of God; for 'The just shall live by faith'" (Gal. 3:11).

Coming into focus in this way is the reality of the saving faith by which the sinner is brought to Christ. The faith by which one believes in Christ is itself the gift of God. Faith and repentance, the Scripture explains, are among the gifts that Christ purchased for his people in his obedience and death, and which are conferred on the sinner by the regenerating work of the Holy Spirit. But what, then, is the content of saving faith, and what are we to understand as the motions of the faculties of the soul as the repentant sinner moves to Christ?

The elements of saving faith are twofold. Faith involves, first, the individual's assent that what God has said in his Word is true. That is in turn based on a newly-endowed knowledge of what God has said regarding the state and condition of man in sin and the remedy that God has provided in Christ. Then secondly, saving faith involves the sinner's commitment of himself in trust to Christ and his claiming the promise that Christ held out when he said "Come unto me, all ye that labour and are heavy laden, and I will give you rest" (Matt. 11:28).

We are saved, the Scriptural record makes clear, by faith. But that statement is to be understood in the context of the grace of God from which the gift of faith emanates. The relation between grace and faith can best be put by observing that the *efficient* cause of our salvation is the grace of God, the *meritorious* cause is the death of Christ, and the *instrumental* cause is our faith. We are saved, if we are saved, by grace alone, through faith alone, because of the death of Christ alone.

That means that the sole object of saving faith is Christ

himself in the performance of the act of redemption on our behalf. The ground on which we are justified in the sight of God and receive the pardon of all our sins is solely the substitutionary obedience and death of Christ. Justification has to do with one's relation to the law of God and his consequent standing before God. The best short definition of justification is that one is "just" insofar as his relation to the law of God is what it ought to be. But the problem is that we all, by virtue of our fallen and sinful state and nature, are in ourselves contrary to that law of God. We stand under the liability to penalty for our repudiation of our obligation to God. How, then, can we be reestablished in a condition of justification in relation to God? That is the problem to which, by his mercy and grace, God has addressed all of his sovereign processes of redemption. The reality is that "Christ died for the ungodly" (Rom. 5:6).

We mean by justification the declarative act of God by which he declares the sinner to be righteous. It is referred to as a "forensic" act, where the word and concept of "forensic" relates to our status in relation to law. God's statement that the sinner is now just or righteous is a statement that, so far as that sinner is concerned, all of the demands of God's law have been met and satisfied. God can and does make that statement because, in the case of those whom Christ redeemed and for whom, therefore, such a statement is true, the sinner is regarded as just and righteous because Christ has acted as his substitute. We must now work out the meaning of that more fully.

We come here to a question that we must face with some care. Why, we can ask again, does any sinner come to Christ in repentance and faith? The answer is because, as we have seen, the Holy Spirit of God brings the sinner to Christ. But it is precisely that movement of faith towards Christ that we must understand. We can regret very much that at this point the preaching and teaching of the evangelical church in general has gone sadly astray. We speak in our churches of Christians being "born again". We have seen from our discussion of regeneration what it means to say that one is born again. But do we say that one is born again because he has faith in Christ? That is what the evangelical church is to a large extent saying. But does that correctly reflect the Scriptural doctrine? Our answer must be that it does not.

One is not born again because he has faith in Christ. The reality is the precise opposite of that. The truth is that one comes to faith in Christ only because he has been born again. We say, then, that regeneration is prior to faith. No person can come to Christ unless and until the Holy Spirit has created new life within him, because up to that time he is, as Paul said, "dead in trespasses and sins" (Eph. 2:1). And of course a dead person cannot do anything. He is simply dead. The issue is beautifully clarified in the record of Paul's meeting with the women who met to worship by the river at Philippi in Macedonia. Lydia, you will recall, came to faith in Christ. But the Scripture does not say that she opened her heart to Christ. She is described, on the contrary, as one "whose heart the Lord opened" (Acts 16:14). The regenerating awakening of the sinner and the opening of the sinner's heart to believe in Christ is the sovereign work of God.

But what, then, is the ground on which God can declare that the sinner who comes to him and expresses repentance and faith in Christ is at that point "just" or "justified" and "righteous"? The only ground is that provided by the substitutionary obedience of Christ.

God declares the repentant sinner righteous because the righteousness of Christ is imputed to him, or is placed to the sinner's account. We come here to the great evangelical doctrine of double or reciprocal imputation. The sinner's sin is imputed to Christ, and Christ's righteousness is imputed to the sinner (2 Cor. 5:21). That declarative, forensic act and statement of God is part of a remarkable process of divine grace.

"God", Paul stated to the Romans, must be "just and the justifier of him which believeth in Jesus" (Rom. 3:26). Whatever action God takes in the justification of the sinner must itself be consistent with God's own righteousness. God himself must be just, as well as the justifier. We may conclude, then, that the justice of God is maintained in three respects in the act that declares the sinner to be righteous. First, by virtue of the substitutionary redemptive work of Christ, the demands of God's holy wrath against sin are satisfied, and God's action in justification can therefore be a freely unconstrained act. Second, as God himself must be "just", "the judgment of God is", as

Turretin puts it, "according to truth".[3] That means that what God says is true. Turretin is saying quite rightly that because God is eternally righteous he cannot utter a lie. Therefore, if God says that the sinner is righteous, the sinner must, in fact, *be* righteous. But, we may ask, how can that be so? The sinner is a sinner. And it is only because, and after, he is turned to Christ that he is declared righteous. But we are here saying that in order to be himself righteous, God can and does declare the sinner to be righteous only because the sinner is in fact righteous. What, then, is the explanation of our doctrine at this critically important point?

In order for God to declare that the sinner is righteous, he actually constitutes him righteous. God first of all gives to a sinner a righteousness that the sinner did not himself possess. When God in that way constitutes the sinner righteous, the sinner is then said to possess constitutive righteousness. How is that possible, we may well ask? The answer is that God gives to the sinner the righteousness of Christ and it is thereby the sinner's own righteousness. As Turretin observes, "the obedience of Christ rendered in our name to God the Father is so given to us by God that it is reckoned to be truly ours".[4]

Turretin has summed up the doctrine in this way. "God cannot show favor to, nor justify anyone without a perfect righteousness. For since the judgment of God is according to truth, he cannot pronounce anyone just who is not really just.... By the righteousness and obedience of one, Christ, we are constituted righteous (Rom. 5:19).... Justification takes place on account of the suretyship of Christ and the payment made for us by him".[5]

Turretin's statement of the doctrine is clear. "Christ by his obedience is rightly said 'to constitute' us 'righteous', not by an inherent but by an imputed righteousness".[6] John Murray has argued at length to the same effect. "Justification", he says, "is a constitutive act, not barely declarative. And this constitutive act

---

[3] Francis Turretin, *Institutes of Elenctic Theology*, Phillipsburg: P&R Publishing, 1994, Vol. 2., 647.

[4] Ibid., 648.

[5] Ibid., 647, 651, 653.

[6] Ibid., 644.

consists in our being placed in the category of righteous persons by reason of our relation to Christ".[7] Again, "Justification ... is constitutive in order that it may be truly declarative. God must constitute the new relationship as well as declare it to be. The constitutive act consists in the imputation to us of the obedience and righteousness of Christ. The obedience of Christ must therefore be regarded as the ground of justification; it is the righteousness which God not only takes into account but reckons to our account when he justifies the ungodly".[8]

But the righteousness of God in this remarkable transaction is maintained in a third way. To summarize, God is righteous in declaring the sinner righteous, first because the demands of his holy justice have been satisfied; secondly because the sinner has been given the righteousness of Christ and thereby possesses a constitutive righteousness; and now thirdly, because the sinner's guilt has been given to Christ. Just as God cannot declare the sinner righteous until he is righteous by imputation, so God cannot declare his Son guilty until his Son *is* guilty. God has declared his Son guilty because of sin - not his own sin, but our sin. That was because God laid the guilt of our sin upon his own Son when the Son gave his life for us. God punished sin in Christ because he transferred our guilt to him. The amazing fact of redemption is that God punished One who was guilty, not of his own sin, but of ours. R.C. Sproul has rightly said that "the Son willingly bears for his people sins that are imputed or transferred to him. Here is imputation with a vengeance - indeed divine vengeance".[9]

Again the doctrine has been clearly stated by a longer line of theologians, writing in the tradition of the theology of the Reformation, than we can adduce at this point. To take an example from the English Puritan theologians of the seventeenth century, Matthew Poole has observed that "Our sins were reckoned to him [Christ]; so as though personally he was no sinner, yet by imputation he was, and God dealt with him as

---

[7] John Murray, *The Epistle to the Romans*, Grand Rapids: Eerdmans, 1959, Vol. 1, 205.

[8] John Murray, *Redemption: Accomplished and Applied*, 154-55.

[9] R.C. Sproul, *Faith Alone: The Evangelical Doctrine of Justification*, Grand Rapids: Baker Books, 1995, 104.

such; for he was made a sacrifice for our sins".[10] Or to quote
Turretin again, "Justification takes place on account of the
suretyship of Christ and the payment made for us by him -
which cannot be done without imputation....because [of] the
curse and punishment of sin which he received upon himself in
our stead ... as our sins are imputed to him, so in turn his
obedience and righteousness are imputed to us".[11]

At the risk of some repetition, we may sum up the question
of the sinner's justification as follows. By the imputation of
Christ's righteousness to the sinner, the sinner is constituted, or
made, righteous. The sinner is given a *forensic righteousness*
and God looks on him as having satisfied the demands of his
law. Similarly, and by parallel argument, by the imputation of
the guilt of the sinner's sin to Christ, Christ is made guilty. God
placed on Christ a *forensic guilt*, the counterpart of the sinner's
forensic righteousness, and he looked on Christ as guilty for the
sins of his people who had broken God's holy law.

The conclusion is that the ones whom God declares to be
righteous are righteous, because God has made them righteous
by imputation. And the One whom God declares to be guilty is
guilty, and he therefore bears the punishment of that guilt,
because God has made him guilty, again by imputation.

The process and means of sanctification

"Sanctification", the Catechism states, "is the work of God's free
grace, whereby we are renewed, in the whole man after the
image of God, and are enabled more and more to die unto sin
and live unto righteousness".[12] That brings before us quite
clearly what is involved in the redemptive office of the Holy
Spirit. He applies to those for whom Christ died the benefits of
the redemption that Christ accomplished, and by his sovereign
grace the Holy Spirit conducts them to glory.

The Christian's sanctification, the fact and the process of it,
is to be considered in two important respects. It is in the first

---

[10] Matthew Poole, *A Commentary on the Holy Bible*, London: Banner of
Truth [1685] 1963, Vol. III, 616.
[11] Turretin, op. cit., Vol. 2, 653.
[12] *Westminster Shorter Catechism*, Question 35.

place, to use the very good language of John Murray, "definitive".[13] By that we mean that by virtue of the regenerating work
of the Holy Spirit in the soul, the sinner is definitively, once-
and-for-all, set apart as holy for God. He is separated definitively from the slavery to the old life of sin and the sinful state
in which he previously lived. Paul the apostle described that to
the Colossians by saying that God has "delivered us from the
power of darkness, and hath translated us into the kingdom of
his dear Son" (Col. 1:13). That translation has been effected
once-for-all. The sinner is now the new person we have already
described. The only way to describe him is in terms of the
radically new characteristics of nature to which the faculties of
his soul have been transformed.

But sanctification is also to be understood, as the Catechism
question stated, as that sovereign work of the Holy Spirit within
the regenerate person by which he is progressively transformed,
in all parts of his life and thoughts and actions, to consistency
with the holiness and the righteousness of God. That process we
refer to as progressive sanctification. A number of things are to
be said about it.

First, God, by the ministry of his Holy Spirit, is sovereign in
the Christian's sanctification. God makes Christ to be to us, Paul
states to the Corinthians, "wisdom, and righteousness, and
sanctification, and redemption" (1 Cor. 1:30). The full-orbed
meaning of what God has purposed for the church that he
redeemed in Christ is summed up by saying that against our
ignorance, guilt, pollution, and misery Christ is made our
wisdom and righteousness and sanctification and redemption.
The compass of what God has purposed and guaranteed to us is
wide and deep and will consummate at last in the Christian's
perfection and his eternal glory.

Because God, by his Spirit, is sovereign in our sanctification, we rely on his covenantal promise that he will complete
the work that he has begun (Phil. 1:6). Our redemption is a
covenantal redemption that rests for its security on the oath of

---

[13] John Murray, *Collected Writings of John Murray*, Edinburgh: Banner of
Truth, 1977, Vol. 2, 277, reprinted from *Calvin Theological Journal*, Vol. 2,
No. 1, April 1967.

faithfulness that God has sworn. When we read, as Paul said to the Thessalonians, that "this is the will of God, even your sanctification" (I Thess. 4:3) we are entitled to see in that more than a statement that it is the preceptive will of God that we should be sanctified. We should see also that it is his decretive will that we should be sanctified. For that reason he will, by means of the Holy Spirit's work within us, deal with us in such a way that we shall be brought at last to the perfection of holiness that he has decreed we should attain as his redeemed people.

Secondly, while our sanctification is all the sovereign work of God by his Holy Spirit, from another perspective the work of sanctification is our work. Because we are new people in Christ Jesus, we are responsible to pursue the means of grace that God has provided to us and to progress thereby in the realization of holiness. There are two sides to what we can and should do in order to achieve that progress.

Because we have been created anew in Christ Jesus, and because we are no longer dead in sin but are alive to God, we now have abilities that we did not previously possess or understand. We must therefore work towards holiness, without which, the writer to the Hebrews has said, "no man shall see the Lord" (Heb. 12:14). The two sides of our working as redeemed people can be referred to as the positive use of the means of sanctifying grace, on the one hand, and the work of mortifying our sinful proclivities and inclinations on the other. There will be no progress in sanctification unless there is progress in the mortification of sin.[14] We are told that if we "through the Spirit mortify the deeds of the body, [we] shall live" (Rom. 8:13).

It is the Christian's duty to be engaged in the work of mortifying sin, or what we saw Owen refer to in the previous chapter as the "contrary habitual principle", the indwelling sin that remains in the believer. The Christian is to aim at putting to death that principle of sin, through the habitual weakening of it, even though what is aimed at cannot be fully accomplished in this life. But as Paul's statement to the Romans has made clear,

---

[14] On the important question of the mortification of sin see John Owen, *Of the Mortification of Sin in Believers*, in *The Works of John Owen*, Edinburgh: Banner of Truth, Vol. 6, 1967. See also the discussion in Sinclair Ferguson, *John Owen on the Christian Life*, Edinburgh: Banner of Truth, 1987, 125-53.

that work of mortification is not a work that can be accomplished by man-made means. The latter lead only to a condition of self-righteousness and spiritual self-deception, the very antithesis of the true life in Christ of which mortification of sin is the accompaniment. It is "through the Spirit", or by virtue of the power and grace of the Holy Spirit who works in the Christian by virtue of his union with Christ, that the work is to be done. We are not alone now that we have been joined to Christ. His Spirit ministers to us and calls us repeatedly and consistently to be aware of his presence and his working in our lives.

But what are we to say if, as is so often the case, we as Christian people are careless and delinquent in pursuing the means of grace that are designed for our sanctification? At that point we must see again the sovereignty of the Holy Spirit. The twelfth chapter of the letter to the Hebrews is eloquent on the fact that if we are delinquent, God in his providence will deal with us in such a way by his Holy Spirit that we will be aware of his discipline in our lives. It is the work of the Holy Spirit to exercise that discipline and the chastisement that goes along with it. If we are his people, he will do in us and for us what he has already guaranteed to the Father and the Son that he will accomplish.

What, then, are the means of grace to which we should attend and which we should cultivate? They are more extensive, and they have been more lavishly provided for us, than we can refer to at length at this time. They take up primarily the Holy Spirit's use of the Word of God to educate us and to mold us and to lead us into progressively higher realizations of his will for us. Our Lord himself prayed to the Father for us and said, "Sanctify them through thy truth; thy word is truth" (John 17:17). The means of grace include our attention to the high privilege of not only reading the Word of God, but of reflecting and meditating upon it, and welcoming the conviction of the Holy Spirit as he communicates to us the meaning and the relevance of it. He has said to us that "I stand at the door and knock; if any man hear my voice, and open the door, I will come in to him, and will sup with him, and he with me" (Rev. 3:20). He makes that statement, not to the unregenerate sinner whose heart is dead to the things of God, but to us who have the new life that gives us the privilege and responsibility of opening our heart to him again and again.

The means of sanctifying grace include the covenant privilege of communion with God in prayer, directed and supported by the working of the Holy Spirit in our lives and in the manner and the matter of our prayer. They include also the Christian's participation in the sacraments that God has provided as signs and seals of our covenantal union with Christ and our sharing in the benefits of the redemption that he accomplished. The means of grace extend also to include the privilege of fellowship with God's people who, with us, are joined to him in Christ. We are brought to Christ one by one. But we are never alone. We are members of his body, the church, and we stand in a new solidarity with all of the people of God.

Christian ethics

We have said, in relation to the Christian's knowledge of God, that knowledge is ethical. To know God truly is to love God, and to love God is to obey God. Our Lord has stated clearly, "If ye love me, keep my commandments" (John 14:15). And in his first epistle John has elevated the keeping of the commandments to a test of our standing in the faith. "Hereby we know that we know him", John says, "if we keep his commandments" (1 John 2:3).

In the language of what we referred to in chapter 1 as "Triad 3", we consider now the respects in which the Christian's transition from wrath to grace carries with it significance for the ethical quality of all of his subsequent actions.

The question of ethical criteria, or the formulation of canons of human behavior, has attracted a long discussion in the history of both secular and theological thought.[15] The basic questions

---

[15] An entry to the literature of ethical or moral philosophy is provided in Peter Singer, *A Companion to Ethics*, Oxford: Blackwell, 1993. An extensive and insightful treatment from the perspectives of this present book is contained in John Murray, *Principles of Conduct*, Grand Rapids: Eerdmans, 1957. Carl F.H. Henry, who was referred to above as one of the principal architects of the neo-evangelical theological movement, has published *Christian Personal*

that ethics addresses have been described as: "How can I know what is right? What is the ultimate criterion of right action? Why should I do what is right? What ought I to do? How ought I to live?"[16] Or as Francis Schaeffer has put the question in his brief but ambitious survey of "the rise and decline of western thought and culture", "How should we then live?"[17] The "then" in Schaeffer's question implies that the manner or conduct of life follows consequentially from the antecedent character of Christian life, or the life that the Christian possesses by virtue of his identification with Christ.

To make that statement is to stand aside from much of contemporary opinion. In her discussion of "The origin of ethics", Mary Midgley, a philosopher who has written extensively on the relation between ethics and evolutionary hypotheses, has distinguished between the answers to the ethical question that came from parts of the history of secular thought and that which has come from Christian belief and doctrine. Christian belief, in Midgley's view, "explains morality as our necessary attempt to bring our imperfect nature in line with the will of God. Its origin-myth is the Fall of Man, which has produced that imperfection in our nature in the way described - again symbolically - in the Book of Genesis". But what Midgley then goes on to call the "simplicity" of the Christian answer will, she says, not do. It "cannot really ...deal with our questions".[18] Our position, on the contrary, is distinguished from Midgley's "myth" by being based on the significance of the actual historical reality, not the "origin-myth", of Adam's Fall. The Christian's ethical aspirations are not to be understood, as

---

Ethics, and *Aspects of Christian Social Ethics*, Grand Rapids: Eerdmans, 1957 and 1964. For a recent attempt to clarify the relevance of ethical theory to the social sciences see Douglas Vickers, *Economics and Ethics: An Introduction to Theory, Institutions, and Policy*, Westport, CT.: Praeger, 1997.

[16] Peter Singer, op,cit, vi, vii.

[17] Francis A. Schaeffer, *How Should We Then Live? The Rise and Decline of Western Thought and Culture*, Old Tappan, N.J.: Revell, 1976.

[18] Mary Midgley, "The origin of ethics", in Peter Singer, op. cit., 3-4. See also in the same volume, Jonathan Berg, "How could ethics depend on religion", 525ff., where the author examines "grounds for holding [the] belief ... that without God there can be no morality", ibid., xiii.

Midgley's argument suggests, as those of an autonomous individual attempting autonomously to bring his "imperfect nature in line with the will of God".

The Christian answer to the ethical question turns on the understanding of the newness of life in Christ that regeneration by God's Holy Spirit involves, and on the implications of that for individual behavior. When Peter clarified the fact that the church is now the "holy nation", replacing in the purpose and ordination of God the older theocratic nation of Israel, he stated that the purpose of redemption was that his people "should show forth the praises of him who hath called you out of darkness into his marvellous light" (1 Peter 2:9). The apostle Paul repeatedly advanced the same proposition. The Christian's identification with Christ, he says, is for the purpose that "we should walk in newness of life" (Rom. 6:4), and that, as he stated to the Ephesians, "we should be holy and without blame before him ... to the praise of the glory of his grace" (Eph. 1:4,6). To the Colossians Paul explained the Christian walk by telling them that his prayer for them was that they "might walk worthy of the Lord unto all pleasing, being fruitful in every good work" (Col. 1:10). And he reinforced that with the admonition, "As ye have therefore received Christ Jesus the Lord, so walk ye in him" (Col. 2:6). In the light of their calling in Christ, Peter says again, "what manner of persons ought ye to be in all holy conversation [or conduct] and godliness" (2 Peter 3:11). The Scriptural directives as to Christian conduct could be multiplied.

God set forth his law at the beginning in its threefold dimensions of the moral law, the ceremonial law, and the civil or judicial law. The imperatives of the moral law, the Decalogue that contained the canons or rules of behavior that would conform God's people to the requirements of his own perfections, first came to expression in the institutional arrangements that described and constituted the ceremonial and civil laws. The ceremonial law, in the form in which God at first gave it to his people of old, has passed away by virtue of its fulfillment in the coming and the substitutionary work of Christ. He is the high priest of the Christian profession who, as the antitype, fulfilled all of the types that preceded and anticipated him under the older Mosaic administration. The letter to the Hebrews is eloquent in a highly sustained manner on that reality. The older Mosaic civil law has also passed away, as to the form in which it was originally given and implemented. What does remain of the civil law is, as the *Westminster Confession* has stated it, "the general equity thereof".[19]

The significance of the older ceremonial and civil laws rests in the fact that they were each, in their respective ways and on their own levels of relevance for God's people, applications of what God had set forth in the moral law. That moral law, which is embodied in the Ten Commandments, is a republication of what God had communicated to Adam at the beginning. We hold to the sanctity and perpetuity of the moral law. But by virtue of God's culmination of his purposes in Christ, we do not, and under the Scriptures we cannot, hold to the perpetuity of the institutional forms in which, under the ceremonial and civil laws, the implications of the moral law first came to expression.

It is in the moral law that we discover the answer to the question of ethical criteria. At the very beginning, when God first gave his law to his people, he summarized its mandates by stating, "thou shalt love the Lord thy God with all thine heart, and with all thy soul, and with all thy might" (Deut. 6:5). And that was in turn the manner in which Christ himself summed up the matter when a Pharisaic lawyer approached him with the question, "which is the great commandment in the law?" (Matt. 22:34-40). "Love", Paul said to the Romans, "is the fulfilling of the law" (Rom. 13:10), meaning thereby that to love God truly is to love his law and to wish to live in such a way as to honor and obey it.

The ethical aspects of the Christian life

It is beyond our present objective to discuss all of the ways and respects in which this ethical mandate comes, or should come, to expression in the Christian life.[20] But we may consider briefly some aspects of the Christian life as it precedes and determines Christian behavior. That follows from the fact that the condition

---

[19] *Westminster Confession*, Ch.19:4.
[20] See the works of John Murray and Carl F.H. Henry cited in n.13 above.

of the individual in the state of sin has been changed to that of his union with Christ.

The reality of that union imposed its burden on the mind of our Lord to such an extent that much of the discourse that he gave to his disciples on the night on which he was betrayed was taken up with it. It is spread throughout the thirteenth to the seventeenth chapters of John's gospel, culminating in our Lord's high priestly prayer on that occasion. In that prayer he made clear that our union with him, that is effected by the coming to us of his Holy Spirit, implies and carries along with it union with the triune Persons of the Godhead. Here, indeed, is "the highest privilege that the gospel offers".[21]

The benefits of redemption that the Spirit of God communicates to the Christian involve, as we have seen in this chapter, his progress in sanctification. That implies the need to consider the extent to which, and the manner in which, the Christian does in fact achieve the ethical standards that the moral law of God presents to him.

Here we confront the paradox of the Christian life. By virtue of the regeneration that is effected in the soul by the Holy Spirit, the sinner is in every respect made a new person, joined to Christ is a vital, organic, spiritual, and indissoluble union. The new-born person is a saint. That is the precise language in which the apostle refers to him in the salutations in his letters to the Ephesians, the Philippians, and the Colossians (Eph. 1:1; Phil. 1:1; Col. 1:2). He is a saint, and yet he is a sinner.

The meaning of the Christian person's sanctification is that he is thereby enabled, as the Catechism has put it, "more and more to die unto sin, and live unto righteousness". What is at issue is that Christian regeneration does not imply the immediate achievement of a state of moral perfection. A new principle, we have seen, is implanted in the soul, the faculties are endowed with new abilities and capacities, and new aspirations for conformity to the pattern of holiness that God has set forth are created. But there is a progress involved that will, at last,

---

[21] J.I. Packer, *Knowing God*, Downers Grove: InterVarsity Press, 1973, 186. See also the very perceptive discussion of "Union with Christ" in John Murray, *Redemption Accomplished and Applied*, 201-13.

accomplish the objectives of holiness that the purpose of God has contemplated.

Sanctification means progressive conformity to the ethical standards of the moral law. But the realities of the Christian's position is that he sins. He keeps the perfect law of God only imperfectly. The apostle John understood that completely when, as he wrote under the inspiration of the Holy Spirit, he argued the case in his first epistle. "If we say that we have no sin, we deceive ourselves", John said. But then the glory of the evangel appears again. "If we confess our sins, he is faithful and just to forgive us our sins, and to cleanse us from all unrighteousness" (1 John 1:8-9). While the Christian's standing in union with Christ is eternally secure, while it is clearly guaranteed that Christ will complete in him the work of grace that he has begun (Phil. 1:6), and while he has the assurance that nothing will be able to pluck him from the hands of Christ (John 10:28; Rom. 8:38-39), yet it is all too true that in this life the Christian person lives below the standards of moral excellence to which he has been called.

At issue, therefore, is not simply or only the degree of conformity to the law of righteousness that the Christian person has or has not achieved. At issue, rather, is the question of whether the professing Christian loves the law of God, and whether he lives with a passion and determination that, by the grace of God, he will seek after righteousness. The redemptive office of the Holy Spirit of God, which he undertook in the determinate council of the Godhead before the foundation of the world, is to bring to glory, perfected at last, those for whom Christ died. He has given the Christian his guarantee that he will not fail in that assignment.

The Christian can embrace, with the confidence born of his newly-endowed knowledge of God, the promise that at the last day, "when Christ, who is our life, shall appear, then shall ye also appear with him in glory" (Col. 3:4). The Christian understands with a new-born perception the truth warranted to him by the inspired argument of the apostle John: "Now are we the sons of God, and it doth not yet appear what we shall be; but we know that, when he shall appear, we shall be like him; for we shall see him as he is" (1 John 3:2).

Let the Christian pursue with all diligence the means of progress in sanctification that God has provided to him. Let him "through the Spirit, mortify the deeds of the body" (Rom. 8:13); let him "give all diligence to make his calling and election sure" to himself (2 Peter 1:10); let him "work out [his] salvation with fear and trembling", knowing that "God ... is working in [him] both to will and to do of his good pleasure" (Phil. 2:12-13). Once he was far from Christ, the slave of Satan and sin. He was a God-hater (Rom. 1:30), desiring nothing that conformed to the righteousness of God, and unable to do anything to turn to God. But now he is alive in Christ. Let him therefore be active in pursuing the righteousness to which he has been called.

A theology of hope

The third of the elements envisaged under our "Triad 3" referred to the Christian's eschatological hope. That takes up what has been referred to doctrinally as the perseverance of the saints. It refers to the certainty that the Christian will be preserved in the state of salvation until he is brought, by the grace of God and the ministry of the Holy Spirit, to his resurrection state.

The Catechism alerts us to the benefits that accompany, "or flow from", justification, adoption, and sanctification. They include "assurance of God's love, peace of conscience, joy in the Holy Ghost, increase of grace, and perseverance therein to the end".[22] Here explicitly is the promise of the grace of perseverance. In the light of what has already been said, it is necessary to refer to only two brief points in connection with it.

First, the Christian is an eschatological person. He holds the prospect that he will be brought at last to eternity with Christ. Secondly, a significant implication follows in this respect from the Christian's union with Christ. At issue now is the organic aspect of that union.

When we say that the union contemplated is an organic union, we have in view the fact that the Christian person, by reason of his union with Christ, has been assumed into membership of the church of which Christ is the head. The

---

[22] *Westminster Shorter Catechism*, Question 36.

church is an organic entity, an organism, a living structure or orgnization, that is what it is by virtue of the contemplation of it in the mind of God, and by reason of his election of it, before the foundation of the world. Now, in actual historical time, those whom God elected before time began have been brought into the church. Their actual incorporation into the church, in both its visible and its invisible aspects, has been effected and has conferred upon them its attendant benefits. The church is the organic entity that exists and draws its life and its energies from Christ, its head. It exists in a vital union with Christ.

But because the Christian is incorporated into that organic entity, the church, his eschatological prospect and hope also have an organic dimension. The Christian's hope is not only or simply his hope and prospect of his personal perseverance. At issue also is the prospect he now holds for the eschatological condition and the eternal preservation of the church into which, by the grace of God, he has been incorporated.

The Scriptural data that bear on the point are copious and do not call for extensive exploration at this stage. Suffice it to say that the apostle alerted his readers to the eschatological prospect of the church when, writing to the Ephesians, he contemplated the purposes of God in relation to it. He concludes that "in the dispensation of the fulness of times he [will] gather together in one all things in Christ ... in whom also we have obtained an inheritance, being predestinated according to the purpose of him who worketh all things after the counsel of his own will" (Eph. 1:10-11).

The Christian embraces the certain hope that, joined as he is to Christ in an indissoluble union, he will at last participate in the glorious reality of the eternal kingdom of grace that God has established in Christ. The conclusion follows that the evangel, whose terms and scope we set out to elucidate, presents us with a theology of hope. It is a hope that is founded on the faithfulness of God who, transcendent above all that he has made, is yet immanent in the world of history and time. It is a theology of hope that is informed by the realization that God has ordered all things, and supervises the history of all things, in the interest of his church that he has redeemed to himself at so great a price.

Index of Scripture References

Index of Names

Index of Subjects

active, 100, 126-128
passive, 100, 126, 129
oblation of, 130
Person of, 28, 38, 40, 55,
69, 70-75, 77
pre-existence of, 111
priestly office of, 77, 101,
108, 109, 114, 138, 141,
142, 221
satisfaction of, 117, 125,
188
shepherd, 34, 114, 138
temptation of, 30
See also Atonement
Christological interpretation,
See also Facts
Christological settlement, 72
Church, 15, 61, 124, 139, 142,
145, 185, 217, 223, 224
Circumcision, 122
Commingling, 70, 75-77
Common grace, 96
Communion with God, 99,
217
Contingency, 60
Continuity, principle of, 167,
168
Copernican revolution, 157
Cosmological proof, 172
Council of Chalcedon, 28, 72
Council of Nicea, 72
Council of the Godhead, 109,
111, 114, 119
Covenantal objectives, 31
Covenantal obligations, 120,
132, 139, 166, 181
Covenantal promise, 122, 123
Covenant-breaker, 93
Covenant of creation, 126, 139
Covenant of Grace, 123
Covenant of Redemption, 68,
106, 109-111, 119,
120, 126, 133, 138

Creation, 17, 18, 39, 63, 172,
184, 188
Creation covenant, 41
Creation mandate, 94, 166,
185
Creation ordinances, 166
Creator-creature relation, 44,
167, 171, 191
Creaturehood, 32, 97
Criteria of belief, 155
Criteria of knowledge, 181
Cultural accommodation, 156
Cultural consensus, 153
Cultural hegemony, 14

Death of God, 160, 181
Death of man, 182
Decalogue, 89, 219
Deism, 173, 180
Depravation, 91, 100
Deprivation, 91
Dereliction, 124
Devil, 92, 96, 203
Dialectical idealism, 178
Dialectical materialism, 178
Dialecticism, 167-169
Disarray of faith, 22, 145, 188
Discontinuity, principle of,
167, 168
Divine mind, 67
Donum superadditum, 195
Dualism, 87

Effectual calling, 17, 35-37,
189, 194
Eleatics, 175
Election, 112
Empiricism, 173, 178, 183-4
Enlightenment, 158, 173, 179
Epistemic capacity, 65
Epistemic status, 150, 182,
183
Epistemological data, 165